Architektur und Baudetails /
Architecture and Construction Details

Renzo Piano Building Workshop

Architektur und Baudetails /
Architecture and Construction Details

Renzo Piano Building Workshop

Edition **DETAIL**

Diese Veröffentlichung basiert auf Beiträgen, die in den Jahren 2001 bis 2017 in den Fachzeitschriften DETAIL und DETAIL structure erschienen sind. / This publication is based on articles published in the journals DETAIL and DETAIL structure between 2001 and 2017.

Herausgeber /
Editor:
Dr. Sandra Hofmeister

Projektleitung /
Project Manager:
Nicola Brower, Steffi Lenzen

Englischübersetzungen /
Translation into English:
Elise Feiersinger, Peter Green, Mark Kammerbauer, Alisa Kotmair, Roderick O'Donovan, Raymond Peat, Almut Pohl, Stefan Widdess

Korrektorat deutsch /
Proofreading (German):
Sandra Leitte, Valley City

Korrektorat englisch /
Proofreading (English):
Stefan Widdess, Berlin

Gestaltung /
Design:
strobo B M (Matthias Friederich, Samuel Hinterholzer, Julian von Klier), München / Munich

Zeichnungen /
Drawings:
DETAIL Business Information GmbH München / Munich

Redaktionelle Mitarbeit /
Editorial team:
Duy Mac

Druck und Bindung /
Printing and binding:
Grafisches Centrum Cuno GmbH & Co. KG, Calbe

Bibliografische Information der Deutschen Nationalbibliothek Die Deutsche Nationalbibliothek verzeichnet diese Publikation in der Deutschen Nationalbibliografie; detaillierte bibliografische Daten sind im Internet über http://dnb.d-nb.de abrufbar.

Bibliographic information published by the German National Library. The German National Library lists this publication in the Deutsche Nationalbibliografie; detailed bibliographic data is available on the Internet at http://dnb.d-nb.de.

© 2018, 1. Auflage / 1st Edition
DETAIL Business Information GmbH
München / Munich
www.detail.de

Dieses Werk ist urheberrechtlich geschützt. Die dadurch begründeten Rechte, insbesondere die der Übersetzung, des Nachdrucks, des Vortrags, der Entnahme von Abbildungen und Tabellen, der Funksendung, der Mikroverfilmung oder der Vervielfältigung auf anderen Wegen und der Speicherung in Datenverarbeitungsanlagen, bleiben, auch bei nur auszugsweiser Verwertung, vorbehalten. Eine Vervielfältigung dieses Werks ist auch im Einzelfall nur in den Grenzen der gesetzlichen Bestimmungen des Urheberrechtsgesetzes in der jeweils geltenden Fassung zulässig. Sie ist grundsätzlich vergütungspflichtig. Zuwiderhandlungen unterliegen den Strafbestimmungen des Urheberrechts. / This work is subject to copyright. All rights reserved, whether the whole or part of the material is concerned, specifically the rights of translation, reprinting, citation, reuse of illustrations and tables, broadcasting, reproduction on microfilm or in other ways and storage in data processing systems. Reproduction of any part of this work in individual cases, too, is only permitted within the limits of the provisions of the valid edition of the copyright law. A charge will be levied. Infringements will be subject to the penalty clauses of the copyright law.

ISBN 978-3-95553-421-9 (Print)
ISBN 978-3-95553-422-6 (E-Book)
ISBN 978-3-95553-423-3 (Bundle)

Impressum / Imprint

007
Vorwort /
Preface

010
The Whitney Museum
of American Art
at Gansevoort,
New York,
USA

020
Intesa Sanpaolo
Office Building,
Turin,
IT

036
Valletta City Gate,
Valletta,
MT

050
Jérôme Seydoux-
Pathé Foundation,
Paris,
FR

064
Kimbell Art Museum
Expansion,
Fort Worth,
USA

074
Auditorium
del Parco,
L'Aquila,
IT

086
Chicago Art Institute
– The Modern Wing,
Chicago,
USA

094
The New York Times
Building,
New York,
USA

128
Maison Hermès,
Tokyo / Tokio,
JP

136
Zentrum Paul Klee,
Bern,
CH

146
High Museum
Expansion,
Atlanta,
USA

156
Padre Pio Pilgrimage
Church,
San Giovanni Rotondo,
IT

164
Partner /
Partners
RPBW Architects

166
Projektbeteiligte /
Project Credits

168
Bildnachweis /
Picture Credits

Inhalt / Index

Als das Centre Pompidou im Januar 1977 eröffnete, war Paris um eine architektonische Attraktion reicher. Die radikale Architektur der ungewöhnlichen Kulturmaschine avancierte in kürzester Zeit zum Publikumsmagneten – und ist es bis heute geblieben. Der Entwurf der damals wenig erfahrenen Architekten Renzo Piano und Richard Rogers sollte Geschichte schreiben. Viele Gebäude, die Renzo Piano seit dem Wettbewerb des Beaubourg entwarf, haben ebenfalls architektonische Maßstäbe gesetzt. Der gebürtige Genueser gründete 1981 sein Architekturbüro Renzo Piano Building Workshop (RPBW), das von Paris, Genua und New York aus in verschiedenen Ländern und auf mehreren Kontinenten weltbekannte Museen und Bürohochhäuser, Auditorien und Parlamentsgebäude plant. Das gekonnte Zusammenspiel von funktionalen, technischen und ästhetischen Aspekten gehört zum Markenzeichen von Renzo Piano Building Workshop. Dass sich die architektonische Sprache dabei nie wiederholt, sondern sich stets neu erfindet und wandelt, ist ein weiteres Charakteristikum und macht das Werk von Renzo Piano einzigartig. Als Meister der Bautechnik bekannt, setzen der Pritzker-Preisträger und sein Team, zu dem heute elf Partner zählen, auf die unterschiedlichsten Materialien, Formen und Bauweisen, die stark vom Standort und der jeweiligen Funktion inspiriert sind. Die Gebäude von Renzo Piano Building Workshop sind technisch versiert und sorgfältig bis ins Detail geplant, gleichzeitig jedoch mit Bedacht auf den Menschen entworfen und reagieren gezielt auf den städtebaulichen Kontext. Diese Monografie stellt zwölf Gebäude des vielseitigen Werks von Renzo Piano zusammen, die in der Zeitschrift Detail veröffentlicht wurden. Die Projekte sind mit Fotos, Plänen und Texten dokumentiert. Zusätzlich geben Detailschnitte im Maßstab 1:20 Aufschluss über ihre baukonstruktiven Aspekte.
Die Redaktion

Paris gained an architectural attraction when the Centre Pompidou opened in January 1977. With its radical architecture, the unusual cultural machine quickly became a crowd-puller, and it has remained so until today. The design by then little-experienced architects Renzo Piano and Richard Rogers was to make history. Many other buildings developed by Renzo Piano since the Beaubourg competition also set architectural benchmarks. Born in Genoa, he founded his architectural firm Renzo Piano Building Workshop (RPBW) in 1981. Its Paris, Genoa and New York offices went on to plan world-famous museums and office towers, auditoriums and parliamentary buildings in many countries and on several continents. One of the Renzo Piano Building Workshop trademarks is the skilful interplay of functional, technical and aesthetic aspects. The fact that the architectural language is never repeated but always reinvented and transformed is another characteristic distinguishing Renzo Piano's work. Known for his mastery of construction technology, the Pritzker Prize laureate and his team, which consists of eleven partners today, use a wide variety of materials, shapes and construction methods that are heavily inspired by the location and their respective function. Renzo Piano Building Workshop buildings are technically well-crafted and carefully planned down to the last detail but always designed with the human being in mind and specifically react to the urban context. This monograph compiles twelve buildings from Renzo Piano's versatile oeuvre that were published in the Detail magazine. The projects are documented with pictures, plans and text. In addition, detailed cross sections on a scale of 1:20 provide information about constructional aspects.
The Editors

Vorwort / Preface

Projekte / Projects

The Whitney Museum of American Art at Gansevoort, New York, NY, USA

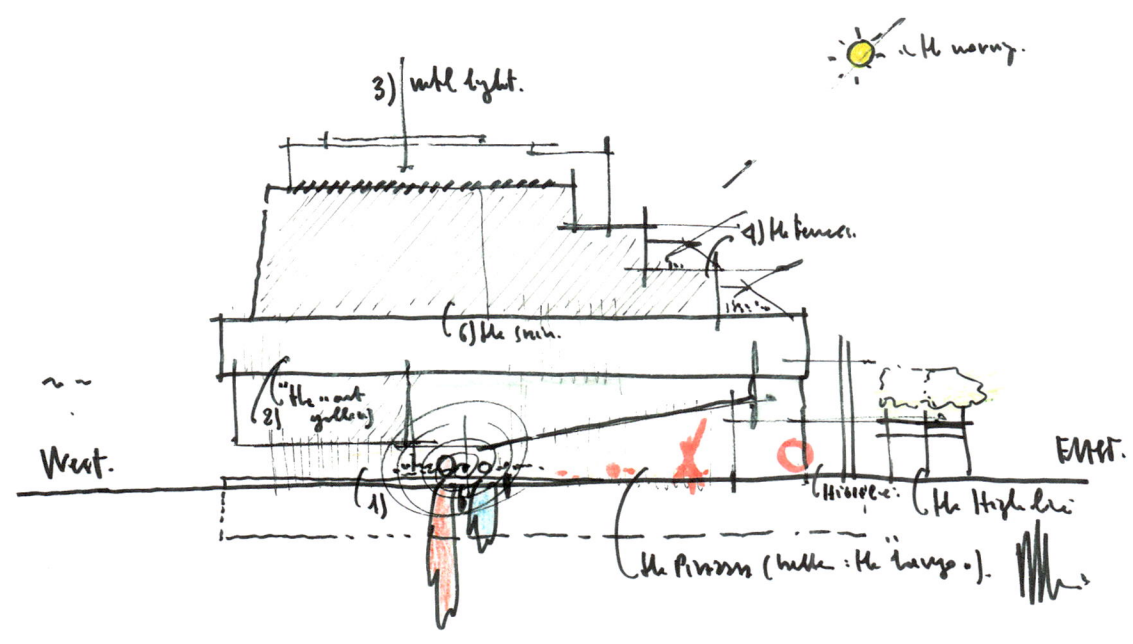

Entwurfsskizze von Renzo Piano / Design sketch by Renzo Piano

Hochwasserschutz für das Whitney Museum in New York City

Im Juli 2004 wurde Renzo Piano Building Workshop mit der Planung für das neue Whitney Museum of American Art in New York City beauftragt. Das ausgewählte Grundstück liegt im Meatpacking District am Ende der Highline in Downtown Manhattan. Das neue Museum löst den an der Upper East Side gelegenen Bau von Marcel Breuer aus dem Jahr 1966 ab. Mit seinen großen lichten Galerien bietet das Gebäude ein beeindruckendes Panorama über den Hudson River und Manhattan. Der gläserne Eingangsbereich, der sich zur Gansevoort Street hin orientiert, ist vom Straßenniveau abgehoben und über eine großzügige Außentreppe erreichbar.

In der Nacht des 29. Oktobers 2012 verursachte der Hurrikan Sandy eine enorme Flutwelle, die über das sich im Bau befindende Museum und ganz New York hereinbrach. Die Sturmflut mit einer Höhe von 2,94 m übertraf im Bereich der Baustelle den zugrunde liegenden Bemessungswasserstand der FEMA (Federal Emergency Management Agency) für ein 100-jährliches Hochwasserereignis und überschwemmte den Rohbau. Das Museum war mit einem wasserdichten Sockel bis + 3,05 m geplant, über dem sich der offene und transparente Eingangsbereich mit seinem großen Vorplatz, dem Largo, anschloss. Nun zeigte sich, dass diese Maßnahme für das Museum mit seiner unschätzbar wertvollen Kunstsammlung nicht ausreichen würde.

Der Bau des Museums war jedoch bereits so weit fortgeschritten, dass eine umfassende Neuplanung nicht mehr möglich war. Es stellte sich zum einen die Frage, bis zu welchem Wasserstand ein Flutschutz erforderlich ist, da die alten Bemessungswerte augenscheinlich nicht ausreichen und neue erst durch die FEMA ermittelt werden mussten, und zum anderen wie dieser Flutschutz in den Entwurf des Architekten integriert werden konnte. Ziel war es, einen im Alltag unsichtbaren Hochwasserschutz zu entwerfen. Mit dieser Aufgabe wurden WTM Engineers International beauftragt, unterstützt durch das Franzius Institut für Wasserbau, Ästuar- und Küsteningenieurwesen in Hannover.

Flood Mitigation for the Whitney Museum in New York City

In July 2004, Renzo Piano Building Workshop was commissioned to design the new Whitney Museum of American Art in New York City. The selected site is located in the Meatpacking District at the end of the High Line in Manhattan. The new museum serves as replacement for Marcel Breuer's 1966 building in the Upper East Side. With its ample and bright galleries, it offers an impressive panorama of Manhattan and across the Hudson River. Generous exterior stairs lead to an elevated plaza and the glazed entrance area facing Gansevoort Street.

However, the designers couldn't foresee the flood disaster that impacted the museum construction site as well as the entire city of New York during the night of 29 October 2012. Originating in the Caribbean Sea, Hurricane Sandy steered directly towards New York City, accompanied by a huge storm surge. The surge reached a height of 2.94 m and surpassed the base flood level in the area of the construction site that FEMA (Federal Emergency Management Agency) had determined for a 100-year flood event. The museum had been designed with a waterproof base up to 3.05 m. An open and transparent entrance area with a large plaza, the Largo, was situated above it. Yet now it became apparent that this measure offered insufficient flood protection for the museum.

The construction of the new museum had already proceeded so far that a comprehensive redesign was no longer possible. The old base flood levels were obviously no longer sufficient and new levels had yet to be determined by FEMA, so a decision had to be made on how to fit a sufficient flood protection system into the architect's design. The aim was to develop a type of flood mitigation that was invisible during everyday operation. WTM Engineers International in collaboration with the Franzius Institut for Hydraulic, Estuarine and Coastal Engineering in Hanover, Germany, were commissioned for this task.

Bestimmung des Schutzziels

Um Sturmflutstände unterschiedlicher Eintrittswahrscheinlichkeit zu berechnen, wurden umfangreiche Datensätze berücksichtigt, wie z. B. die Ganglinien des Pegels im Battery-Park an der Südspitze Manhattans über einen Zeitraum von über 90 Jahren und Simulationsergebnisse möglicher Hurrikanereignisse der NOAA (National Oceanic and Atmospheric Administration). Dabei kamen verschiedene Rechenansätze zum Einsatz (Einzelwert-, Vergleichswert- und Extremwertverfahren), wie sie auch bei der Ermittlung von möglichen Hochwasserständen an den deutschen Küsten eingesetzt werden. Zusätzlich berücksichtigten WTM Engineers die maximalen Wasserstände von Sturmfluten der Hurrikankategorien 1 bis 4. Diesen Sturmflutständen wurde die Widerstandsfähigkeit des Bauwerks gegenübergestellt. Neben der Erfordernis, Öffnungen auch oberhalb des bisher angesetzten Bemessungswasserstands zu schließen, musste auch der vorhandene Kellerkasten höherem Wasserdruck und Auftrieb widerstehen. Da der Rohbau bereits fertig gestellt war, waren höhere Bemessungswasserstände nur unter Ausnutzung von Systemreserven und lokalen Ertüchtigungsmaßnahmen bis zu einem Grenzwert wirtschaftlich.

Das Ergebnis dieser Optimierung war eine Lösung, die sowohl 250-jährliche Hochwasserereignisse als auch Sturmfluten einschließlich eines Hurrikans der Kategorie 2 sicher abdeckt. Damit liegt das Schutzniveau des neuen Whitney Museums of American Art 1,22 m höher, als es die überarbeiteten neuen Bemessungswasserstände der FEMA für ein 100-jährliches Ereignis mit 3,66 m vorsehen.

Schutzmaßnahmen

Nach Festlegung des Schutzziels und der Analyse des bestehenden Rohbaus entwickelten WTM Engineers Maßnahmen, die das Bauwerk auf das höhere Schutzniveau bringen sollten:
1. Wasserdichte und druckstabile Ausbildung und Erhöhung von Außenwänden, Verstärkung der Kellerdecke
2. Anordnung von Flutschutztoren und -türen vor den Öffnungen unterhalb der neuen Hochwasserschutzlinie
3. Dammbalkensystem zum Schutz des Vorplatzes und der offenen Eingangsbereiche im Erdgeschoss
4. Verschließbarkeit aller weiteren Öffnungen (Lüftung, Medien) unterhalb des neuen Schutzniveaus

Außenwände

Oberhalb des alten Bemessungswasserstands war das Gebäude als Stahlskelett mit vorgehängten, großformatigen Betonfertigteilplatten oder Blechfassadenelementen ausgebildet – eine Konstruktionsweise, die keine Anforderungen an die Wasserdichtigkeit erfüllte.

Aus diesem Grund musste nachträglich hinter die Fassadenplatten und die Dämmung eine Dichtung und eine druckstabile Stahlbetonwand eingezogen werden. Infolge der begrenzten Zugänglichkeit konnte diese Wand teilweise nur in kleinen Abschnitten erstellt werden. An den Übergängen zu den Flutschutztoren konnten die Wände nach innen verzogen und direkt mit den Rahmen der Tore

Verschluss Flutschutztor /
Closing mechanism, flood gate

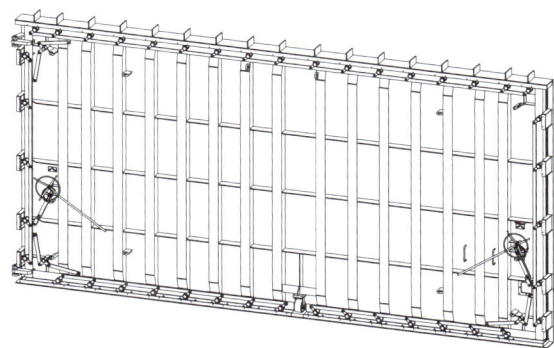

Isometrie Flutschutztür /
Isometric drawing, flood gate

Determining mitigation goals

In order to calculate different storm surge heights, extensive data sets were taken into consideration. These included the hydrographic gauge in Battery Park along Manhattan's southern tip across 90 years, as well as simulation results for possible hurricane events according to the NOAA (National Oceanic and Atmospheric Administration). Different calculation approaches were employed that are typically used to identify possible flood levels in German coastal regions. In addition, the maximum water levels of storm surges of Category 1 to 4 hurricanes were taken into account. These storm surge levels were used to test the resilience of the building. Aside from the requirement of closing openings located above the previously known base flood level, the existing basement structure needed to be able to resist higher levels of water pressure and hydrostatic uplift. Since the shell had already been completed, adapting to higher base flood levels was economically feasible only to a limited degree and only by employing all system reserves and local reinforcing measures.

The result of this optimisation is a solution that offers flood proofing for 250-year flood events as well as storm surges of Category 2 hurricanes. The mitigation measures in the new Whitney Museum of American Art add 1.22 m to FEMA's revised new base flood level of 3.66 m for a 100-year flood event.

Mitigative measures

After determining the mitigation goals and analysing the existing shell construction, measures were developed to provide the building with the envisioned higher level of flood proofing:
1. Water- and pressure-proof design, raised exterior walls, reinforcement of basement ceiling slab
2. Arrangement of flood gates and doors for openings beneath the new mitigation level
3. Stop-log system for flood proofing of plaza and open ground floor entrance area
4. Closing capacity of all other openings (ventilation, media) beneath the new mitigation level

Exterior walls

Above the previous base flood elevation the building was designed as a steel frame with a curtain wall consisting of large prefabricated concrete panels and sheet metal elements. This construction type didn't meet any waterproofing requirements. It therefore required retrofitting with a sealant layer and a pressure-proof reinforced concrete wall located behind the facade panels and the insulation. Along the transitions to the flood gates the walls were modified to directly connect to the gate frames. Ducts were avoided as far as possible by redistributing them or waterproofing them.

Flood gates and doors

Along the western facade, entrances and loading areas were provided with lockable flood doors and gates that resist not only water pressure but also impact from floating debris. A clear width of 8,50 m was required for loading areas

Nachträglich einzuziehende Wand mit Frischbetonverbundabdichtung und Bewehrung /
Retrofit wall, concrete waterproofing built-up system, reinforcement

verbunden werden. Leitungsdurchdringungen wurden, wenn möglich, durch Verlegung vermieden oder wasserdicht ausgeführt.

Flutschutztore und -türen
An der Westfassade planten WTM Engineers die Zugänge und den Anlieferungsbereich mit verschließbaren Flutschutztüren und -toren, die neben dem Wasserdruck auch Treibgutstoß widerstehen. Die Anlieferung benötigt eine lichte Breite von 8,5 m, die Zugänge von ca. 2,5 m.

Infolge des Baufortschritts und des gestalterischen Anspruchs konnten weder sichtbare Tore noch Schiebe- und Hubtore realisiert werden. Die einzig umsetzbare Lösung waren nach innen aufschlagende Tore und Türen, die sich im offenen Zustand in die Wandverkleidung der Innenwand integrieren lassen. Damit schlagen sie jedoch gegen den Wasserdruck zu und bedingen daher einen Verriegelungsmechanismus, der die Dichtung fest in den Rahmen drücken muss. Umgesetzt wurde diese Lösung durch die in New York ansässige Firma Walz + Krenzer, die über umfangreiche Erfahrung bei diesen Konstruktionen aus dem Schiffbau verfügt. In enger Zusammenarbeit zwischen Planern, Rohbaufirma und Torlieferant war es möglich, die Tore so präzise einzubauen, dass deren Verschluss auch bei manueller Bedienung gewährleistet ist. Auch das 6 t schwere Flutschutztor vor dem Anlieferungsbereich schließt und verriegelt sich ohne Motorunterstützung.

Beim Schließen läuft das Tor mit einer einzelnen Stahlrolle auf einem im Boden eingelassenen Stahlband. Dieses Stahlband ist mit Kopfbolzen im Aufbeton verankert und musste beim Betoniervorgang mit hoher Präzision waagrecht eingebaut werden. Das Tor ist so konstruiert, dass es im Gleichgewicht auf der Rolle liegt und keine Vertikallasten in die Angeln einbringt. Seine Verriegelung erfolgt durch ein Drehrad mit Zahnradübersetzung, sodass die Riegel die Dichtung in den Rahmen drücken.

Das Drehrad setzt eine Mechanik in Bewegung, die alle angeschlossenen Riegel zeitgleich schließt. Das große Flutschutztor ist in zwei Bereiche geteilt, die separat über zwei Drehräder verriegelt werden können.

Dammbalkensystem
Der Vorplatz und der Eingangsbereich müssen höchsten ästhetischen Anforderungen genügen. Sowohl die Wandbereiche, an denen das Dammbalkensystem anschließt, als auch die Bodenausbildung des Vorplatzes sollten nicht durch Anschlusskonstruktionen beeinträchtigt werden.

Mögliche Anschlusspunkte stellten Schraubmuffen in den Sichtbetonfassadenelementen dar, die ohnehin für deren Befestigung am Bauwerk vorhanden waren. Den Wandanschluss konnten wir durch Endpfosten mit Dichtungsband ausbilden, die sich in die vorhandenen Anschlusspunkte der Sichtbetonfassade verschrauben ließen. Die betroffenen Fassadenelemente wurden auf ihrer Rückseite statisch ertüchtigt und kraftschlüssig sowie wasserdicht an die neuen Stahlbetonwände angeschlossen, um Hinterläufigkeiten auszuschließen. Dadurch konnte jegliche Änderung der geplanten Gestaltung der Wandansichten vermieden werden.

Das Dammbalkensystem planten WTM Engineers klassisch mit stranggepressten Aluminiumpfosten und Aluminiumbalken. Wegen des hohen Wasserdrucks und des zu berücksichtigenden Treibgutstoßes erhielten die Pfosten eine Absteifung nach hinten.

Die anfangs vorgesehenen Einbauplatten im Boden des Vorplatzes für die Pfosten des Dammbalkensystems ließen sich nicht mit dem ästhetischen Anspruch an die Freifläche vereinbaren. In einem langwierigen und aufwendigen Abstimmungsprozess zwischen Planern, Architekten, Statikern und ausführender Firma wurden die Einbauplatten so modifiziert, dass nur noch verschließbare Hülsen in der Betonoberfläche sichtbar waren. Diese können die Verschraubung der Pfosten für das Einspannmoment und die Querkraft aufnehmen. Durch den oberflächenbündigen Einbau der Verschlusskappen bleiben die Anschlusspunkte des Dammbalkensystems schließlich kaum wahrnehmbar. Der Aufbau des kompletten Dammbalkensystems erfolgt innerhalb von sechs Stunden, was bei einer Alarmierungszeit von über drei Tagen eine zuverlässige Umsetzung sicherstellt.

Karl Morgen, Beratender Ingenieur und Prüfingenieur, ist seit 1988 als Geschäftsführer von WTM Engineers verantwortlich für Projekte im In- und Ausland mit Schwerpunkten bei der Tragwerksplanung von Hochbauprojekten sowie der Gesamt- und Fachplanung im Wasserbau und Ingenieurbau.

Dipl.-Ing. Friedrich Hilgenstock ist seit 1995 bei WTM Engineers und seit 2010 als Prokurist bei WTM Engineers International verantwortlich für internationale Projekte.

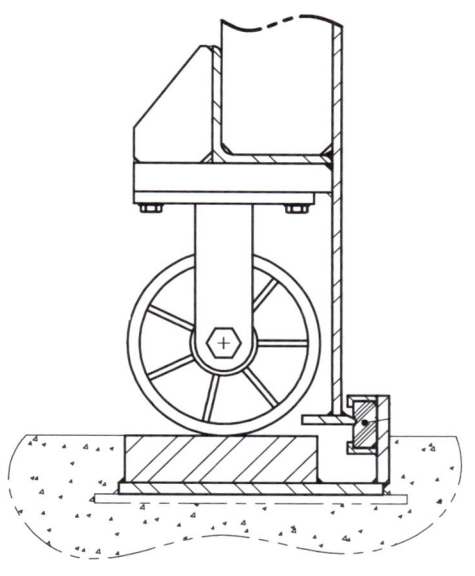

Seitenansicht Stahlrolle /
Elevation, steel wheel

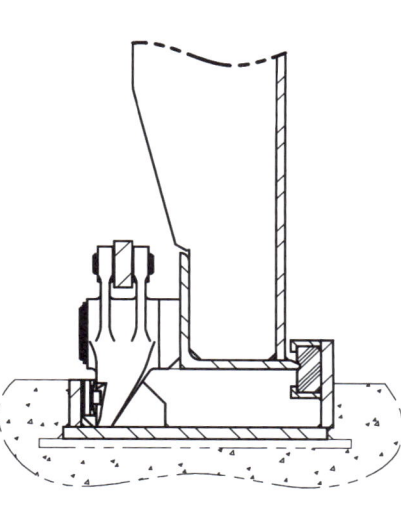

Detail Verriegelung /
Detail, lock mechanism

Mechanik für Anschluss
Zahnrad an Riegel /
Mechanism, gear wheel
connection to latches

Detail Laufrolle
aus Stahl /
Detail, steel wheel

and roughly 2,50 m for doors. The design called for near-invisible gates and doors that open inward and integrate into the wall cladding of the interior wall while open. This meant that the gates and doors would have to be closed facing the water pressure. As result, a locking mechanism was required that would tightly press the gasket into the frame. This solution was implemented by the New York-based firm Walz + Krenzer. In close cooperation with the designers and contractors, it was possible to integrate the gates in such a precise manner as to guarantee that they could be locked even when operated manually. The gate runs on a single steel wheel led by a steel band integrated into the floor. Locking is enabled by a handwheel with gear transmission and by latches that press the gasket against the frame simultaneously.

Stop log gate system

The plaza and the entrance area had to meet highest aesthetic requirements, connections were to remain near-invisible, and changes to the design were avoided. Bolt sockets serve as connection points that were already in place in the exposed concrete facades. A wall connection with an end post and a sealing strip was created and bolted to the existing connection points of the exposed concrete facade. Related facade areas were strengthened along their reverse side and feature load-bearing and waterproof connections to the new reinforced concrete walls. The stop log system is comprised of a typical construction with extruded aluminium posts and aluminium logs. Due to the expected high water pressure and possible impact from floating debris, the posts received additional bracing on their reverse side. The initially planned imbeds could not be reconciled with the design intent. Setting up the complete stop log system requires 6 hours.

Karl Morgen is a consulting and test engineer, and has been managing director of WTM Engineers since 1988. He is responsible for projects in Germany and abroad, focusing on structural design of building construction projects as well as overall and technical planning in hydraulic engineering and civil engineering.

Friedrich Hilgenstock joined WTM Engineers in 1995 as a graduate engineer (Dipl.-Ing.). He has been responsible for international projects as authorised representative of WTM Engineers International since 2010.

New York, 2007–2015

Standard- und Eck-
elemente Dammbalken-
system /
Standard and corner elements, stop log system

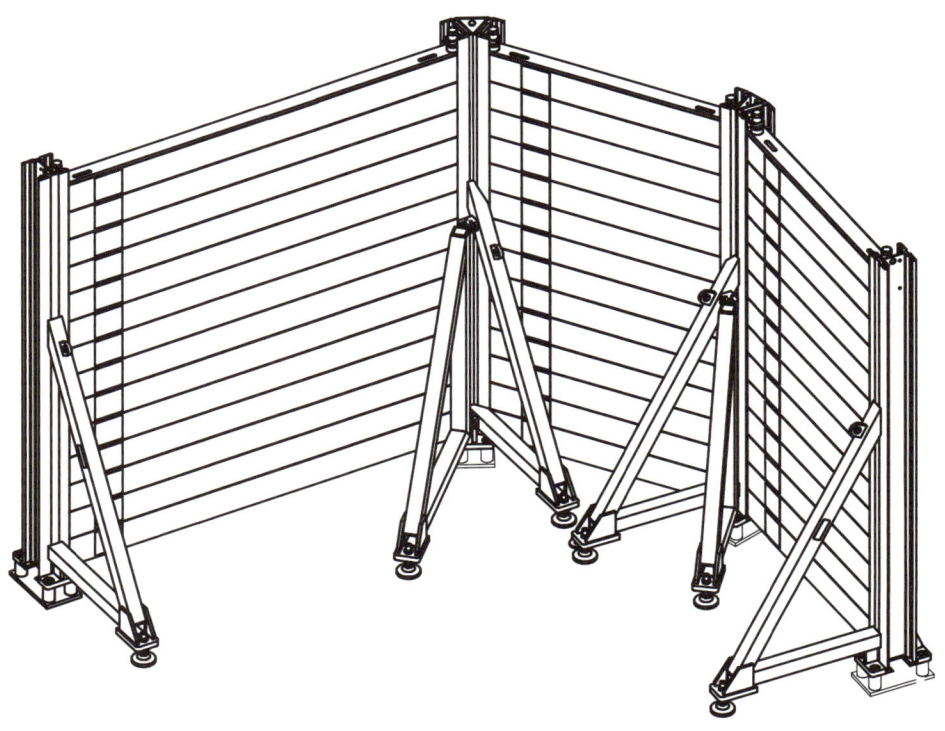

Anschlusspunkte
Endpfosten an
Betonwand /
Connections, end post to
concrete wall

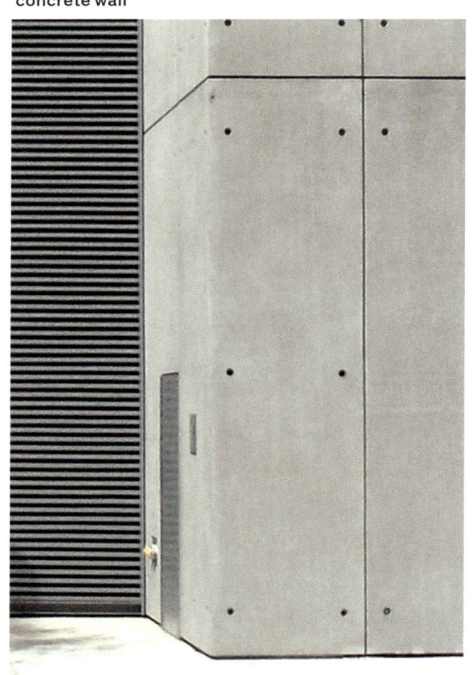

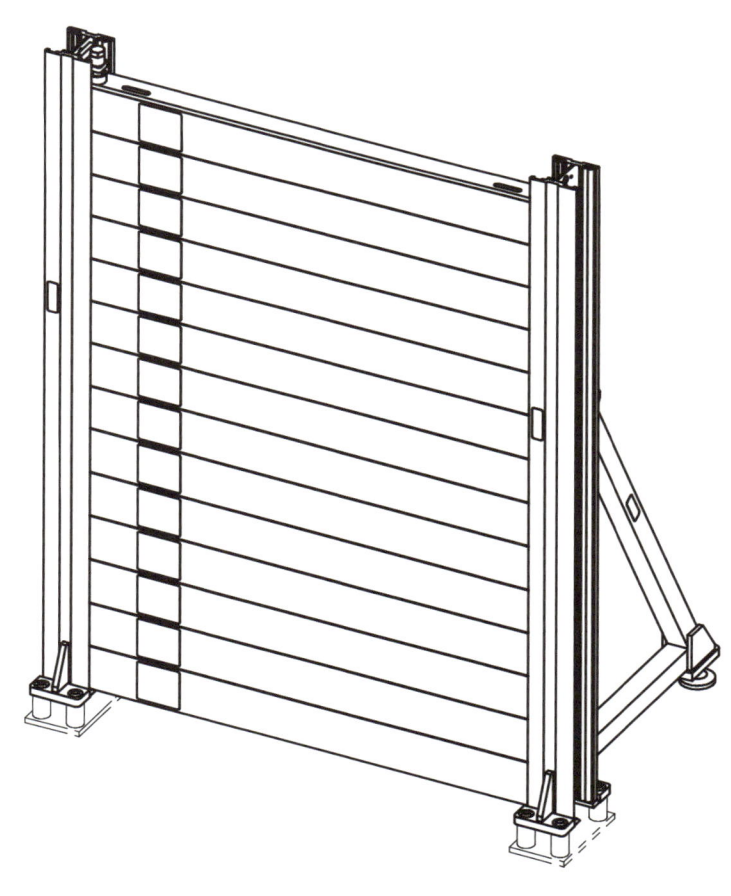

016 The Whitney Museum of American Art

Schnitt durch Stützenfuß und Fußplatte /
Section, post, connector plate

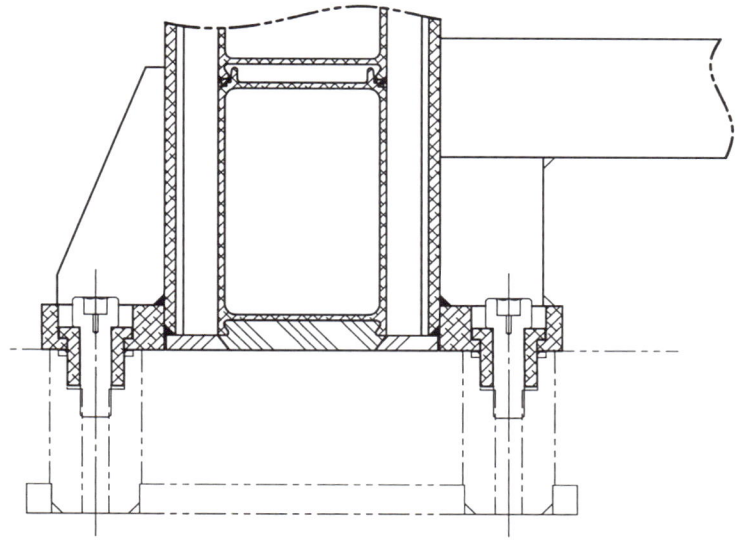

Fertig aufgebautes Dammbalkensystem /
Completed stop log system

Dammbalken vor der Montage /
Stop logs before assembly

New York, 2007–2015

The Whitney Museum of American Art

New York, 2007–2015

Intesa Sanpaolo Office Building, Turin, IT

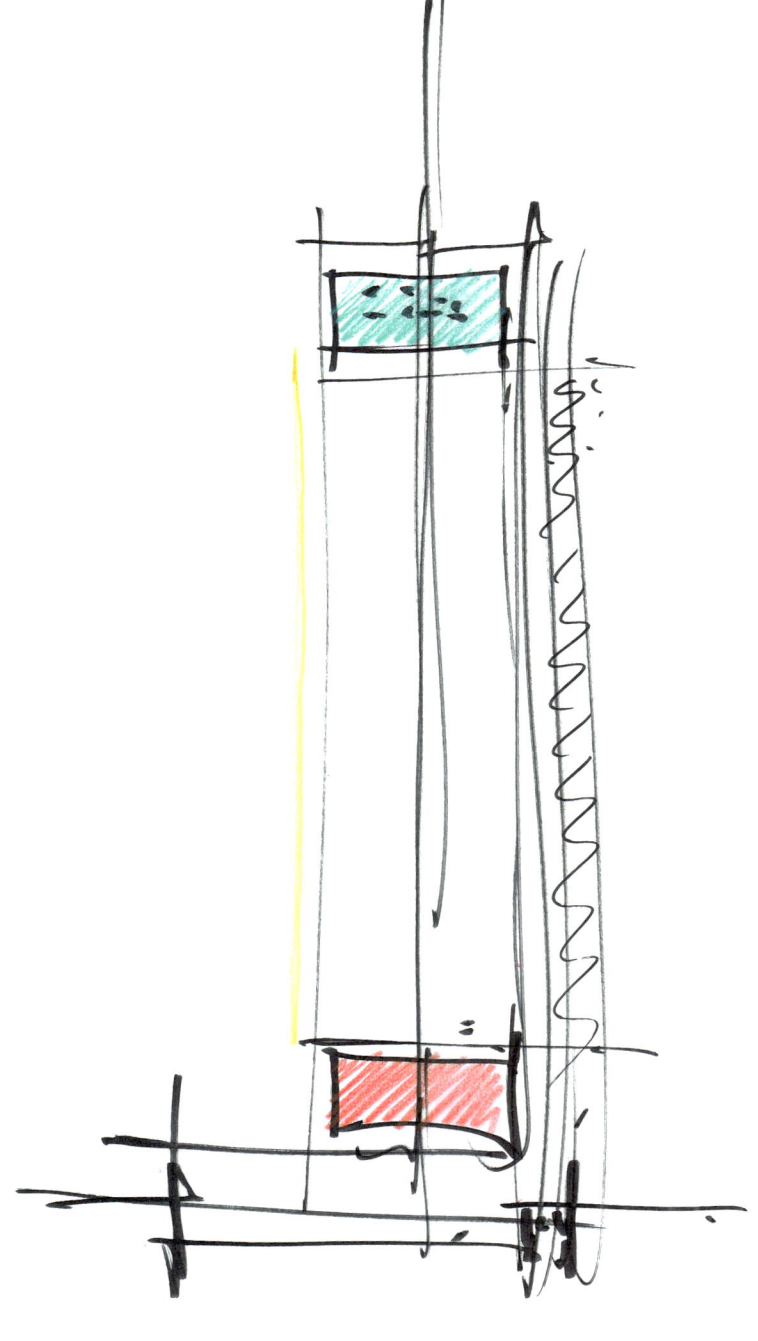

Skizze des Architekten zum grundlegenden Konzept des Hochhauses / The architect's sketch describing the concept of the tower

Hochhaus in Turin

Der transparente Solitär setzt mit 166 m Höhe einen klaren Akzent im Turiner Stadtbild, nur knapp überragt von der 1,50 m höheren Spitze des Wahrzeichens »Mole Antelliana«, dem nationalen Filmmuseum. Sein strahlend weißes Tragwerk – sich verjüngende, über diagonale Zug- und horizontale Druckstäbe verbundene Pfeiler – schimmert als zentrales Gestaltungselement durch die gläserne Doppelfassade. Durch enge Verknüpfung mit dem öffentlichen Raum soll der neue Sitz einer der größten italienischen Banken Teil des täglichen Lebens der Stadtbewohner werden und verspricht damit mehr als ein Zurschaustellen monetärer Stärke des Bankenwesens.

Bewusst unter Nachhaltigkeitsaspekten geplant und mittlerweile mit LEED-Platin ausgezeichnet, ragt der markante Bau mitten aus dem neu gestalteten Nicola Grosa Park empor. Er ruht auf einem Fundament aus Parkflächen und Versorgungsräumen sowie einem Restaurant und einem Kindergarten mit Innenhof. Leicht abgesetzt schwebt über der Erdgeschosszone ein multifunktionales Auditorium, das für öffentliche Vorträge und Ausstellungen genutzt werden kann und über 350 Personen Platz bietet. Darüber erstrecken sich 27 Büroetagen mit nach Norden gerichteten Besprechungs- und Fortbildungsräumen. Ein aussteifender Erschließungskern aus Stahlbeton an der Nordseite und die außen liegenden Stahlpfeiler ermöglichen offene und flexible Bürogrundrisse, orientiert nach Westen und Osten mit großzügiger Belichtung über die filigrane Doppelfassade. Die Südfassade liefert durch integrierte Photovoltaikelemente einen wichtigen Beitrag zur Stromversorgung des Gebäudes – nur ein Baustein des umfassenden Energiekonzepts mit Nachtauskühlung und natürlicher Belüftung der Fassade sowie Grund- und Regenwassernutzung.

Das der Fassade vorgehängte, mit Kletterpflanzen begrünte Treppenhaus im Süden dient zudem wie ein Wintergarten der Filterung des Sonnenlichts und der direkten bürointernen Verbindung. Den Abschluss des Hochhauses bildet ein für jedermann frei zugänglicher Dachpavillon, inspiriert durch die viktorianischen Glaspaläste. Als mehrgeschossiger Dachgarten mit Restaurant und Ausstellungsbereich bietet dieser einen einzigartigen Ausblick auf die Stadt und das Turiner Alpenpanorama.

High-Rise Block in Turin

At 166 metres, the tower is a distinctive feature in the Turin cityscape in which its height is surpassed only just by the tip of the historic "Mole Antonelliana", the national film museum. Its brilliant white load-bearing structure – tapering columns connected by diagonal and horizontal ties – appears to shimmer as the defining design element through the glazed double facade. Through the close linking with the surrounding public open space, the new seat of one of Italy's biggest banks becomes part of the daily lives of the city's inhabitants, promising more than an extravagant expression of the banking industry's financial powers:

Designed specifically with sustainability in mind, and since awarded the LEED Platinum certificate, the striking structure rises from the centre of the newly designed Nicola Grosa Park and rests on a foundation of parking garages and utility services rooms, a restaurant and a children's nursery with an internal courtyard. Slightly offset and with seats for more than 350, a multifunctional auditorium that can be used for public presentations and exhibitions floats above the ground plane. Twenty-seven office floors with north-facing meeting and training rooms extend above this level. A reinforced concrete circulation core to the north end of the floor plate and external steel columns allow open, flexible office floor layouts oriented to the west and east with plenty of natural light entering the spaces through a slender-framed double facade. The integrated photovoltaic arrays on the southern facade make a significant contribution to the power required to operate the building – and are only one component of the comprehensive energy concept, with night cooling and natural ventilation through the facade, and the use of ground and rain water.

A glazed stair cantilevers from the south elevation and contains climbing plants. Like a conservatory, it filters sunlight and provides a direct connection between the office floors. The tower is topped by a roof pavilion, inspired by the great glasshouses of the 19th century and can be accessed by the general public. This multistorey roof garden with a restaurant and exhibition area offers a unique view of the Turin Alpine panorama.

Grundrisse,
Maßstab 1:1000 /
Floor plans,
scale 1:1,000

Schnitt,
Maßstab 1:1500 /
Section,
scale 1:1,500

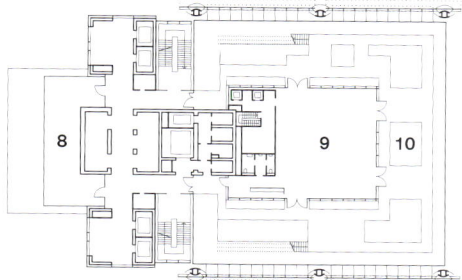

35. Obergeschoss /
35th floor

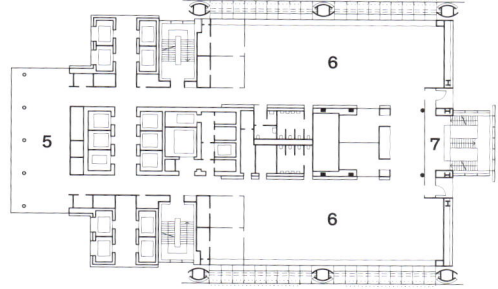

9. Obergeschoss /
9th floor

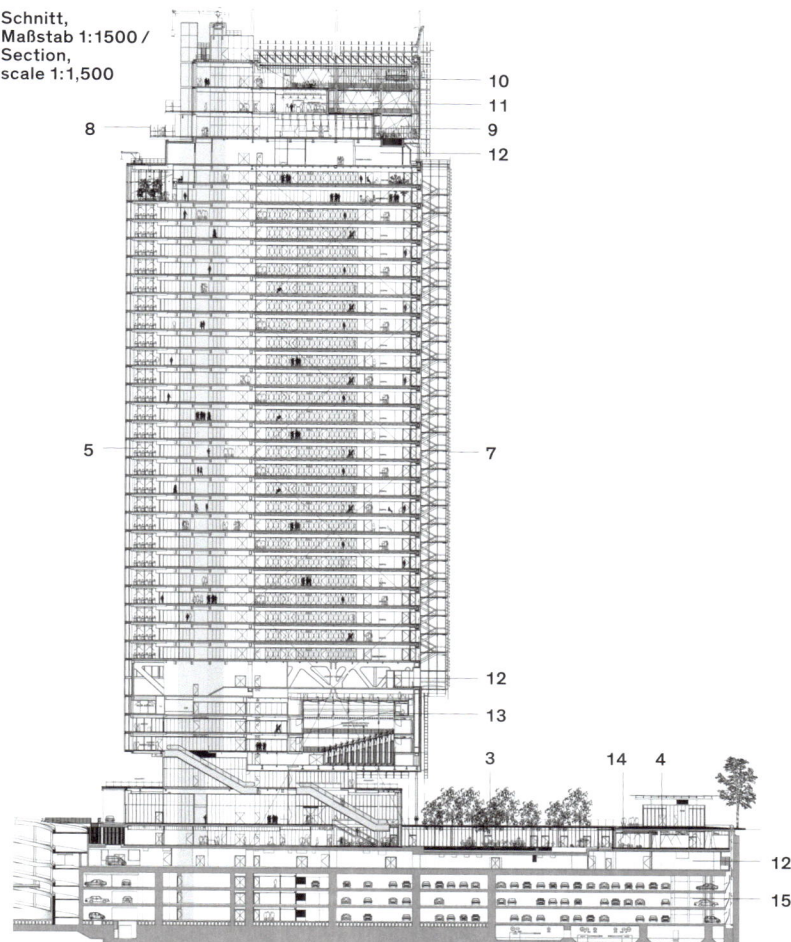

aa

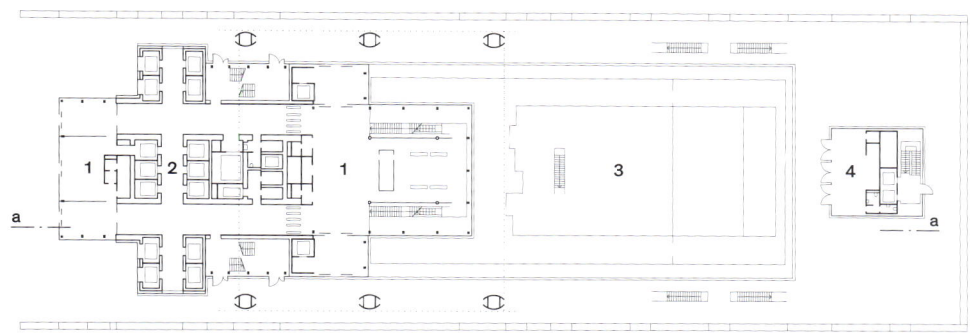

Erdgeschoss /
Ground floor

1	Empfang	Reception
2	Erschließungskern	Circulation core
3	Innenhof	Courtyard
4	Café	Café
5	Besprechungsraum	Meeting room
6	Büro	Office
7	Begrünte Südtreppe	Planted south stairwell
8	Dachterrasse	Roof terrace
9	Restaurant	Restaurant
10	Dachgarten	Roof garden
11	Ausstellung	Exhibition area
12	Technikebene	Building services floors
13	Auditorium	Auditorium
14	Kindergarten	Children's nursery
15	Parkgarage	Underground parking

Turin, 2006–2015

Text: Julia Ratcliffe
DETAIL structure
1/2016

Das Tragwerk des Hochhauses

Renzo Piano Building Workshop und Expedition Engineering entwarfen das Hochhaus in Turin im Jahr 2006 im Rahmen eines beschränkten internationalen Wettbewerbs. Ein zentrales Merkmal des Entwurfs war es, das Hauptvolumen des Turms von der Erdgeschosszone abzuheben und so eine Verbindung zwischen der Straße – dem Corso Inghilterra – und dem angrenzenden öffentlichen Park zu schaffen. Diese Entscheidung hatte großen Einfluss auf die Entwicklung der primären Tragkonstruktion. Das Planungsteam erarbeitete auf Grundlage dieses Konzepts eine komplexe Hierarchie der Tragwerkselemente und ihrer Ausbildung im Detail. Diese ist ablesbar von den massigen Stahlpfeilern bis zum filigranen Dachgarten. Jedes Element wurde anhand ästhetischer und funktionaler Kriterien in enger Zusammenarbeit aller beteiligten Planer genau geprüft, um in der Ausführung höchste technische Standards zu erfüllen. Die sichtbare Konstruktion wurde in der Regel aus Stahlblechelementen gefertigt, um eine durchgängige Architektursprache im gesamten Gebäude zu erreichen und die Entwicklung aufeinander abgestimmter Verbindungsdetails zu erleichtern.

An der Ost- und Westseite befindet sich jeweils ein mit Zugstäben verspanntes Außenskelett mit drei enormen Hauptpfeilern von je 16,5 m Achsabstand. Die sechs 175 m hohen Pfeiler verjüngen sich ab dem Stahlbetonfundament auf der Ebene 2 von 2800 × 1970

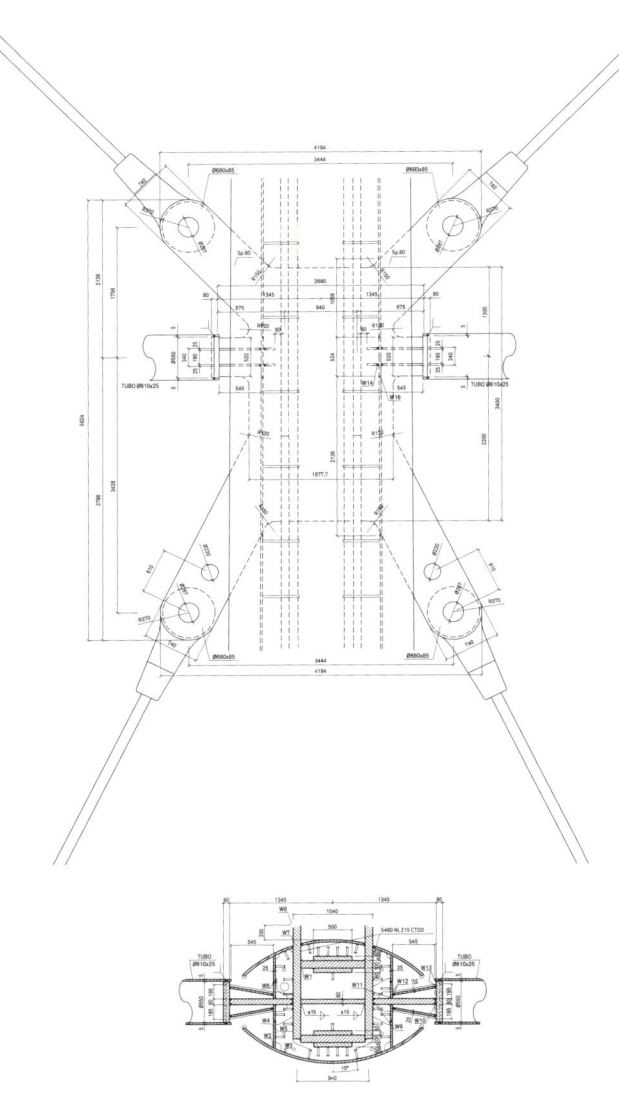

Anschlusspunkt der diagonalen Verspannungen an den mittleren Pfeiler, Maßstab 1:100 /
Connection of the diagonal struts at the central megacolumn, scale 1:100

026 Intesa Sanpaolo Office Building

Schematische Darstellung der Tragstruktur, Maßstab 1:1500 / Schematic of the primary structure, scale 1:1,500

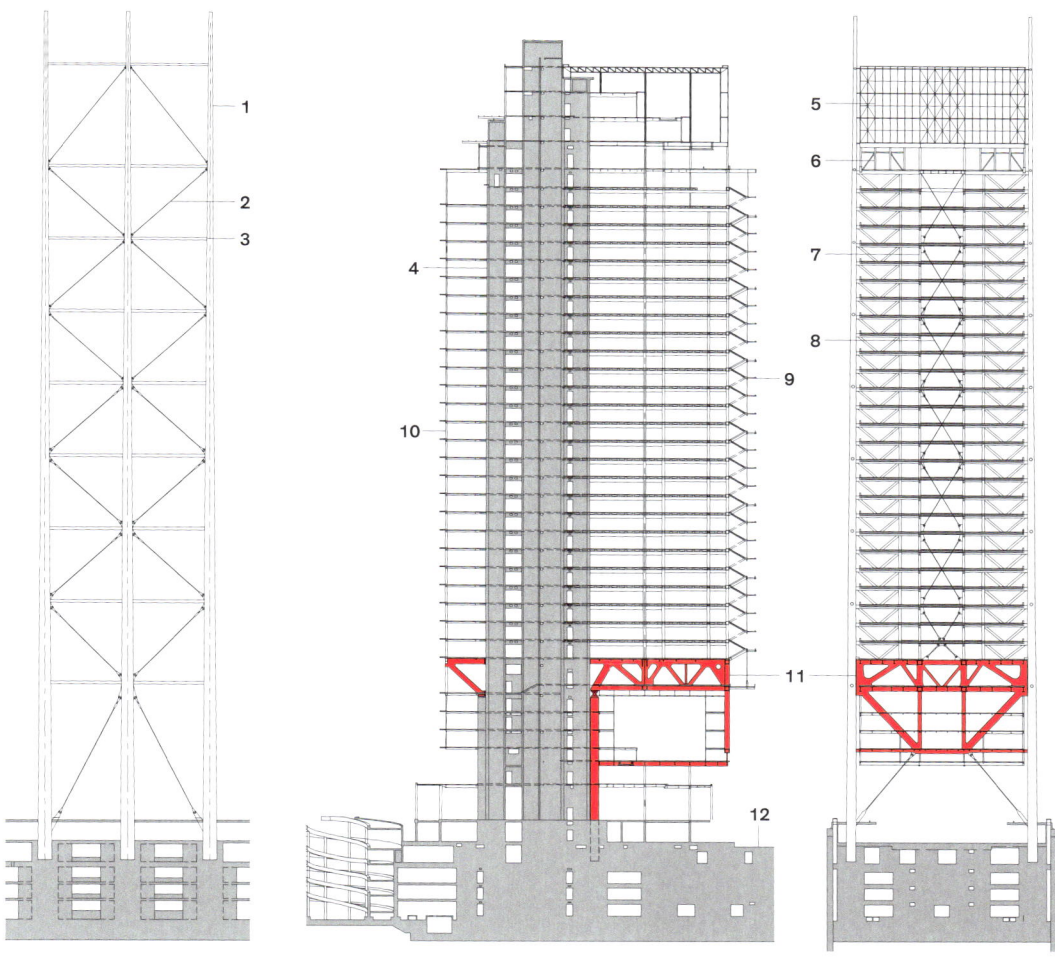

1	Hauptpfeiler	Megacolumn
2	Diagonale Verspannung der West- und Ostseiten	Diagonal bracing on west and east elevations
3	Horizontalstreben zur Lastabtragung der äußeren Hülle der Doppelfassade	Horizontal bracing struts supporting the double facade's outer skin
4	Stahlbetonkern zur Erschließung und Aufnahme der Quer- und Torsionskräfte	Reinforced concrete vertical circulation core
5	Dachpavillon aus filigranen Stahlprofilen	Glass roof pavilion
6	Fachwerkträger als Sockel für den Dachpavillon	Truss supporting the roof pavilion
7	Innen liegende Stützen	Internal columns
8	Diagonale Verspannung der Stützen an der Südseite	Diagonal bracing on the south elevation
9	Auskragendes Südtreppenhaus	Cantilevering south stairs
10	Auskragende Besprechungsräume im Norden	Meeting rooms on the north side supported on cantilever truss
11	Fachwerkträger zur Umlenkung der Geschosslasten auf die Pfeiler und den Kern	Transfer trusses spanning onto the megacolumns and core
12	Stahlbetonfundament	Reinforced concrete substructures

Text: Julia Ratcliffe
DETAIL structure
1/2016

The tower structure

The tower design was conceived in 2006 by Renzo Piano Building Workshop and Expedition Engineering in response to an invited international competition. A fundamental principle of the winning scheme was to lift the main volume of the tower above the ground to create a connection between the main street – Corso Inghilterra – and the adjacent public park. This feature was a major influence on the development of the tower's primary load-bearing frame and stability system. On the basis of this concept, the design team developed a complex hierarchy of structural elements and detailing. This is legible from the massive megacolumns to the filigree of the rooftop glasshouse. Each element was carefully developed and tested against aesthetic and functional criteria with the close collaboration of all the designers to ensure the details could be realised to the highest technical standards. The exposed steelwork framing was formed from steel plate for consistency of architectural language throughout the building and to assist with development of complementary connection detailing.

The east and west elevations feature a braced exoskeleton with three megacolumns spaced 16.50 m apart on each side. The six 175 m high columns taper from 2,800 × 1,970 mm at the second basement level, where they are supported on the reinforced concrete substructure, to 700 × 600 mm at the top of the tower. In 2007, the engineers

Turin, 2006–2015

Intesa Sanpaolo Office Building

auf 700 × 600 mm an der Spitze. Die Planer arbeiteten dafür bereits im Jahr 2007 mit einem Vorläufer der Software Grasshopper für parametrische Konstruktionen, um die Geometrie der Pfeiler aus einfach gekrümmten Blechen zu formen. Horizontale Aussteifungen zwischen den Hauptpfeilern in jedem vierten Geschoss tragen zugleich die äußere Hülle der Doppelfassade. Die Tragkonstruktion muss sowohl seitlichen Windkräften, seismischen Einwirkungen sowie ständigen Kippmomenten durch die auskragenden Besprechungsräume an der Nordseite standhalten. Ursprünglich war angedacht, den zentralen Erschließungskern ebenfalls als reine Stahlkonstruktion zu realisieren, um die Herstellung und den Bauablauf zu vereinfachen. Ein Anstieg der Stahlpreise während der mehrjährigen Entwurfsphase führte dazu, die Planungen hin zu einem Stahlbetonkern zu ändern. Dies hat den zusätzlichen Vorteil, dass die Biegesteifigkeit verbessert und damit auch für den Nutzer wahrnehmbare Schwingungen – ausgelöst durch seitliche Windkräfte – verhindert werden konnten. Ein massereicher Schwingungstilger, der sowohl höhere Kosten bedeutet, als auch räumliche Auswirkungen gehabt hätte, war dadurch obsolet geworden.

Eine der großen Herausforderungen dieser vergleichsweise späten Änderung war es, Modelle zu entwickeln für das langfristige unterschiedliche Kriech- und Schwindverhalten des Kerns relativ zur umfassenden verspannten Stahlkonstruktion. Zudem mussten

Finite-Elemente-Studie zur maximalen Zugbelastung des Fachwerkträgers / Finite element analysis of the two-way transfer trusses

Oasys-GSA-Analysemodell zur Knickbeanspruchung des Hochhauses / Oasys GSA model for tower buckling analysis

used a forerunner of the Grasshopper software package for the parametric design to arrive at the geometry of the columns based on single curvature plates. Horizontal bracing struts between the megacolumns at every fourth storey support the outer skin of the double facade. The structure has to withstand lateral wind forces, seismic effects and permanent overturning moments from the cantilevering conference rooms on its northern side. The central circulation core was originally intended to be of steel to simplify procurement and construction sequencing. An increase in steel prices during the design period was a prime driver in the decision to change to a reinforced concrete core. This change had the added benefit of increasing the lateral and torsional stiffness and damping, which led to a reduction in the perceptible accelerations due to lateral wind forces. This meant that there was no longer a need for provision to be made for a high-level tuned mass vibration damper with its associated high cost and space requirements. A major challenge of this comparatively late change was developing models to calculate long-term differential shrinkage and creep of the core relative to the surrounding braced steel structure, and designing modified connection details and a construction sequence to accommodate these movements.

The office floor slabs are constructed from high-quality exposed prestressed, precast concrete channel units with an in-situ concrete topping slab to form 230 mm deep internal

Turin, 2006–2015

die Verbindungsdetails sowie der Bauablauf den Änderungen und diesen Bewegungen angepasst werden.

Die Deckenplatten der Bürogeschosse – vorgespannte Stahlbetonhalbfertigteile – lagern auf Stahlträgern, die geschossweise an den äußeren Pfeilern und innen liegenden Stützen befestigt sind. Über die Doppelfassade wird Außenluft mithilfe des Kamineffekts in 230 mm hohen Deckenkanälen von Ost nach West geleitet und zur Nachtauskühlung in den Sommermonaten genutzt. Die Deckenuntersichten sind als Sichtbetonoberflächen mit integrierten Leuchten ausgeführt. Abgehängte Flächenheizkörper werden mit einer Grundwasserwärmepumpe betrieben.

Der lastenumlenkende Fachwerkträger

Die Lastabtragung aus den 27 Büroetagen über dem Auditorium machte eine in zwei Richtungen spannende, 2350 t schwere Fachwerkkonstruktion zur Umlenkung der Lasten notwendig. Diese spannt bis zu 30 m zwischen den sechs Hauptpfeilern und dem aussteifenden Kern. Der 6,5 m hohe Träger besteht aus vorgefertigten rechteckigen Querschnitten aus hochfesten, bis zu 120 mm dicken Stahlplatten und befindet sich auf der Technikebene im sechsten Obergeschoss. An der Südfassade hat er eine Höhe von bis zu 20 m und wird von der Rückwand des Auditoriums verdeckt. Zunächst auf Erdgeschossniveau zusammengesetzt, wurde der Fachwerkträger Anfang 2012 mit einem Litzenhubsystem angehoben, das auf dem bereits fertigen Teil der Hauptpfeiler installiert war, und anschließend in Position verschweißt.

Für den Fachwerkträger, der die Hauptlasten auf die Pfeiler überträgt, arbeiteten die Planungsbüros eng mit den Baufirmen, Stahlbauern und Schweißspezialisten zusammen, um die Verbindungen aus Schmiedeteilen an den Schnittstellen des in zwei Richtungen spannenden Trägers zu entwickeln. Im Entwurfsprozess nutzte Expedition Engineering die Software Rhino für 3D-Modelle und zur Kommunikation der Tragwerksprinzipien. Exportierte Geometrien aus diesen Modellen bildeten die Grundlage für die ersten Simulationen und wurden schließlich in die Detailplanung und die Gesamtanalysemodelle einbezogen. Abschließend wurde eine Serie von Finite-Elemente-Teilmodellen verwendet, um das Verhalten kritischer Bauteile zu beurteilen. So konnten Belastungskonzentrationen lokalisiert werden – was besonders bei den Schnittpunkten des großen Fachwerkträgers relevant war.

Krönender Dachabschluss: der »Serra«

Der natürlich belüftete Dachpavillon aus Glas, italienisch »Serra«, umhüllt einen öffentlichen, ganzjährigen Garten mit Blick über die Stadt bis zu den Alpen. Er krönt den Turm und reicht über einem 30 × 30 m großen quadratischen Grundriss über drei Geschosse 15 m in die Höhe. Die Konstruktion besteht aus filigranen, verschweißten Stahlstützen und -trägern mit Zugstabelementen. Inspiriert von Paxtons Kristallpalast des 19. Jahrhunderts wurde er von Anfang an als ein Zusammenspiel von leichten Teilen auf einem regelmäßigen Grundrissraster von 1,5 m konzipiert. In der weiteren Ausarbeitung entstand dann ein Systembausatz aus Standardelementen und Verbindungsdetails.

Die Leichtigkeit der Elemente war der architektonische Anspruch: Die umlaufenden, äußeren Stützen sind nicht mehr als 150 mm tief. Horizontale Auskreuzungen der umlaufenden Galerien und des Dachrands stabilisieren die Hüllflächen in Querrichtung. Über vorgespannte hochfeste Stahlstabauskreuzungen der äußeren Fassadenebene werden die Windlasten und die Horizontallasten aus den Hauptpfeilern zur unterstützenden Sockelkonstruktion geleitet. Die Vorgaben für die Detaillierung der paarweise gekoppelten Bleche und Stäbe wurden durchgängig angewandt, um eine Klarheit und Einfachheit mit schlanken Querschnitten zu erreichen, was eine präzise und anspruchsvolle ingenieurstechnische Analyse erforderte.

Das Dach ist als Sheddach ausgebildet, das diffuses Nordlicht einlässt und zur Belüftung genutzt werden kann. Die Träger sind in die Sheds integriert und ihre kompakten Querschnitte maximieren den Lichteinfall. Regenwasser vom Dach wird gesammelt, um die Pflanzen des Gartens zu bewässern.

---

voids. The slabs are supported by steel beams attached to the columns at each floor. Air is naturally drawn through these voids from the east to west elevations thanks to the stack effect to take advantage of night cooling in the summer months. The soffits are exposed and detailed for integration with lighting and suspended radiant panels using energy from ground source heat pumps.

Transfer truss construction

A 2,350-tonne trussed girder construction spanning in two directions was required to transfer the loads from the internal columns supporting the 27 office floors above the auditorium. This structure spans up to 30 m between the six megacolumns and the core. The 6.50 m deep trussed girders consist of rectangular sections fabricated from high-strength steel plates (up to 120 mm thick) and are located within the equipment room level at the 6th floor. On the south facade, the truss is increased to 20 m deep and concealed by the rear wall of the auditorium. Assembled at ground floor level first, the truss was lifted using a strand jack system, which was installed on the already completed parts of the megacolumns, and then welded into position in 2012. For the design of the trusses, which transfer the main loads into the columns, the engineers worked closely with the construction contractors, steel fabricators and welding specialists to develop connection details including using castings at the intersection of the trusses. The engineering designers used the Rhino software package from the outset as a 3D sketching tool to communicate the structural principles and develop key details with the design team. Geometry exported from these models formed the basis for the first analysis simulations. They were subsequently used in the detailed design and in the global analysis models. Then a series of finite element models of critical elements and connections were used to assess their behaviour. This allowed load concentrations to be identified and located, which was particularly relevant to the transfer truss connections.

The "Serra", crowning the tower

A naturally ventilated glass roof pavilion offers a public all-season garden with a view over the city and beyond to the Alps. The Serra crowns the tower and reaches 15 m into the air over three levels from a 30 × 30 m square base floor plan. It is constructed from slender welded steel columns and beams. Inspired by Paxton's 19th century Crystal Palace, it was conceived from the start as an interplay of delicately proportioned components on a regular 1.50 m planning module. The design developed as a system-built structure made out of standard components and connection details. The slenderness of the elements was a significant aesthetic criterion: the perimeter columns are no more than 150 mm in depth. Horizontal rod bracing in the walkways and the roof laterally restrain the wall elements, transferring wind and megacolumn restraint forces into the supporting base structure through diagonally crossed, prestressed, high-strength steel rods on the perimeter elevations.

The requirements for detailing the paired-plate members were consistently applied to achieve clarity and simplicity using slim cross sections, which required precise and meticulous structural engineering analysis. The sawtooth roof profile allows diffuse north light to enter and can be used for ventilation. The roof trusses are integrated into the roof profile and the compact size of the diagonal members maximises the admitted light. Rainwater is collected from the roof and used to water the plants within.

3D-Analysemodell des Dachpavillons bei Belastung durch Südwind /
3D analysis model of the roof pavilion under load from south wind

Julia Ratcliffe ist Ingenieurin und Mitglied der Geschäftsführung von Expedition Engineering (London). Sie war die verantwortliche Projektleiterin im Bereich der Tragwerksplanung. / Julia Ratcliffe is a structural engineer and a director of Expedition Engineering (London). She was the project manager for structural engineering design.

Turin, 2006–2015

Mock-up der Doppelfassade als 1:1-Modell /
Mock-up of double facade 1:1 model

Stahlbetondeckenelement mit Hohlraum für die Nachtauskühlung /
Reinforced concrete ceiling slab with voids for night cooling

Anschluss der äußeren Hülle der Doppelfassade an die Horizontalstreben /
Connection of the outer skin of the double facade to the horizontal bracing struts

Intesa Sanpaolo Office Building

Schnitt Westfassade,
Maßstab 1:20 /
Section of west facade,
scale 1:20

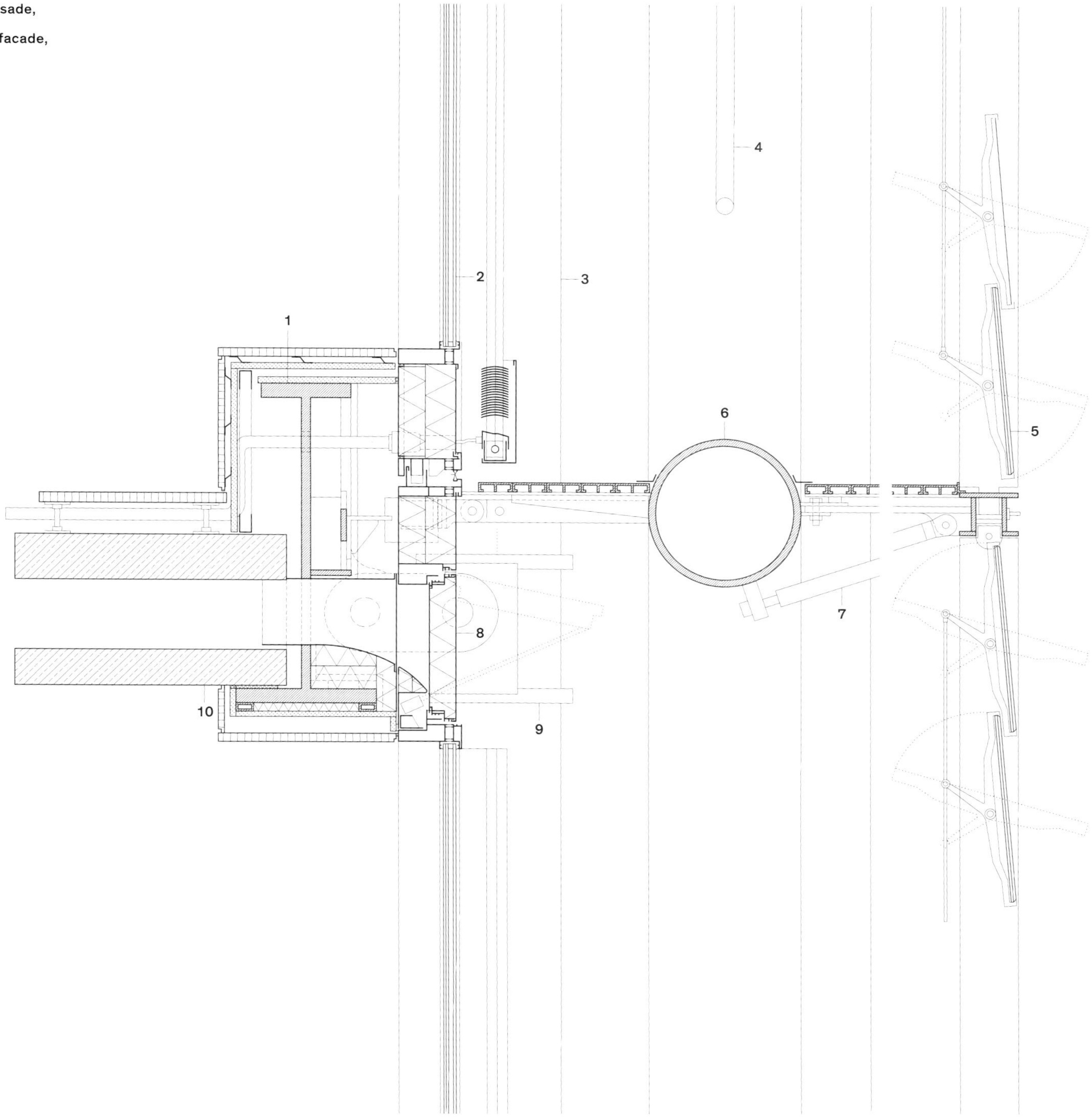

1	Stahlträger I 1100 mm	I 1,100 mm steel beam
2	Isolierverglasung	Double glazing
3	Hauptpfeiler Stahl mit Beton verfüllt (Brandschutz)	Steel megacolumn with concrete fill (fire protection)
4	Diagonaler Zugstab	Diagonal bracing cable
5	Glaslamelle in der äußeren Hülle der Doppelfassade	Operable louvre in outer facade
6	Horizontales Stahlrohr Ø 500 mm	Ø 500 mm horizontal steel bracing strut
7	Anschluss der äußeren Hülle der Doppelfassade an Stahlrohr	Connection of outer facade from bracing strut
8	Öffnungsklappe gedämmt für Nachtauskühlung	Insulated opening flap for night cooling
9	Verbindungsblech Pfeiler an Stahlträger	Megacolumn to steel beam connection
10	Deckenplatte: Stahlbetonhalbfertigteil mit Luftkanal	Exposed soffit of precast concrete floor slab

Profile der umlaufenden Stützen des Dachpavillons /
Sections of typical perimeter columns supporting the roof pavilion

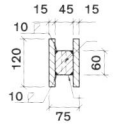

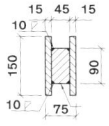

Profil einer inneren kreuzförmigen Stütze /
Section of internal cruciform column

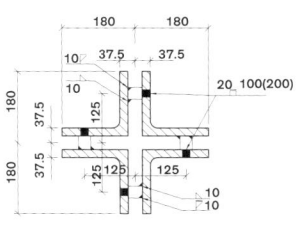

Turin, 2006–2015

Valletta City Gate, Valletta, MT

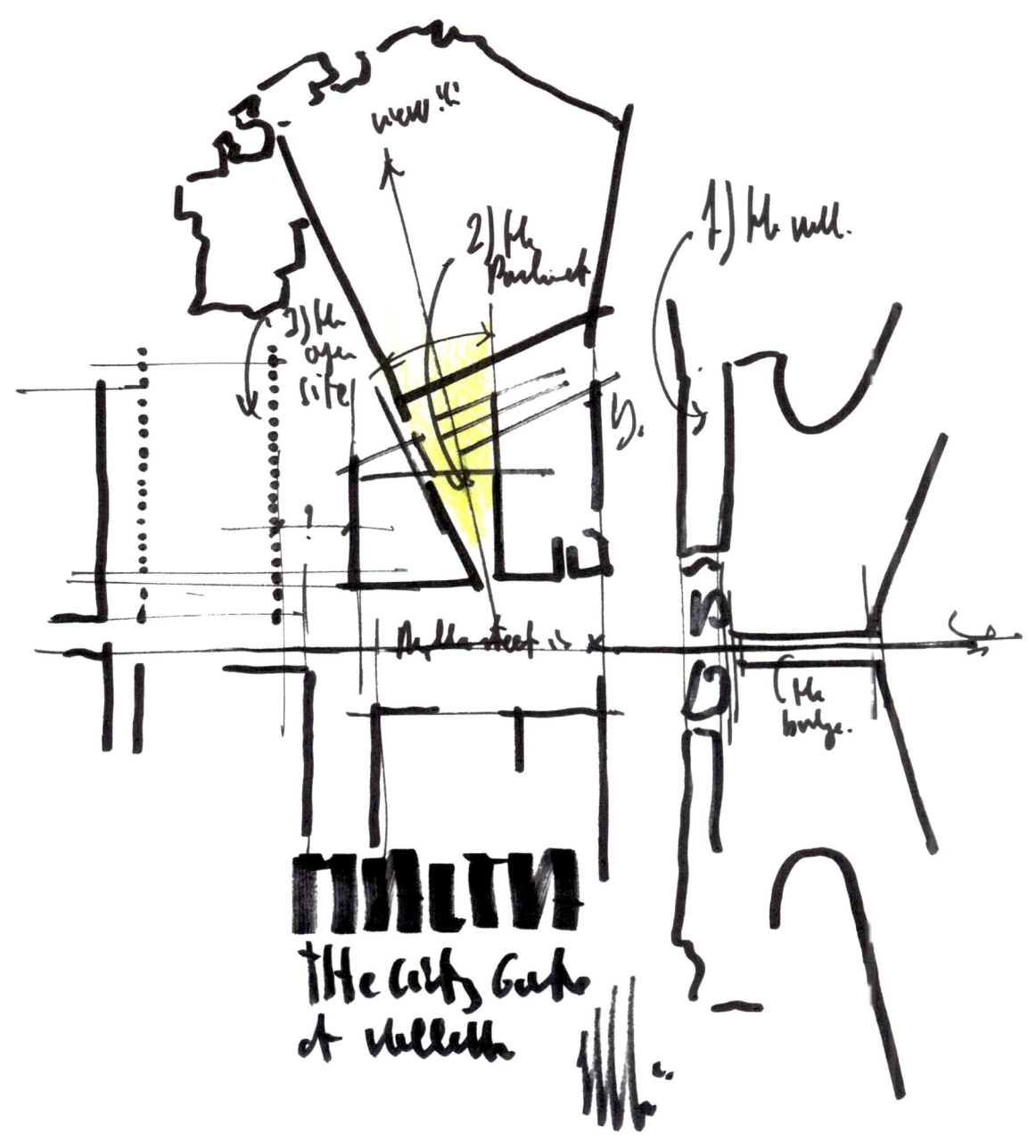

Entwurfsskizze von Renzo Piano / Design sketch by Renzo Piano

Parlamentsgebäude in Valletta

Text: Burkhard Franke
Detail 11/2017

Verwitterungsmuster an den gewaltigen Festungsmauern von Valletta dienen Renzo Piano als Inspiration für die Kalksteinfassade des neuen Parlamentsgebäudes von Malta. Seine Wandflächen sind an den Gebäudekanten glatt und erhalten im Inneren eine reliefartige, für Naturstein ungewöhnlich plastische Textur. Sie wirkt zufällig und natürlich, folgt aber den Gesetzen der Geometrie: Alle Fassaden beruhen auf einem Modul von 100 × 50 mm. Von der äußersten, glatten Fassadenebene treppt sich das Relief in bis zu vier Stufen von je 12 mm nach innen, wo es durch Fensteröffnungen durchbrochen wird. So macht das Muster auch die dahinterliegende Nutzung ablesbar: Kleine, abgetreppte Felder verweisen auf die Loungebereiche in den Gebäudeecken unter dem fensterlosen Plenarsaal, über die gesamte Fläche durchbrochene Fassaden auf dahinterliegende Büros. Auffällig sind die von der Vertiefung ausgesparten, rautenförmigen Stifte, die wie perspektivisch verzerrte Balkenköpfe schräg aus dem Relief ragen. Sie sind nicht nur Ornament, sondern dienen auch der Verschattung der dahinterliegenden Glasflächen.

Der rötliche Korallenkalkstein stammt aus einem Steinbruch auf der Nachbarinsel Gozo. Die komplizierten Formen der Fassadenmodule wurden mithilfe von CNC-Maschinen aus dem vollen Material gesägt bzw. gefräst und vor die Stahlskelettkonstruktion gehängt – die Erdbebengefahr machte eine tragende Steinkonstruktion unmöglich.

Die beiden polygonal geschnittenen Baukörper – einer nimmt den Plenarsaal, der andere die Büros der Parlamentarier auf – sind aufgeständert und erhalten so ein einladendes Entree. Auch das Flugdach über dem verglasten Dachgeschoss des Bürogebäudes und die Brücken über den Innenhof verleihen dem massiven Volumen eine gewisse Leichtigkeit. Im Gegensatz dazu steht der hermetische, sich nach oben verjüngende Erschließungsturm. Er lehnt sich formal an die benachbarten Festungsbauten an und weist in Richtung des ebenfalls durch Renzo Piano Building Workshop umgebauten Stadttors.

Parliament Building in Valletta

Text: Burkhard Franke
Detail 11/2017

Patterns created by weathering on Valletta's mighty fortification walls provided Renzo Piano with the inspiration for the limestone facades of Malta's new Parliament House. At the edges of the building the external walls are smooth, but the inner surfaces have a relief-like sculptural texture, unusual for natural stone. It seems random and natural but in fact obeys the laws of geometry. All the facades are based on a module measuring 100 × 50 mm. From the smooth, outermost plane the relief recedes inwards in four steps, each 12 mm deep, where it is finally interrupted by the glazing. The facade patterns make the function of the spaces behind them legible: for instance, small triangular areas of pattern indicate lounges in the corners of the building, below the otherwise windowless plenary chamber, whereas there are office spaces behind the facades with a regular, continuous texture. Diamond-shaped nibs that resemble beam ends distorted in perspective project at an angle out of the depressions. Not just ornamental, they also shade the areas of glazing behind.

The reddish coral limestone comes from a quarry on the neighbouring island of Gozo. The complicated forms of the facade modules were sawn or milled out of the material with the aid of CNC machines and then mounted on the steel frame structure – the danger of earthquakes made a load-bearing stone structure impossible.

The two polygonal building parts, one of which accommodates the plenary chamber, the other the parliamentarians' offices, are elevated above the street, creating open and inviting entrance areas. The canopy roof above the glazed top storey of the office building and the bridges that cross the internal courtyard lend the massive stone volumes a certain lightness. In contrast, the circulation tower with the pronounced batter that occupies the corner is decidedly hermetic. In formal terms, it employs an idiom similar to the neighbouring fortifications and points along the urban thoroughfare in the direction of the City Gate, also redesigned by Renzo Piano Building Workshop.

Grundrisse,
Schnitt,
Maßstab 1:750 /
Floor plans,
Section
scale 1:750

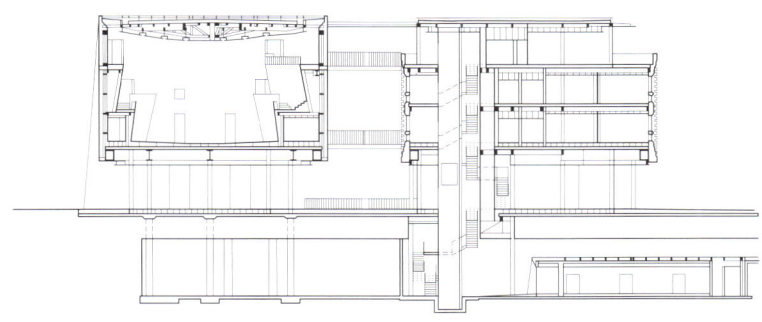

aa

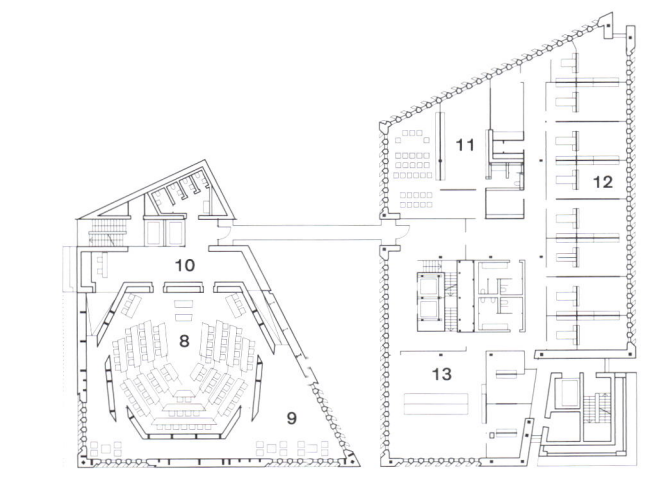

1. Obergeschoss /
First floor

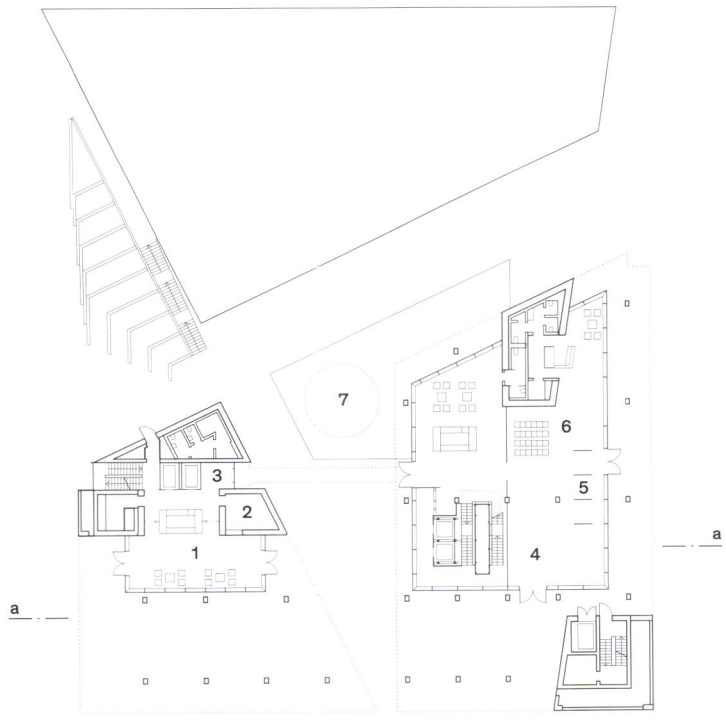

Erdgeschoss /
Ground floor

Lageplan,
Maßstab 1:5000 /
Site plan,
scale 1:5,000

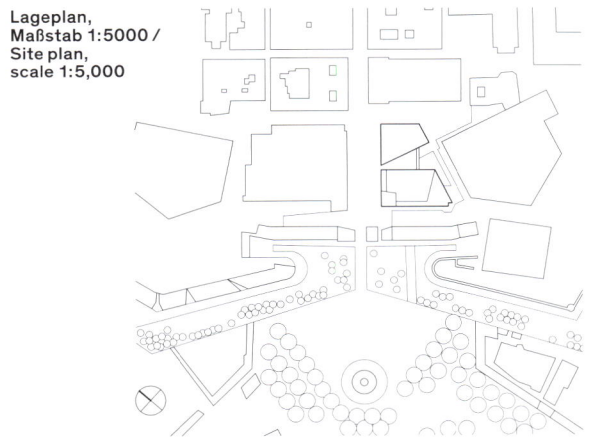

1	Foyer Plenarsaalgebäude	Foyer to plenary chamber building
2	Büro Gebäudesicherheit	Building security office
3	Interview-Bereich	Interview area
4	Foyer Bürogebäude	Foyer to office building
5	Ausstellung	Exhibition
6	Vortragsbereich	Lecture area
7	Luftraum Gartenhof Untergeschoss	Void to sunken garden
8	Plenarsaal	Plenary chamber
9	Abgeordneten-Lounge	Lounge
10	Lobby	Lobby
11	Büro Premierminister	Prime Minister's office
12	Ministerbüro	Minister's office
13	Abgeordnetenbereich	Members of parliament area

Valletta, 2009–2015

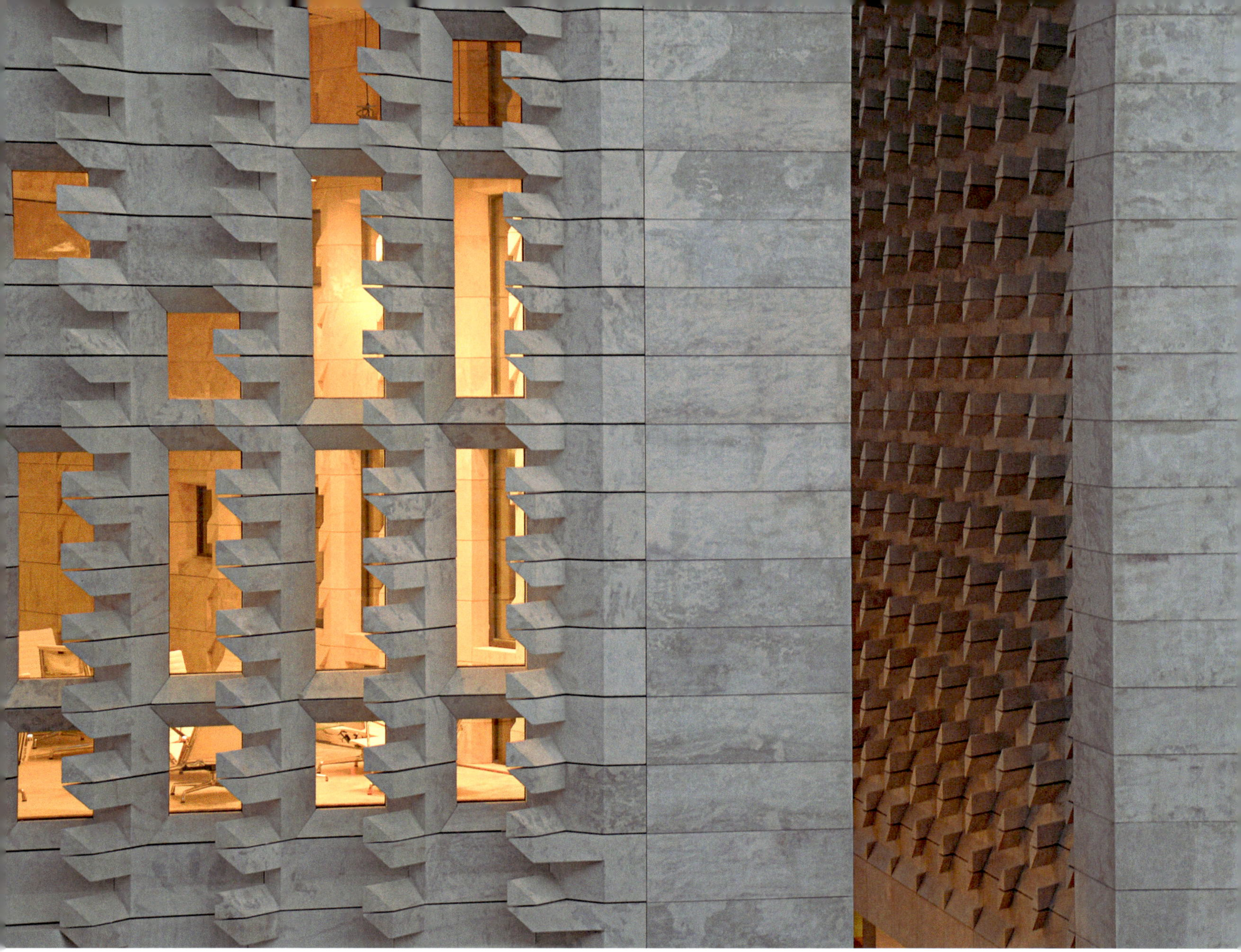

040 Valletta City Gate

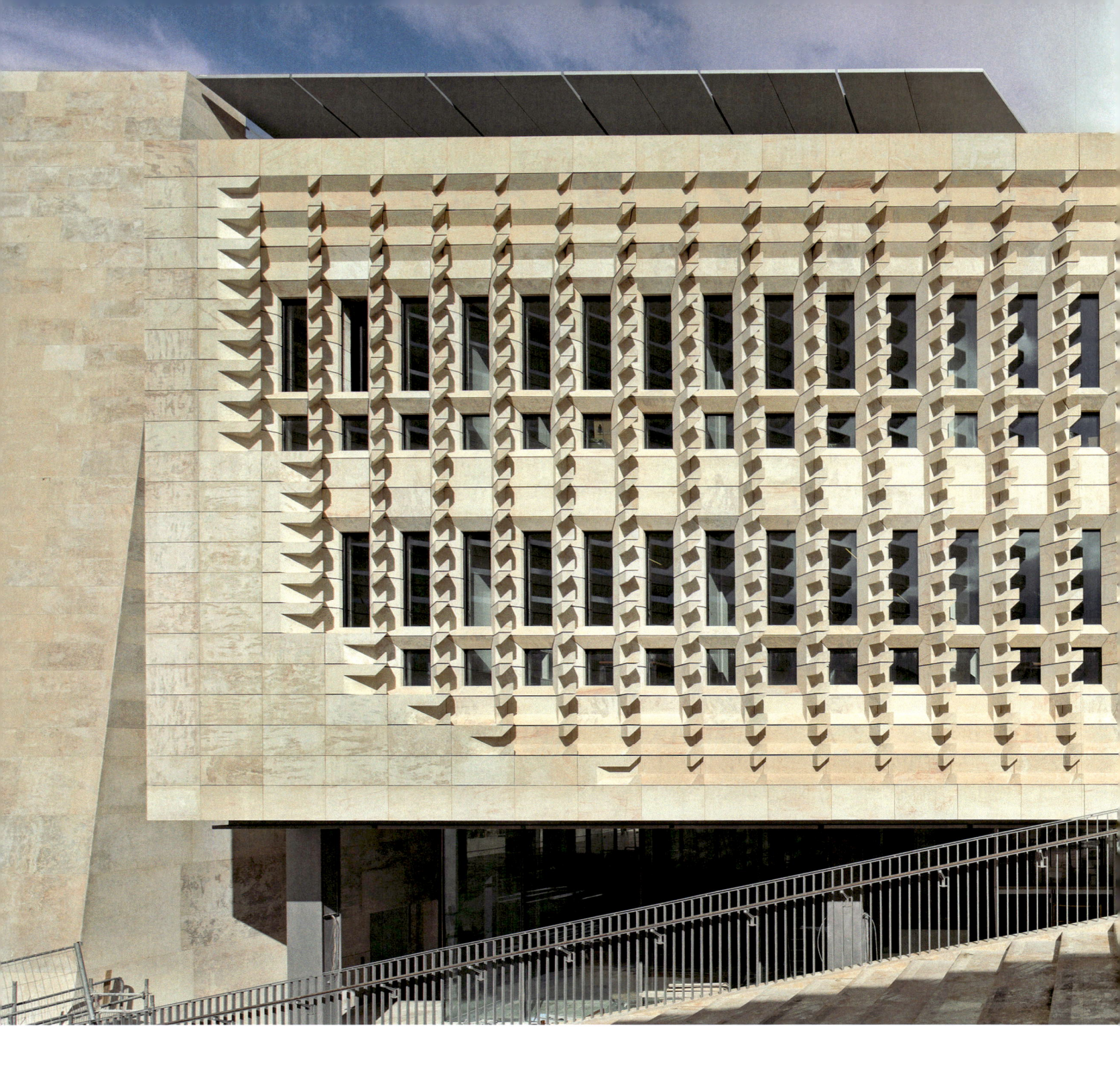

042 Valletta City Gate

Valletta, 2009–2015

1	Oberlicht Plenarsaal	Roof light plenary chamber
2	Aufbau Wand glatt: vorgehängtes Fassadenelement Korallenkalkstein 1000/500/100 mm Hinterlüftung 30 mm Fassadenbahn Wärmedämmung Mineralwolle 80 mm Dampfbremse, Unterkonstruktion Stahlrohr ☐ 150/100 mm Luftzwischenraum 200 mm, Unterkonstruktion Stahlrohr ☐ 150/100 mm, dazwischen Schalldämmung Steinwolle 150 mm Hinterlüftung / Unterkonstruktion 40 mm vorgehängtes Fassadenelement Korallenkalkstein 1000/500/100 mm	Construction smooth wall: 1,000/500/100 mm mounted coral facade element 30 mm back ventilation facade membrane 80 mm mineral wool insulation vapour barrier 150/100 mm steel tube substructure 200 mm cavity 150/100 steel tube substructure with 150 mm rock wool acoustic insulation between 40 mm back ventilation / substructure 1,000/500/100 mm mounted coral limestone facade element mounted on substructure
3	Fenster Abgeordneten-Lounge, Isolierverglasung in Aluminiumrahmen	Window MP lounge thermal glazing in aluminium frame
4	Stahlträger geschweißt 1350/1200 mm	1,350/1,200 mm steel beam welded
5	Aufbau Wand »erodiert«: Korallenkalkstein CNC-gesägt / -gefräst 1000/500/225–555 mm Hinterlüftung 62–290 mm Fassadenbahn Wärmedämmung Mineralwolle 80 mm Dampfbremse Stahlrohr ☐ 200/150mm, Hinterlüftung / Unterkonstruktion 40 mm vorgehängte Wandverkleidung Korallenkalkstein 1000/500/100 mm	Construction of 'eroded' wall: 1,000/500/225–555 mm module coral limestone facade element, CNC sawn /milled; 62–290 mm back ventilation facade membrane; 80 mm mineral wool insulation; vapour barrier; 200/150 mm rectangular section steel tube; 40 mm back ventilation / substructure; 1,000/500/100 mm coral limestone wall cladding

Valletta City Gate

Vertikalschnitt,
Horizontalschnitt,
Plenarsaalgebäude,
Maßstab 1:50 /
Vertical section,
Horizontal section,
Plenary chamber building,
scale 1:50

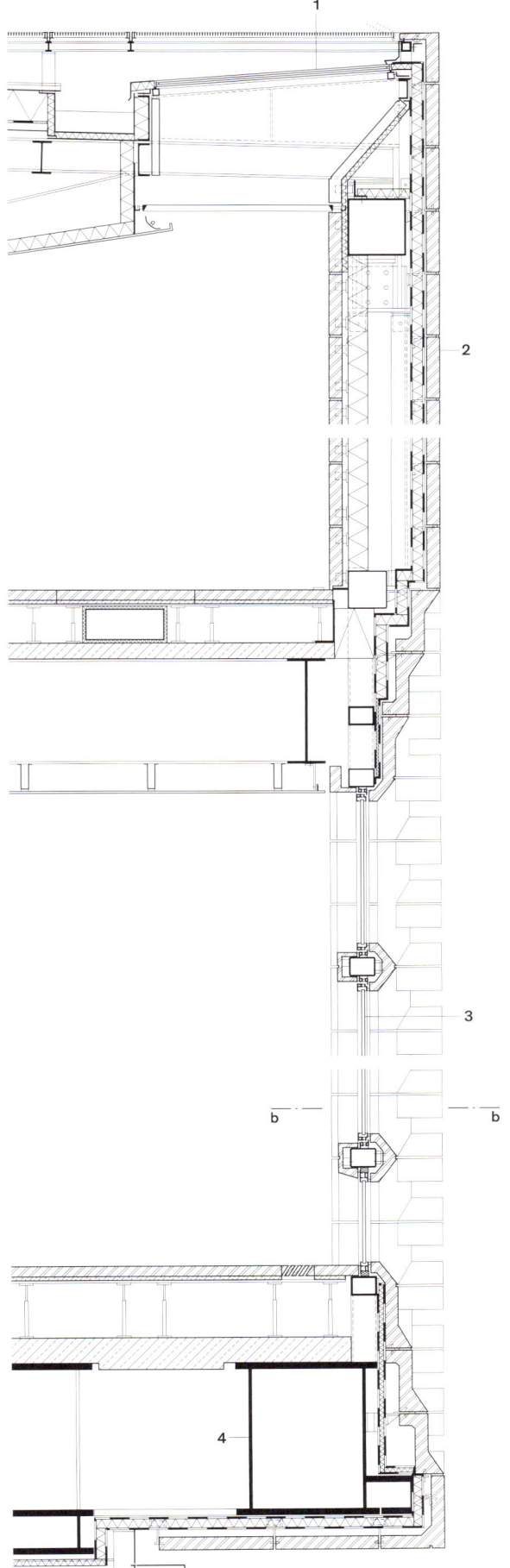

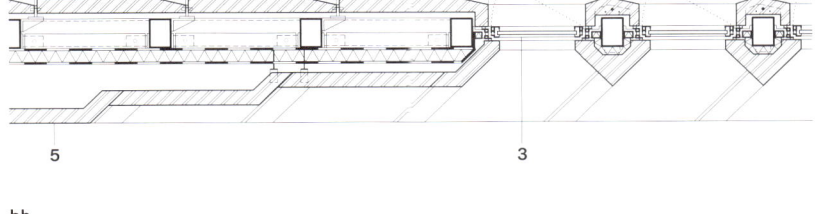

bb

Valletta, 2009–2015

045

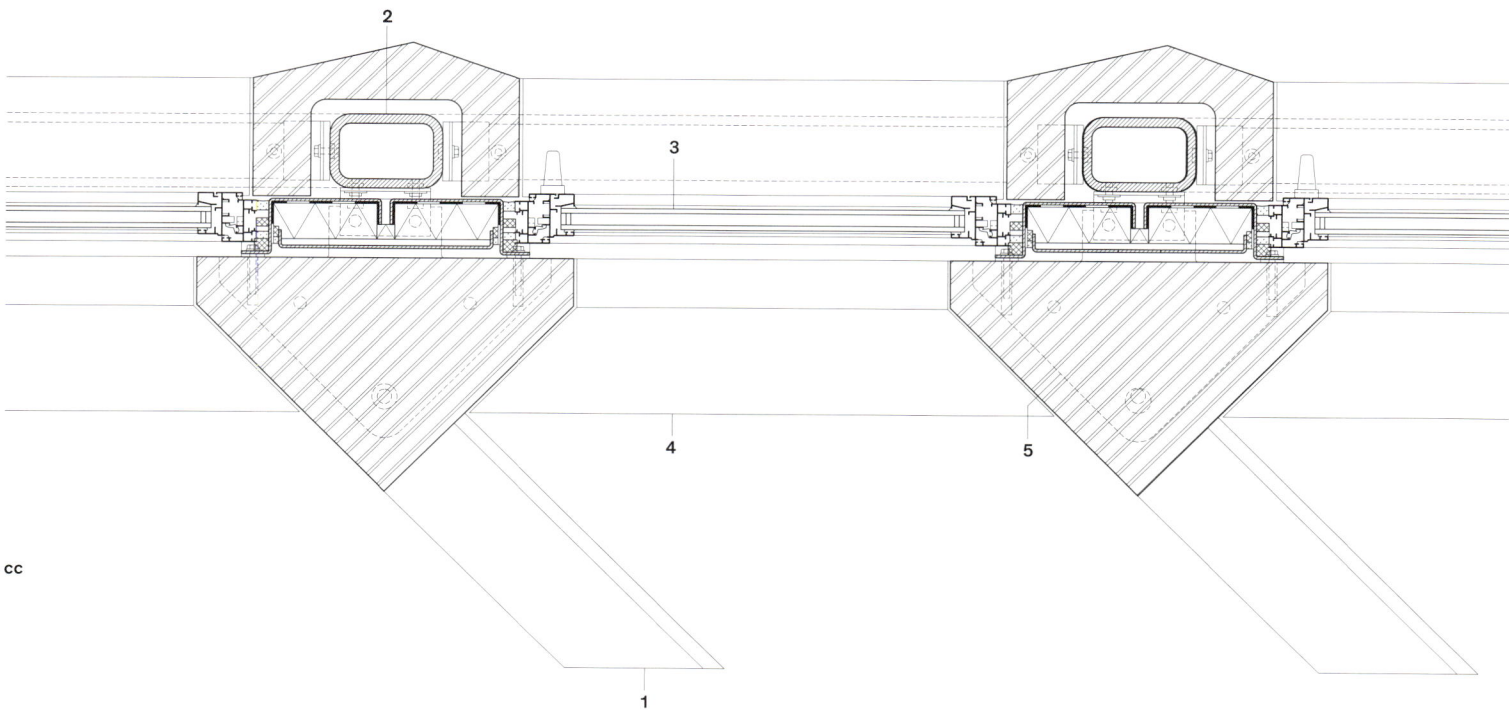

cc

046 Valletta City Gate

Vertikalschnitt,
Horizontalschnitt,
Bürogebäude,
Maßstab 1:10 /
Vertical section,
Horizontal section,
Office building,
scale 1:10

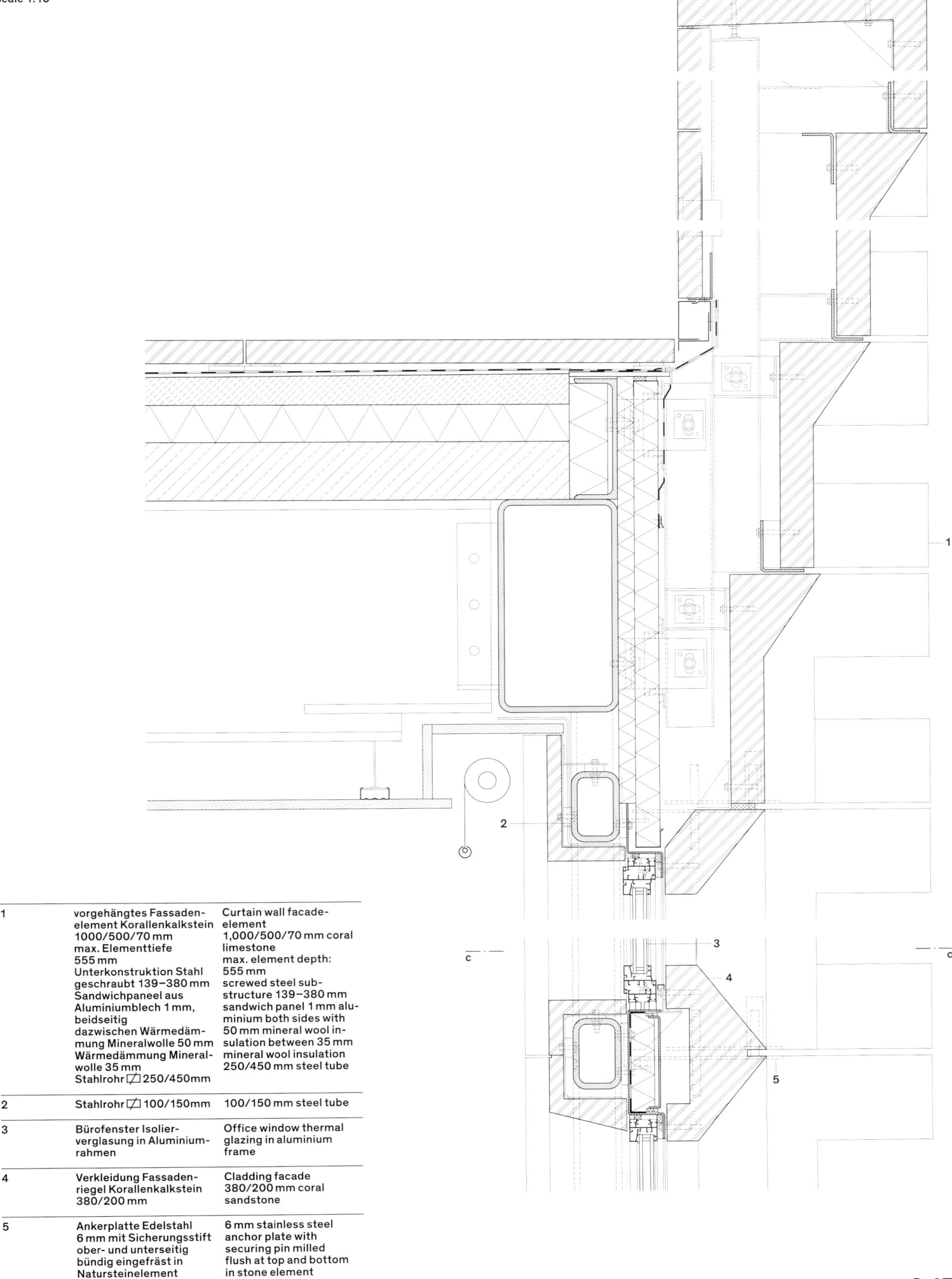

1	vorgehängtes Fassadenelement Korallenkalkstein 1000/500/70 mm max. Elementtiefe 555 mm Unterkonstruktion Stahl geschraubt 139–380 mm Sandwichpaneel aus Aluminiumblech 1 mm, beidseitig dazwischen Wärmedämmung Mineralwolle 50 mm Wärmedämmung Mineralwolle 35 mm Stahlrohr ☐ 250/450mm	Curtain wall facade-element 1,000/500/70 mm coral limestone max. element depth: 555 mm screwed steel substructure 139–380 mm sandwich panel 1 mm aluminium both sides with 50 mm mineral wool insulation between 35 mm mineral wool insulation 250/450 mm steel tube
2	Stahlrohr ☐ 100/150mm	100/150 mm steel tube
3	Bürofenster Isolierverglasung in Aluminiumrahmen	Office window thermal glazing in aluminium frame
4	Verkleidung Fassadenriegel Korallenkalkstein 380/200 mm	Cladding facade 380/200 mm coral sandstone
5	Ankerplatte Edelstahl 6 mm mit Sicherungsstift ober- und unterseitig bündig eingefräst in Natursteinelement	6 mm stainless steel anchor plate with securing pin milled flush at top and bottom in stone element

Valletta, 2009–2015

047

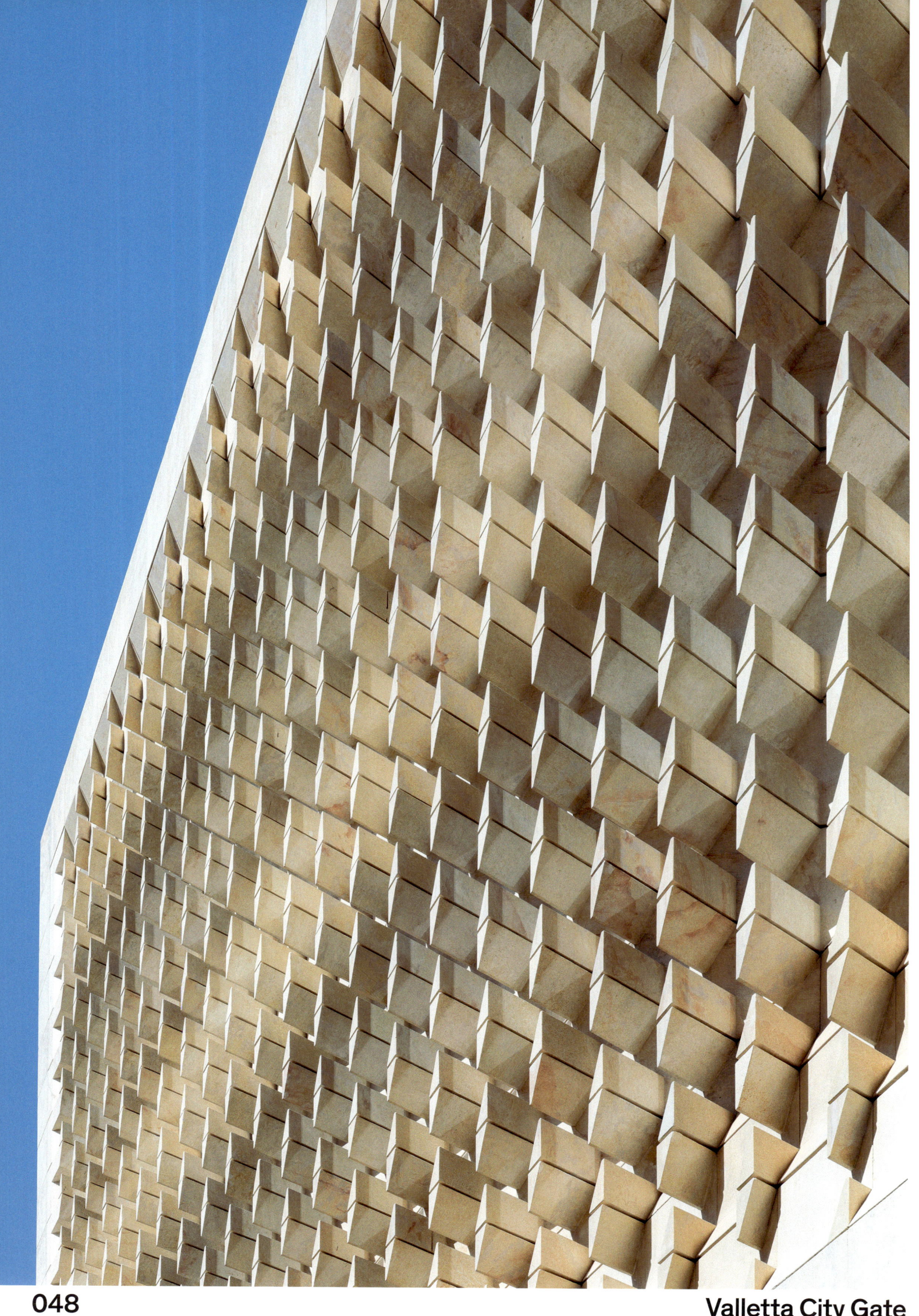

1
Konstruktionsraster und Lage der Fenster / Construction grid and positioning of the windows

2
Ansicht der Südfassade mit reliefartiger Textur / Elevation of the south facade with relief-like texture

3
Tiefenstaffelung des Reliefs in Schritten von 12 mm / The sunken relief is recessed in 12 mm deep steps

1

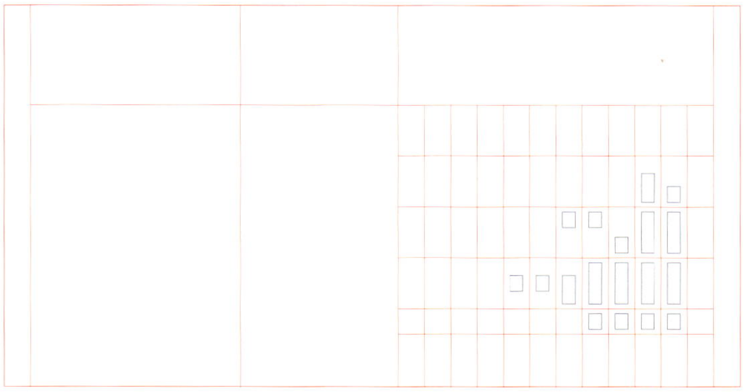

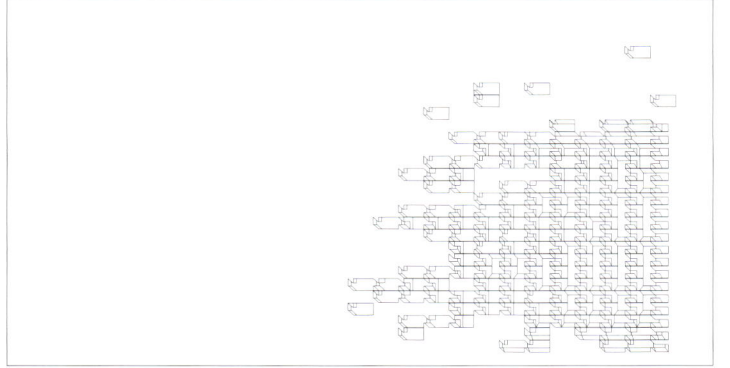

2

3

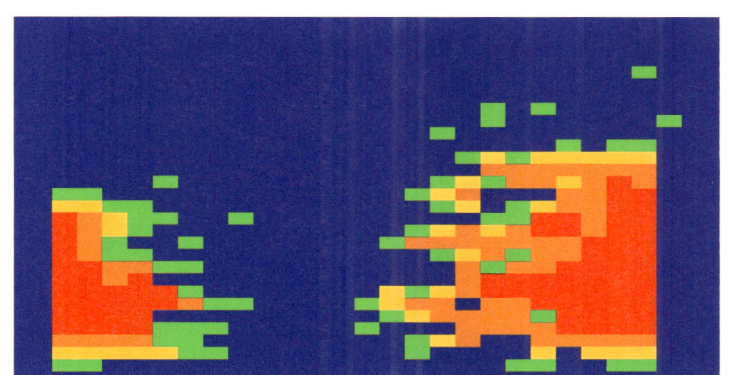

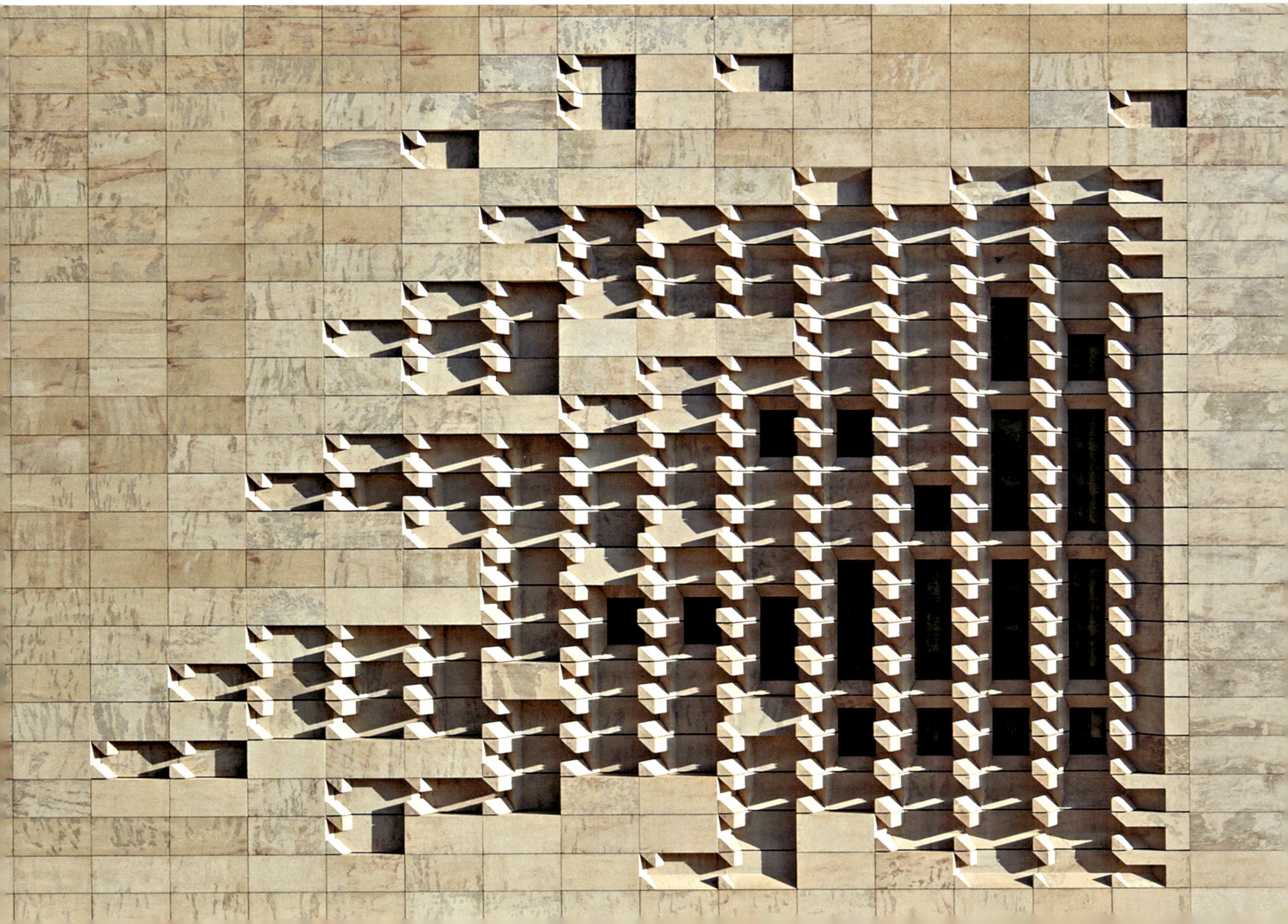

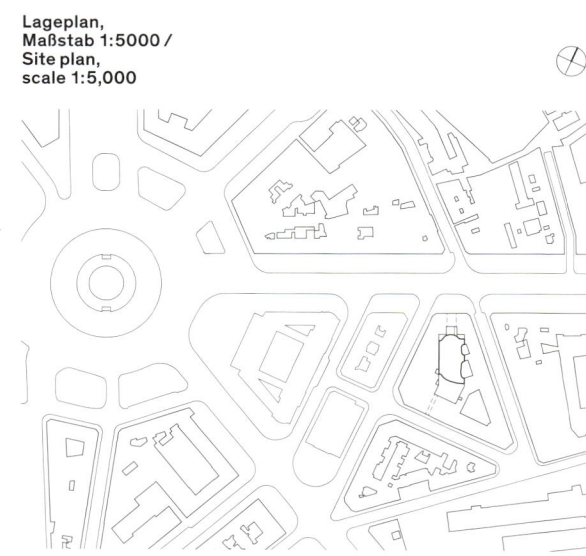

Lageplan,
Maßstab 1:5000 /
Site plan,
scale 1:5,000

050

Jérôme Seydoux-Pathé Foundation, Paris, FR

Entwurfsskizze von Renzo Piano / Design sketch by Renzo Piano

Fondation Pathé in Paris

Text: Andreas Gabriel
Detail 11/2014

Die Fondation Jérôme Seydoux-Pathé bewahrt das Archiv einer der ältesten Firmen des Filmgeschäfts. Der Stiftungshauptsitz fügt sich als neuer Kern in einen dreiecksförmigen Block im 13. Pariser Arrondissement. Die denkmalgeschützte Eingangsfassade wurde behutsam saniert. Dahinter gibt ein gläserner Empfangsraum den Blick auf einen Gartenhof und den organisch geformten Hauptbaukörper frei. Dieser erhebt sich über einem verglasten Erdgeschoss auf wenigen Stützen. Lediglich an der Treppenhausseite und über drei rüsselartige Ausstülpungen dockt er an die Nachbarbebauung an. So gelangt großzügig Luft und Sonne in den Hof und die angrenzenden Häuser.

Neben Archivräumen birgt das Gebäude Ausstellungsflächen, einen Vorführraum für Stummfilme mit Pianobegleitung sowie die Büros der Stiftungsmitarbeiter unter dem Glasdach der beiden oberen Geschosse. Dieses besteht aus drei Schichten: bogenförmigen Brettschichtholzträgern, der Verglasung und einem äußeren Sonnenschutz aus perforierten Aluminiumlamellen. Der Querschnitt der Holzträger variiert je nach Spannweite, Stahlfüße mit Gelenken übertragen die Kräfte an ein umlaufendes Stahlprofil. Die Glasunterkonstruktion besteht aus gebogenen Rundrohren, die zugleich das Tragwerk aussteifen. Die im Warmbiegeverfahren zweiachsig gebogenen Scheiben der Isolierverglasung besitzen jeweils eine individuelle Form. Der außen liegende Sonnenschutz verhindert neben übermäßiger Erwärmung des Innenraums eine zu große Aufheizung der Scheiben, die sonst zum Glasbruch führen könnte. Die gewölbten perforierten Aluminiumlamellen sind auf einer Unterkonstruktion aus Aluminiumrundrohren montiert.

Der 70 mm breite Abstand zwischen Lamellen und Verglasung ermöglicht die Reinigung und Wartung. Als zweite Haut überziehen die Lamellen auch die darunterliegenden Geschosse, die eine massive Außenwand besitzen und verleihen der Gebäudeform so Durchgängigkeit. Ihre obere Kuppe, die tagsüber unauffällig über den Block ragt, leuchtet nachts über den Dächern der Stadt.

Fondation Pathé in Paris

Text: Andreas Gabriel
Detail 11/2014

The Fondation Jérôme Seydoux-Pathé holds the archive of one of the film industry's oldest firms. The foundation's headquarters have been inserted as a new core in a triangular block in Paris's 13th arrondissement. The listed entrance facade was restored with great care. Behind it a glazed reception space presents a view of a garden courtyard and the organic forms of the main building. Resting on just a few columns the latter rises up above a glazed ground storey. It docks onto the neighbouring buildings via the stairway and the three snout-like protrusions. Accordingly, the garden courtyard and the neighbouring buildings are supplied with plentiful fresh air and sunlight.

In addition to the archive rooms, the building contains exhibition spaces, a screening room for silent movies with piano accompaniment, and, beneath the glass roof of the two upper levels, the offices of the foundation employees. The glass roof is made up of three layers: arched glued laminated timber beams, the glazing, and perforated aluminium louvres as external solar control. The cross section of the wood beams changes in response to the span; hinged steel feet transfer the forces to a circumferential steel profile. The glazing is supported by curved circular hollow sections that also serve to stiffen the load-bearing structure. No two of the double-glazed panes, which were double-curved by means of hot-bending, have the same form. The external solar protection keeps the interiors from overheating. But there's another reason: if the panes were to become too hot, the glass might break. The curved, perforated aluminium louvres are mounted on an aluminium supporting structure.

The 70 mm distance between louvres and glazing allows for cleaning and maintenance. As a second skin, the louvres also cloak the storeys below – which have a massive exterior wall – and, in this manner, give the building form its homogeneity. By day the crest peeks out unobtrusively above the urban fabric, and at night it casts a glow that makes it visible from a great distance.

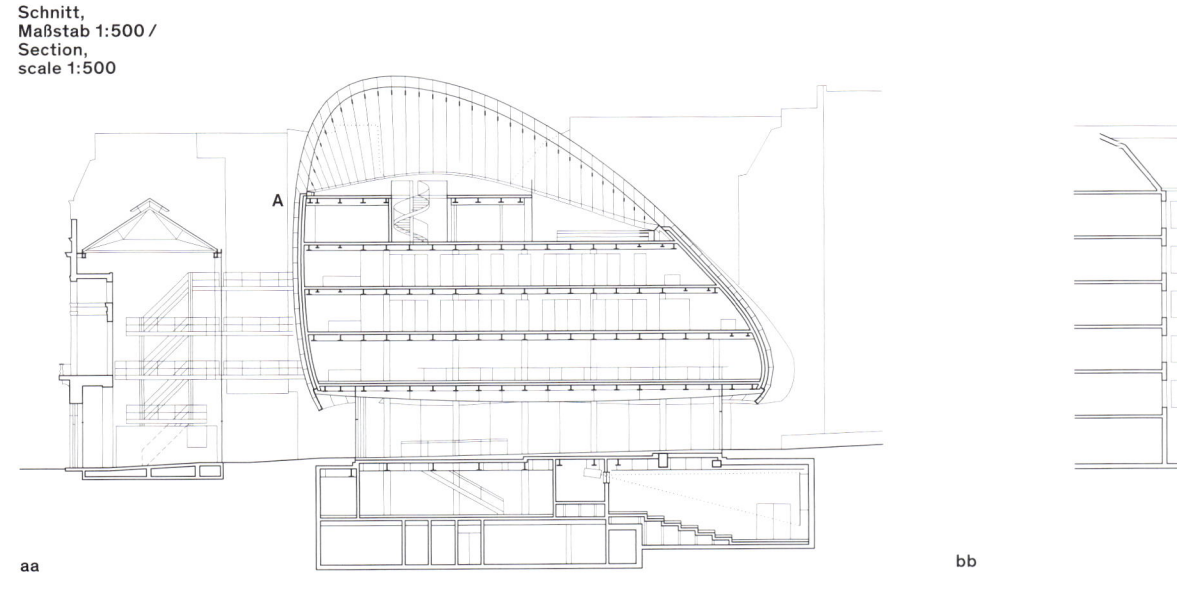

Schnitt,
Maßstab 1:500 /
Section,
scale 1:500

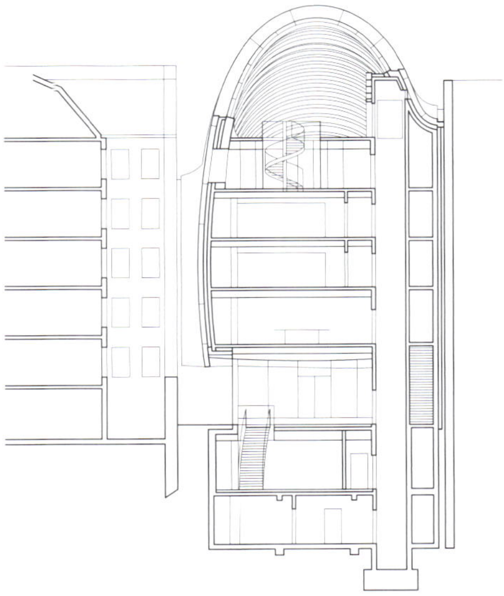

aa

bb

Paris, 2006–2014

053

Grundrisse,
Maßstab 1:500 /
Layout plans,
scale 1:500

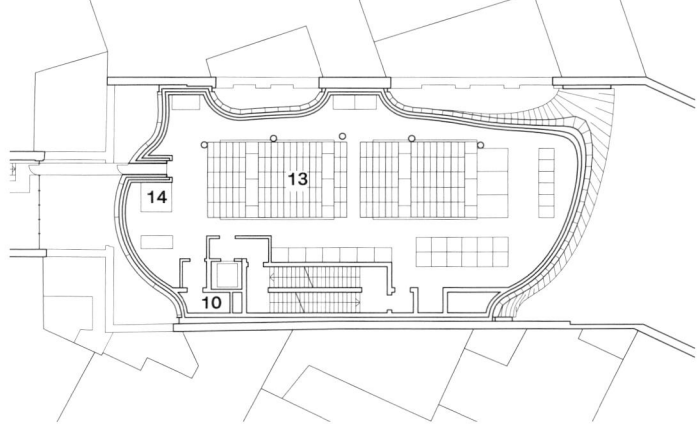

2. Obergeschoss /
Second floor

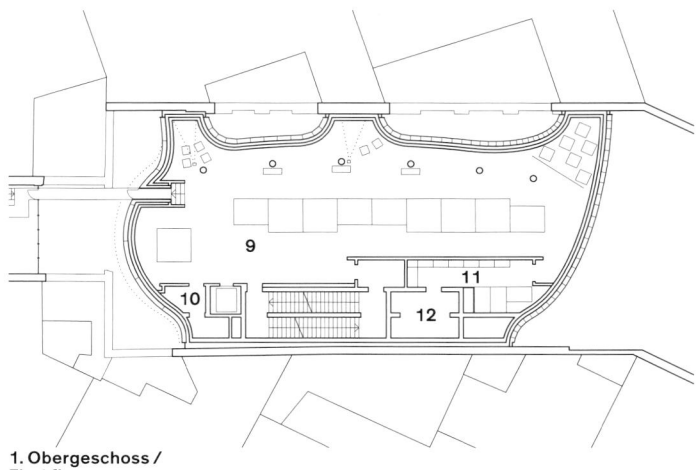

1. Obergeschoss /
First floor

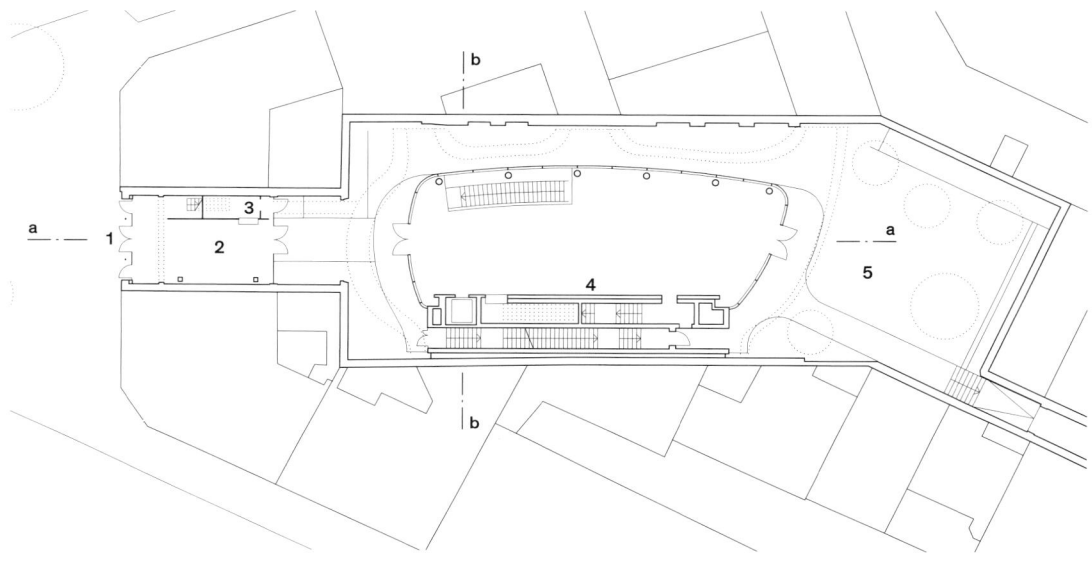

Erdgeschoss /
Ground floor

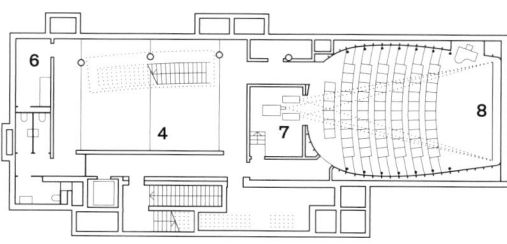

Untergeschoss /
Basement

056　　　　　　　　　　　　　　　　　　　　　　　　Jérôme Seydoux-Pathé Foundation

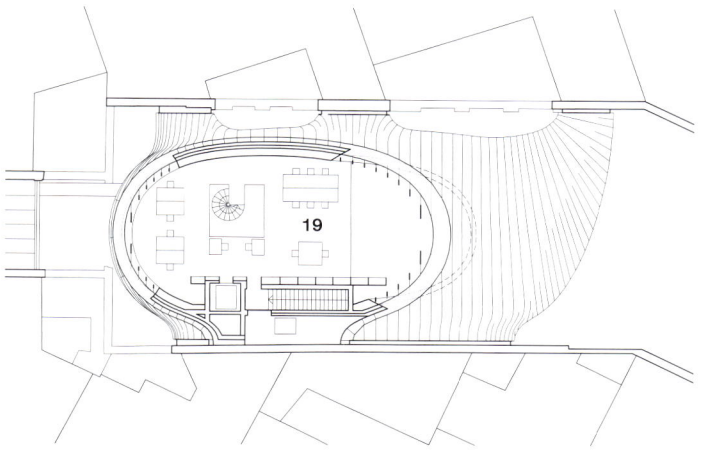

4. Obergeschoss /
Fourth floor

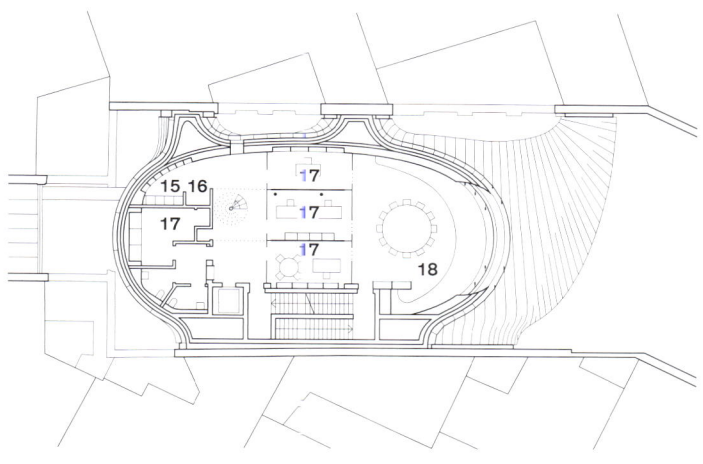

5. Obergeschoss /
Fifth floor

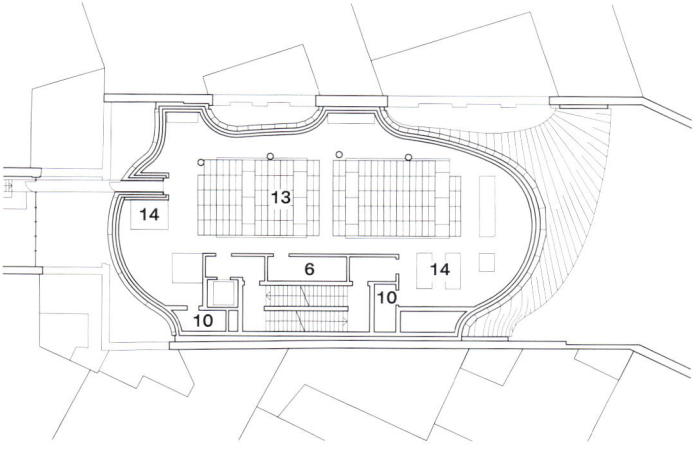

3. Obergeschoss /
Third floor

1	Eingang	Entrance
2	Empfangsraum	Reception
3	Pförtner	Porter
4	Ausstellung temporär	Temporary exhibition
5	Gartenhof	Garden courtyard
6	Lager	Storage
7	Projektionsraum	Projection room
8	Vorführraum	Screening room
9	Dauerausstellung	Permanent exhibition
10	Technikraum	Mechanical services
11	Magazin	Depot
12	Werkstatt	Workshop
13	Archivschränke verfahrbar	Archival cabinets, movable
14	Arbeitstische Archiv	Work table
15	Küche	Kitchen
16	Kopierplatz	Copying
17	Büro	Office
18	Besprechungsraum	Conference
19	Gruppenbüro	Group office

Paris, 2006–2014

Detailschnitt,
Maßstab 1:50 /
Sectional detail,
scale 1:50

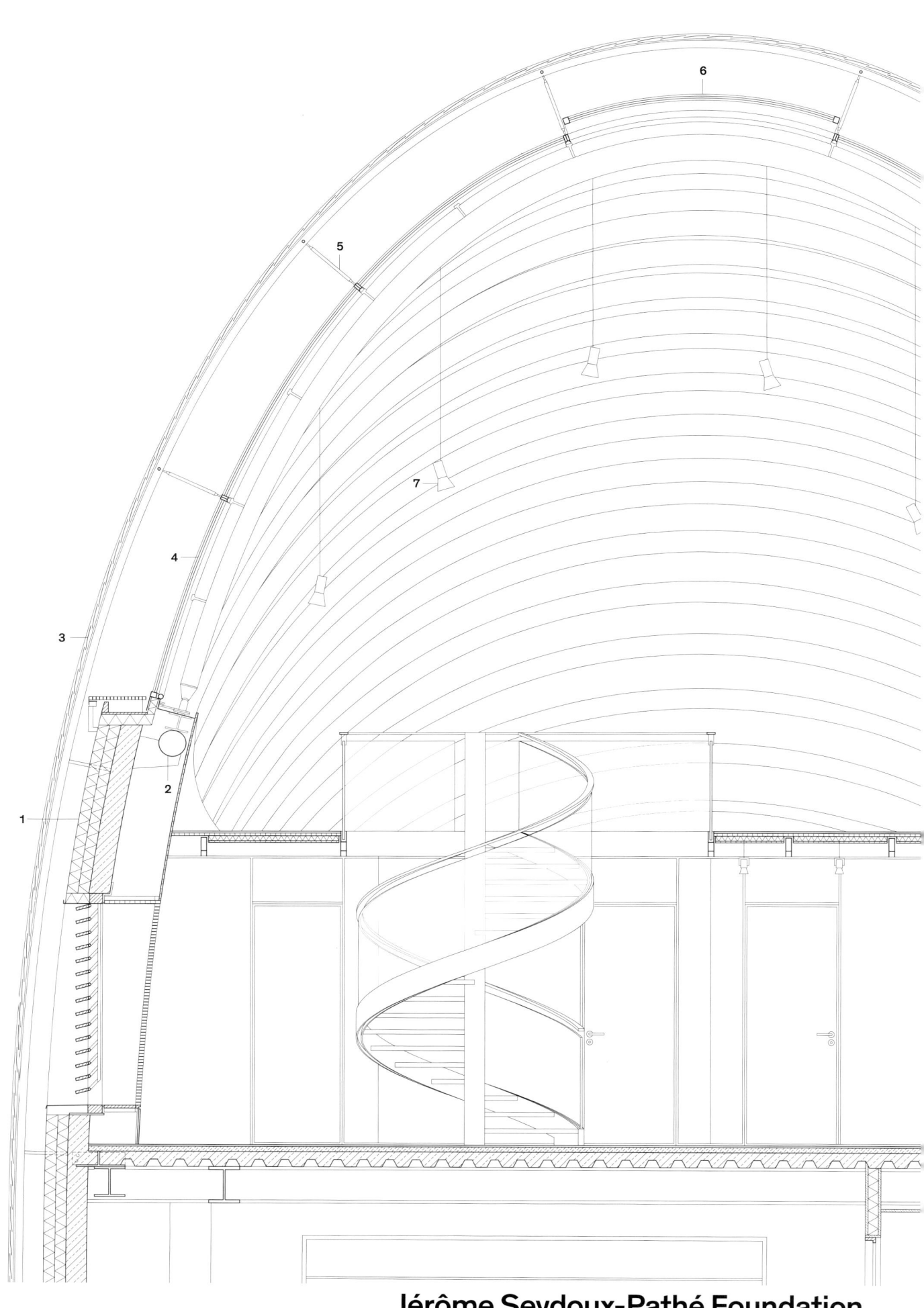

058   Jérôme Seydoux-Pathé Foundation

Die Transparenz der äußeren Aluminiumlamellen variiert in drei Stufen von 30, 40 und 50 %. Zur rationellen Herstellung der über 7000 Lamellen mit jeweils individuellem Zuschnitt diente ein parametrisches 3D Modell (Arnold Walz, Design-to-Production) das jeweils Ausrichtung, Platzierung und Geometrie definierte.

The exterior aluminium louvres have three levels of transparency: 30, 40 and 50 %. A parametric 3D model (Arnold Walz, Design-to-Production) was employed to rationally manufacture the more than 7,000 louvres, each with a shape of its own; the model determined each louvre's placement and geometry.

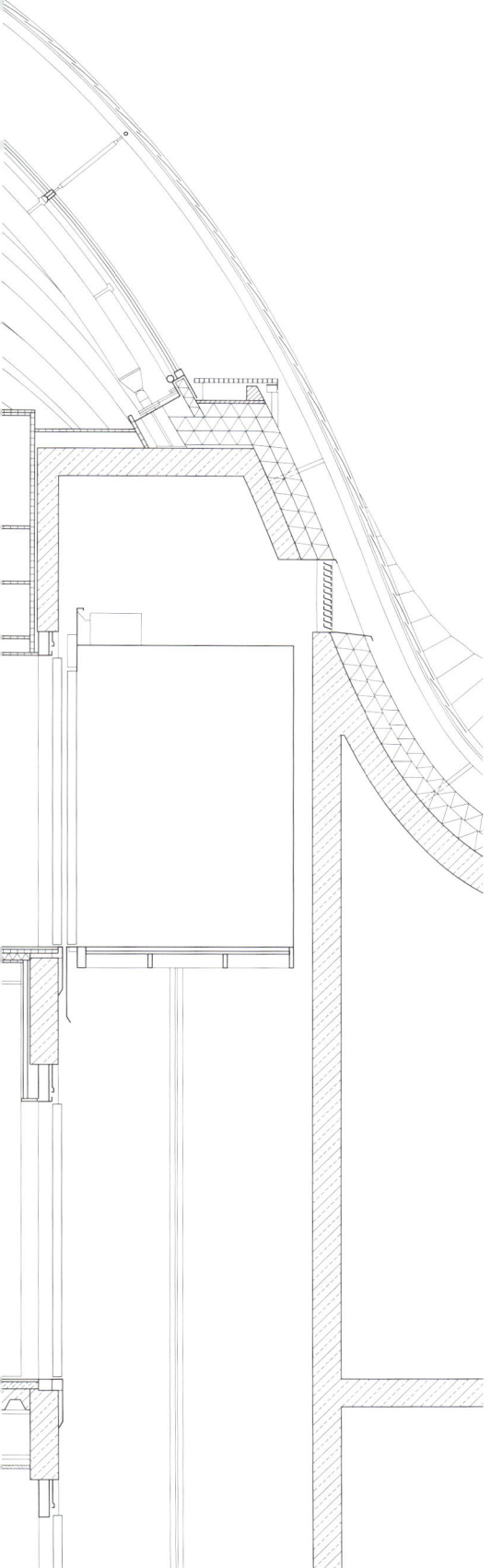

1	Abdichtung EPDM, Wärmedämmung 200 mm Dampfsperre, Stahlbeton 200 mm Luftzwischenraum 465 mm Holzwerkstoffplatte Deckfurnier Eiche 20 mm	EPDM sealant; 200 mm thermal insulation vapour barrier; 200 mm reinforced concrete 465 mm air space 20 mm composite wood board, oak veneer
2	Stahlrohr umlaufend Ø 273/8 mm	Ø 273/8 mm steel CHS, circumferential
3	Aluminiumblech gewölbt, perforiert 3/250 mm Unterkonstruktion Aluminiumrohr Ø 76/8 mm	3/250 mm aluminium sheet, curved, perforated Ø 76/8 mm aluminium CHS supporting structure
4	Isolierverglasung zweiachsig gebogen VSG 2× 6 + SZR 15 + VSG 2× 6 mm Tragkonstruktion Stahlrohr Ø 50/7 mm Abstandhalter Stahl Träger Brettschichtholz 100/180–280 mm	Double-curved double glazing: 2× 6 mm laminated safety glass + 15 mm cavity + 2× 6 mm laminated safety glass Ø 50/7 mm steel CHS load-bearing structure steel distancer: 100/180–280 mm glued laminated timber beam
5	Stahlrohr verzinkt Ø 30/4 mm	Ø 30/4 mm steel CHS, galvanised
6	Verglasungselement motorisch öffenbar	Glazing element, motor operated
7	Leuchte abgehängt	Suspended luminaire

Paris, 2006–2014

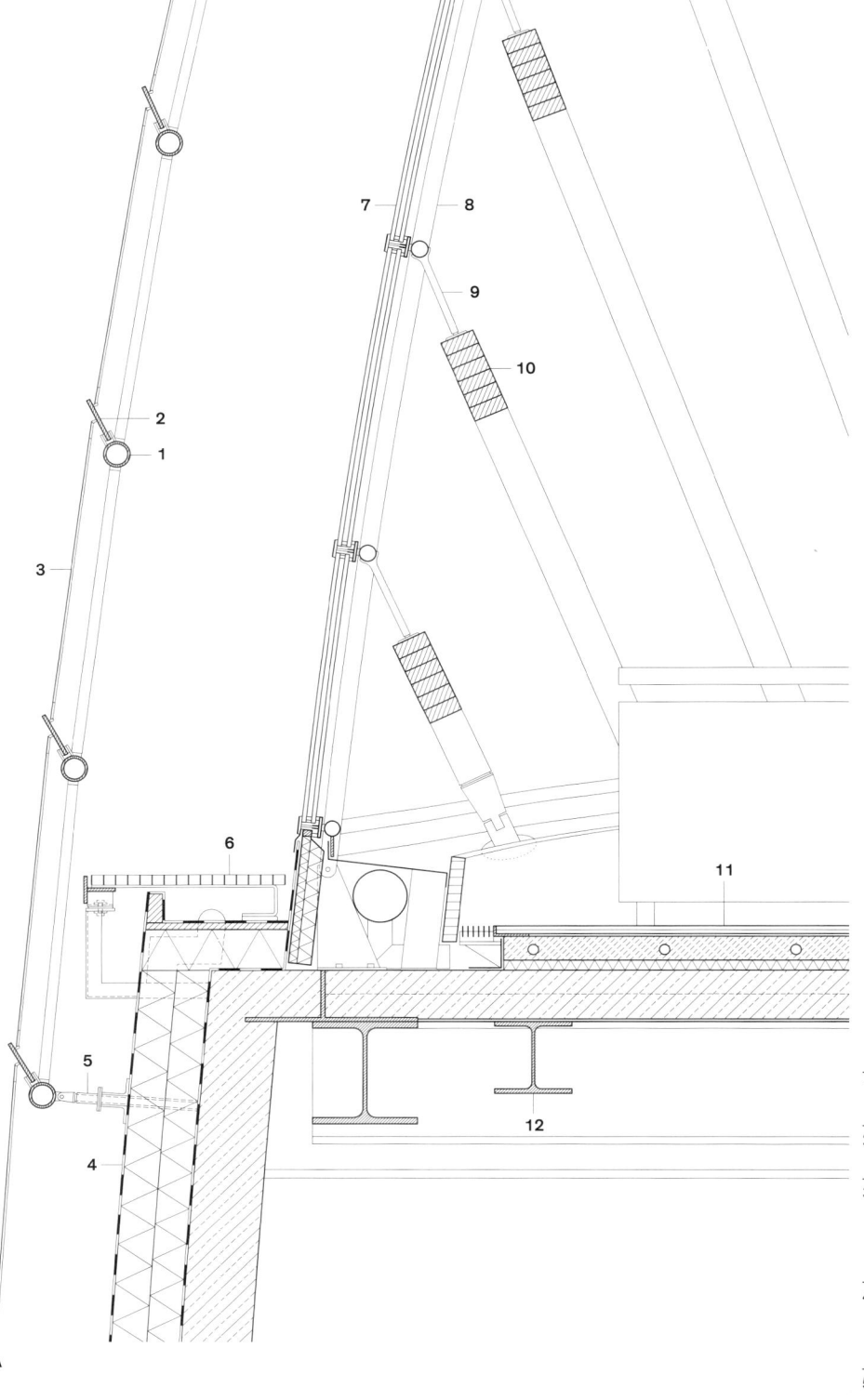

Detailschnitt,
Maßstab 1:20 /
Sectional detail,
scale 1:20

1	Aluminiumrohr ⌀ 76/8 mm	⌀ 76/8 mm aluminium CHS
2	Aluminiumprofil ⌑ 10/variabel mm	Variable / 10 mm aluminium profile
3	Aluminiumblech gewölbt, perforiert 3/250 mm, Lochraster ⌀ 6 mm, Transparenzgrad 30, 40 oder 50 %	3/250 mm aluminium sheet, curved, perforation (⌀ 6 mm grid), degree of transparency: 30, 40 or 50 %
4	Abdichtung EPDM Wärmedämmung 200 mm Dampfsperre Stahlbeton 230 mm	EPDM sealant 200 mm thermal insulation vapour barrier 230 mm reinforced concrete
5	Stahlrohr verzinkt ⌀ 30/4 mm	⌀ 30/4 mm steel CHS, galvanised
6	Gitterrost Aluminium	Aluminium grating
7	Isolierverglasung zweiachsig gebogen: äußere Scheibe metallische Sonnenschutzbeschichtung, innere Scheibe low-E-Beschichtung VSG 2× 6 + SZR 15 + VSG 2× 6 mm	Double-curved double glazing outer pane: metallic solar-control coating; inner pane: low-e coating 2× 6 mm laminated safety glass + 15 mm cavity + 2× 6 mm laminated safety glass
8	Stahlrohr farbbeschichtet ⌀ 50/7 mm	⌀ 50/7 mm steel CHS, colour-coated
9	Abstandhalter Stahl, maschinengeschweißt beschichtet	Steel distancer, automated weld, coated
10	Träger Brettschichtholz bogenförmig 100/180 – 280 mm	100/180–280 mm glued laminated timber beam, arched
11	Parkett Eiche verklebt 30 mm Heizestrich 90 mm Trittschalldämmung 30 mm Stahlbetondecke im Verbund mit Trapezblech 150 mm	30 mm oak parquet, glued 90 mm heating screed 30 mm impact sound insulation 150 mm reinforced concrete deck bonded to corrugated metal
12	Träger Stahlprofil HEB 300	300 mm wide-flange I-beam

Jérôme Seydoux-Pathé Foundation

Aufgrund der individuellen Formgebung konnten die bis zu 3,2 × 0,9 m großen Isoliergläser im Produktionsverfahren nicht vorgespannt werden. Daher besteht auch die äußere Scheibe aus Verbundglas.

On account of the unique shapes of the glazed panels, the double-glazed units, which are up to 3.20 × 0.90 m in size, could not be tempered; therefore, the outer pane is also of laminated safety glass.

Detailschnitt, Maßstab 1:20 / Sectional detail, scale 1:20

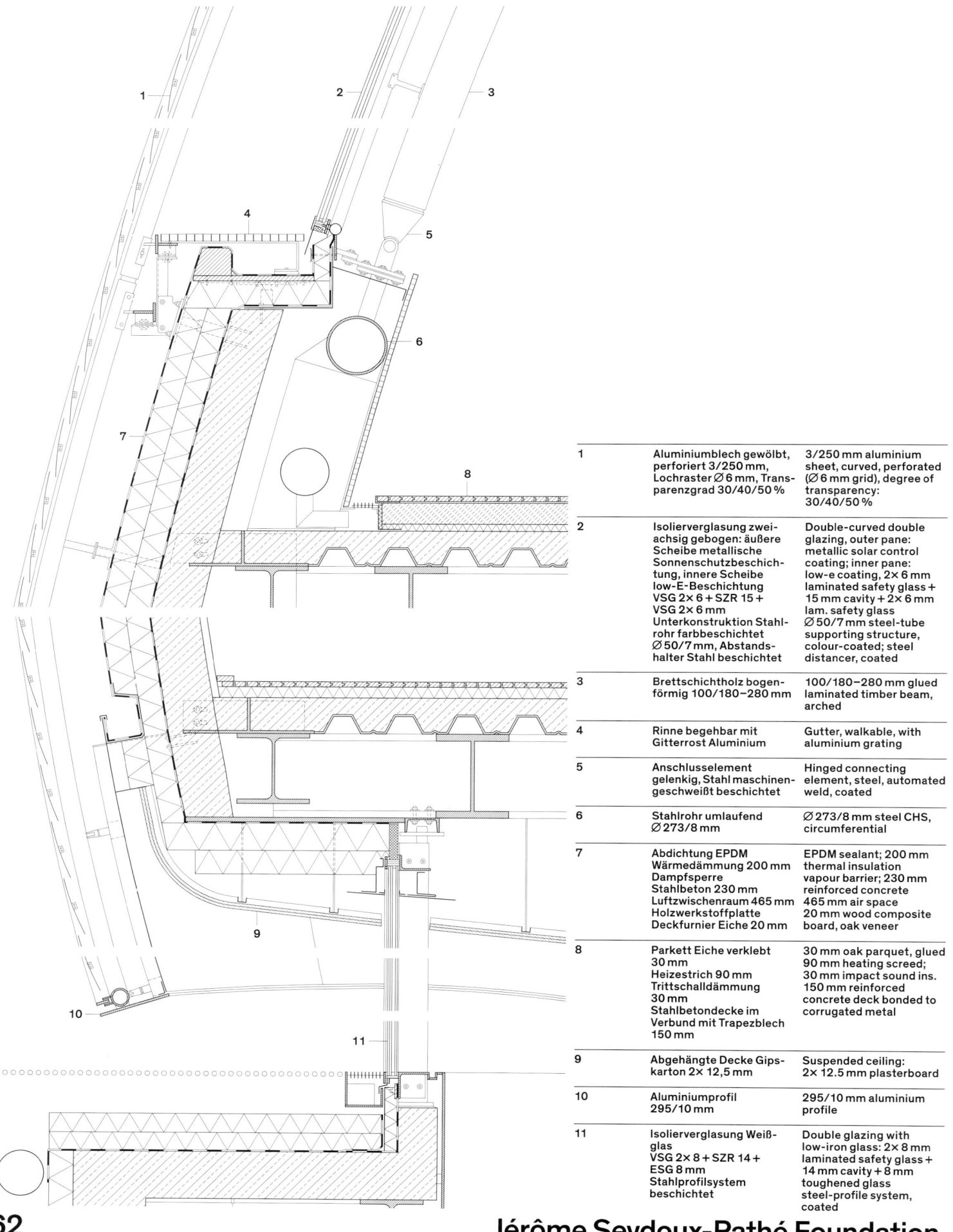

1	Aluminiumblech gewölbt, perforiert 3/250 mm, Lochraster ⌀ 6 mm, Transparenzgrad 30/40/50 %	3/250 mm aluminium sheet, curved, perforated (⌀ 6 mm grid), degree of transparency: 30/40/50 %
2	Isolierverglasung zweiachsig gebogen: äußere Scheibe metallische Sonnenschutzbeschichtung, innere Scheibe low-E-Beschichtung VSG 2× 6 + SZR 15 + VSG 2× 6 mm Unterkonstruktion Stahlrohr farbbeschichtet ⌀ 50/7 mm, Abstandshalter Stahl beschichtet	Double-curved double glazing, outer pane: metallic solar control coating; inner pane: low-e coating, 2× 6 mm laminated safety glass + 15 mm cavity + 2× 6 mm lam. safety glass ⌀ 50/7 mm steel-tube supporting structure, colour-coated; steel distancer, coated
3	Brettschichtholz bogenförmig 100/180–280 mm	100/180–280 mm glued laminated timber beam, arched
4	Rinne begehbar mit Gitterrost Aluminium	Gutter, walkable, with aluminium grating
5	Anschlusselement gelenkig, Stahl maschinengeschweißt beschichtet	Hinged connecting element, steel, automated weld, coated
6	Stahlrohr umlaufend ⌀ 273/8 mm	⌀ 273/8 mm steel CHS, circumferential
7	Abdichtung EPDM Wärmedämmung 200 mm Dampfsperre Stahlbeton 230 mm Luftzwischenraum 465 mm Holzwerkstoffplatte Deckfurnier Eiche 20 mm	EPDM sealant; 200 mm thermal insulation vapour barrier; 230 mm reinforced concrete 465 mm air space 20 mm wood composite board, oak veneer
8	Parkett Eiche verklebt 30 mm Heizestrich 90 mm Trittschalldämmung 30 mm Stahlbetondecke im Verbund mit Trapezblech 150 mm	30 mm oak parquet, glued 90 mm heating screed; 30 mm impact sound ins. 150 mm reinforced concrete deck bonded to corrugated metal
9	Abgehängte Decke Gipskarton 2× 12,5 mm	Suspended ceiling: 2× 12.5 mm plasterboard
10	Aluminiumprofil 295/10 mm	295/10 mm aluminium profile
11	Isolierverglasung Weißglas VSG 2× 8 + SZR 14 + ESG 8 mm Stahlprofilsystem beschichtet	Double glazing with low-iron glass: 2× 8 mm laminated safety glass + 14 mm cavity + 8 mm toughened glass steel-profile system, coated

Jérôme Seydoux-Pathé Foundation

Paris, 2006–2014

Kimbell Art Museum Expansion, Fort Worth, TX, USA

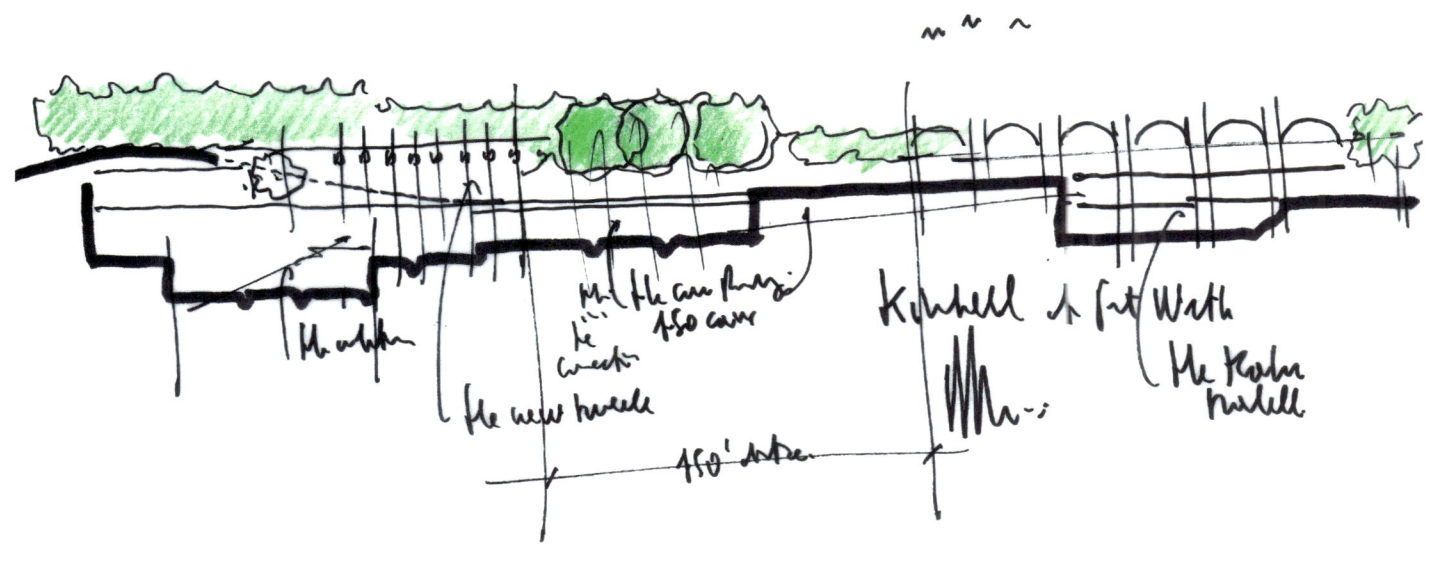

Entwurfsskizze von Renzo Piano /
Design sketch by Renzo Piano

Museumserweiterung in Fort Worth

Text: Burkhard Franke
Detail 1–2/2015

Bei der Erweiterung des Kimbell Art Museums gelingt Renzo Piano die Balance zwischen respektvoller Zurückhaltung gegenüber dem Meisterwerk von Louis Kahn und einem selbstbewussten, durch den großzügigen Einsatz von Glas geprägten architektonischen Auftritt. Städtebaulich spiegelt der Neubau die dreiteilige Gliederung des Kahn-Baus: Zwei Ausstellungsräume liegen zu beiden Seiten eines Foyers, dessen Gebäudesegment etwas zurückgesetzt ist und so den Eingang markiert. Zusätzliche Ausstellungsflächen, Schulungsräume und ein halb unterirdisches Auditorium konnten in einem zweiten, unauffälligen Baukörper auf der Westseite »versteckt« werden. Ein zentraler parkähnlicher Grünzug erschließt beide Häuser und bildet den räumlichen Schwerpunkt des Gesamtensembles.

Die drei etwa gleich großen Räume des Ostflügels werden jeweils von 22 paarweise durch Abstandhalter zu Zangen verbundenen Leimholzbindern überspannt. Diese in Längsrichtung der Räume angeordnete Trägerschar kann strukturell als Referenz an Kahns Stahlbetontonnen gelesen werden — beide Systeme ermöglichen stützenfreie Grundrisse und eine vollständig verglaste Eingangsfassade zwischen den geschlossenen Wänden der Ausstellungsflügel. Vor den transparenten Stirnseiten ruhen die Träger auf einer Kolonnade aus Stahlbetonstützen. Im Dach schichten sich Sprinklerleitungen, Entwässerungsrinnen, gewölbte siebbedruckte Isolierglasscheiben, Wartungsstege und Sonnenschutzlamellen mit integrierten PV-Zellen zu einem sorgfältig geordneten Paket. Aussteifungselemente spannen zwischen den Zangen, in deren Zwischenraum verlaufen die Stromschienen der Beleuchtung. Während dieser Aufbau im Foyer frei einsehbar ist, filtert in den Ausstellungsräumen ein zwischen die Träger gespanntes Textil das Tageslicht und schafft eine ruhige, gebänderte Untersicht. Außerhalb der Klimahülle wechselt die Dachdeckung zu vorgespanntem Sicherheitsglas. Die einzelnen Schichten des Dachaufbaus kragen nach oben hin stufenweise weiter aus und erzeugen in der Ansicht einen eleganten Dachrand, der die Komplexität im Inneren nicht erahnen lässt. So ist dieses weitspannende, gläserne Dach letztlich ein in seiner Durchlässigkeit abgestufter Lichtfilter, ein technisches Instrument, das der Architektur einen Ausdruck von Offenheit und Leichtigkeit verleiht.

Museum Extension in Fort Worth

Text: Burkhard Franke
Detail 1–2/2015

With his design for a new pavilion at the Kimbell Art Museum in Forth Worth, Renzo Piano achieves a balance between deference towards Louis Kahn's masterpiece and a self-confident architectural statement distinguished by large expanses of glass. At the urban scale it mirrors the tripartite structure of Kahn's building: two exhibition spaces flank a foyer, which, to mark the entrance, is slightly recessed. To the west, education rooms, an auditorium (situated partially underground), and additional exhibition spaces are tucked away in a second unobtrusive structure. A central, park-like zone is the spatial centrepiece of the ensemble and provides access to both the original building and the new pavilion.

The spaces of the new pavilion's east wing are nearly equal in size. Eleven pairs of laminated beams – bound together by spacers – span these interiors. They extend the entire length of the wing and can be interpreted as a reference to Kahn's barrel vaults: both systems provide column-free space and facilitate a fully glazed entrance facade between the solid walls of the exhibition wings. The beams rest on a colonnade of reinforced concrete piers situated just beyond the transparent skin. The roof's layers consist of: sprinkler pipes, gutters, arched, silk-screened glazing units, maintenance catwalks, and solar control louvres with integrated photovoltaic cells. Together they constitute a painstakingly arranged package. Bracing members run between the paired beams. Electric channels for the lighting are positioned in the latter's interstitial space. The overall roof assembly is clearly visible in the foyer, but in the exhibition spaces, the fabric mounted between the beams obscures the different components and filters the daylight, creating a serene, striped ceiling. Outside the climatised building envelope the roof surface is made of pre-tensioned safety glass. Each of its layers cantilevers farther than the one below it, creating an elegant roofline that gives little indication of the building's inner complexity. To sum the design up, this translucent glazed roof spanning a considerable length is ultimately analogous to a finely tuned mechanism that generates open, lofty architecture.

Schnitt, Grundriss,
Maßstab 1:750 /
Section, Layout plan
scale 1:750

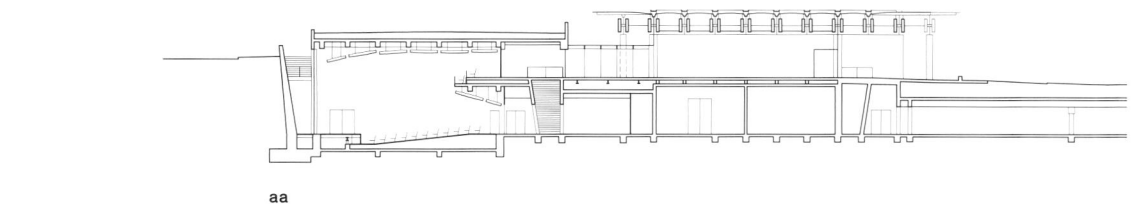

aa

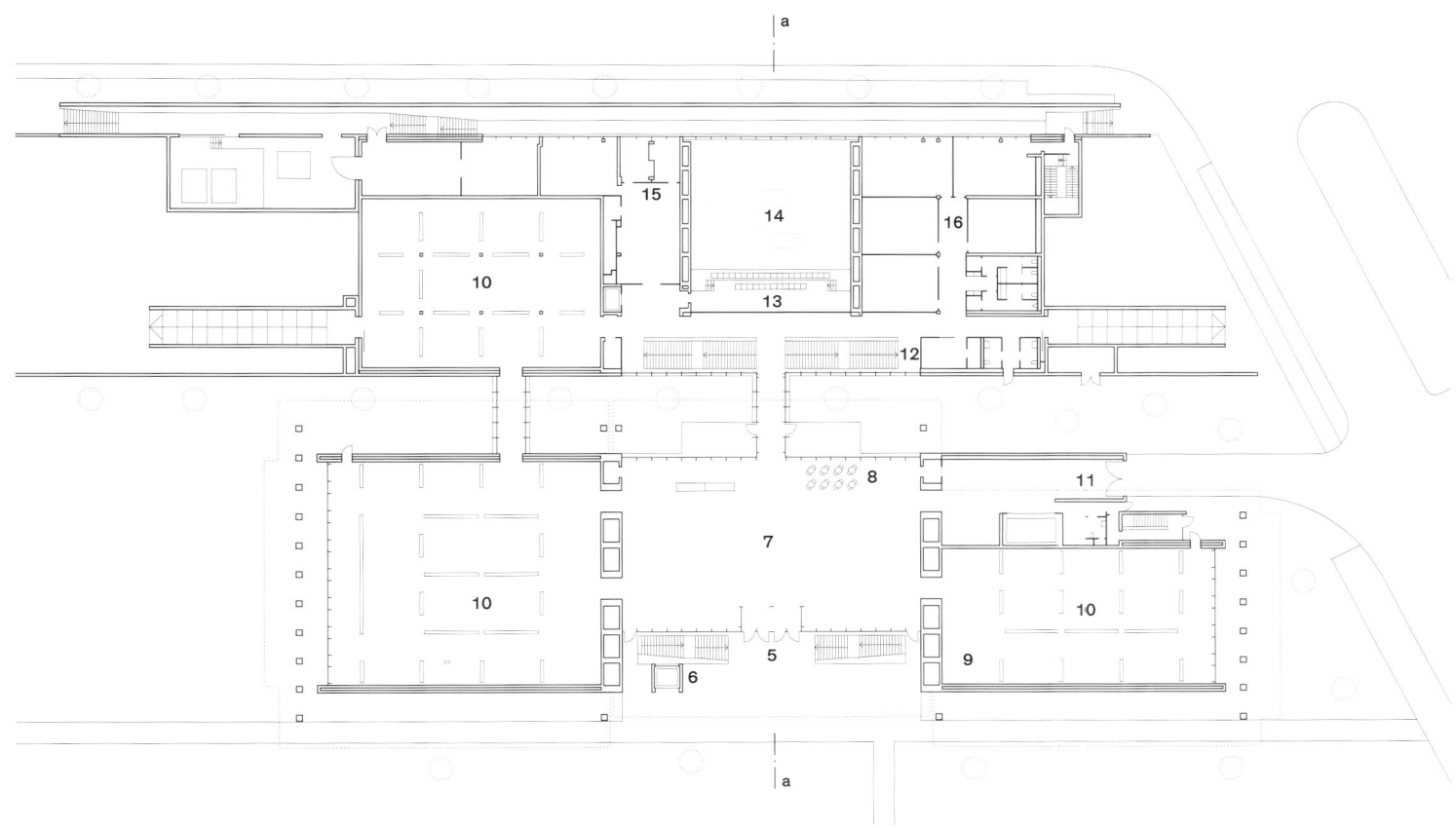

1	Amon Carter Museum Philip Johnson	Amon Carter Museum Philip Johnson
2	KAM-Erweiterung RPBW	KAM extension RPBW
3	Kimbell Art Museum Louis Kahn	Kimbell Art Museum Louis Kahn
4	Modern Art Museum Tadao Ando	Modern Art Museum Tadao Ando
5	Eingang	Entrance
6	Zugang Tiefgarage	Access to parking
7	Foyer	Foyer
8	Café	Café
9	Shop	Shop
10	Ausstellungsraum	Exhibition space
11	Anlieferung	Delivery
12	Zugang UG	Access to basement
13	Galerie Auditorium	Auditorium balcony
14	Luftraum Auditorium	Auditorium void
15	Büro	Office
16	Schulungsräume	Education

Lageplan,
Maßstab 1:7500 /
Site plan,
scale 1:7,500

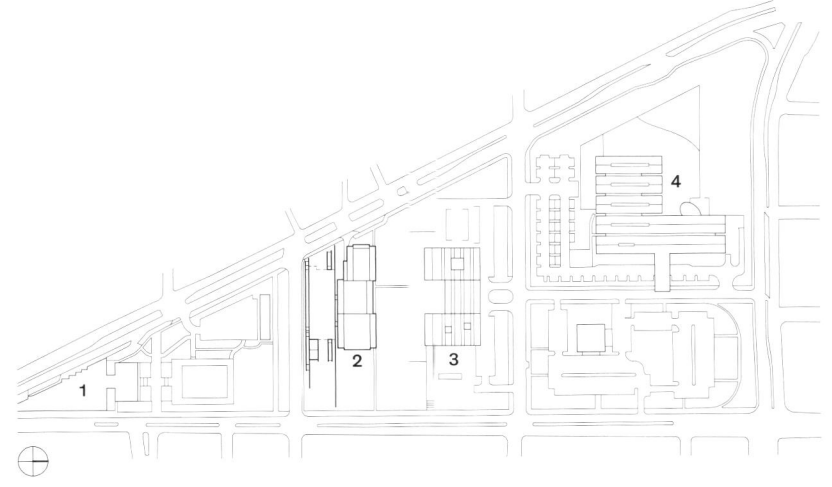

Fort Worth, 2007–2013

#		
1	VSG gebogen aus 2× TVG-Weißglas keramisch bedruckt 10 mm	Laminated safety glass, curved, of 2× 10 mm heat-strengthened, low-iron glass, ceramic frit
2	Kragträger geschweißt aus Flachstahl	Cantilevering beam of welded steel slats
3	Stahlstab Ø 114 mm	Ø 114 mm steel rod
4	Stahlprofil ⌴ 180/70 mm	180/70 mm steel channel
5	Gitterrost Stahl	Steel grating
6	Rinne: PVC-beschichtetes Aluminiumblech 1 mm Wärmedämmung EPS im Gefälle 70 mm Aluminiumblech lackiert 2 mm	Gutter: 1 mm aluminium sheet, PVC-coated 70 mm EPS thermal insulation to falls 2 mm aluminium sheet, lacquered
7	Stahlprofil HEA 100	96 mm wide-flange steel I-beam (HEA 100)
8	Hauptträger Brettschichtholz Douglasie weiß lasiert 1321/203 mm	Primary beam: 1,321/203 mm glued laminated timber Douglas fir, white glaze
9	Verbindungselement Aluminium geschweißt mit thermischer Trennung	Connection element: aluminium, welded, with thermal zoning
10	Paneel: Aluminiumblech 1 mm Wärmedämmung 60 mm Aluminiumblech 1 mm	1 mm aluminium-sheet panel; 60 mm thermal insulation 1 mm aluminium sheet
11	Wärmeschutzverglasung ESG 6 + SZR 16 + VSG aus 2× ESG 5 mm keramisch bedruckt	Thermal glazing: 6 mm toughened glass + 16 mm cavity + laminated safety glass of 2× 5 mm toughened glass, ceramic frit
12	Sonnenschutzlamelle Aluminium schwenkbar mit integriertem Photovoltaik-Modul	Pivoting aluminium solar control louvre, with integrated photovoltaic module
13	Wärmeschutzverglasung Weißglas gebogen, keramisch bedruckt, Lichtdurchlässigkeit 62,5%, ESG 8 + SZR 16 + VSG aus 2× TVG 6 mm	Thermal glazing, curved: 8 mm toughened glass + 16 mm cavity + laminated safety glass of 2× 6 mm heat-strengthened glass, all low-iron glass, ceramic frit, light permeability: 62.5%
14	Sprinklerleitung	Sprinkler pipe
15	Aussteifung / Träger abgehängte Decke: Druckstab Stahlrohr Ø 60 mm	Bracing / beam suspended ceiling (compression member): 60 mm steel CHS
16	Aussteifung Zugstab Stahl Ø 14 mm	Bracing (tension member): Ø 14 mm steel rod
17	abgehängte Decke: Polyestertextil in Aluminiumrahmen	Suspended ceiling: polyester fabric in aluminium frame
18	Stahlbeton 250 mm Wärmedämmung EPS 127 mm Dampfbremse Stahlbetonfertigteil 80 mm Systemträger Stahl Stahlbeton 250 mm	250 mm reinforced concrete; 127 mm EPS thermal insulation; vapour retarder; 80 mm precast concrete; unit steel studs; 250 mm reinforced concrete

Kimbell Art Museum Expansion

Schnitt,
Maßstab 1:20 /
Section,
scale 1:20

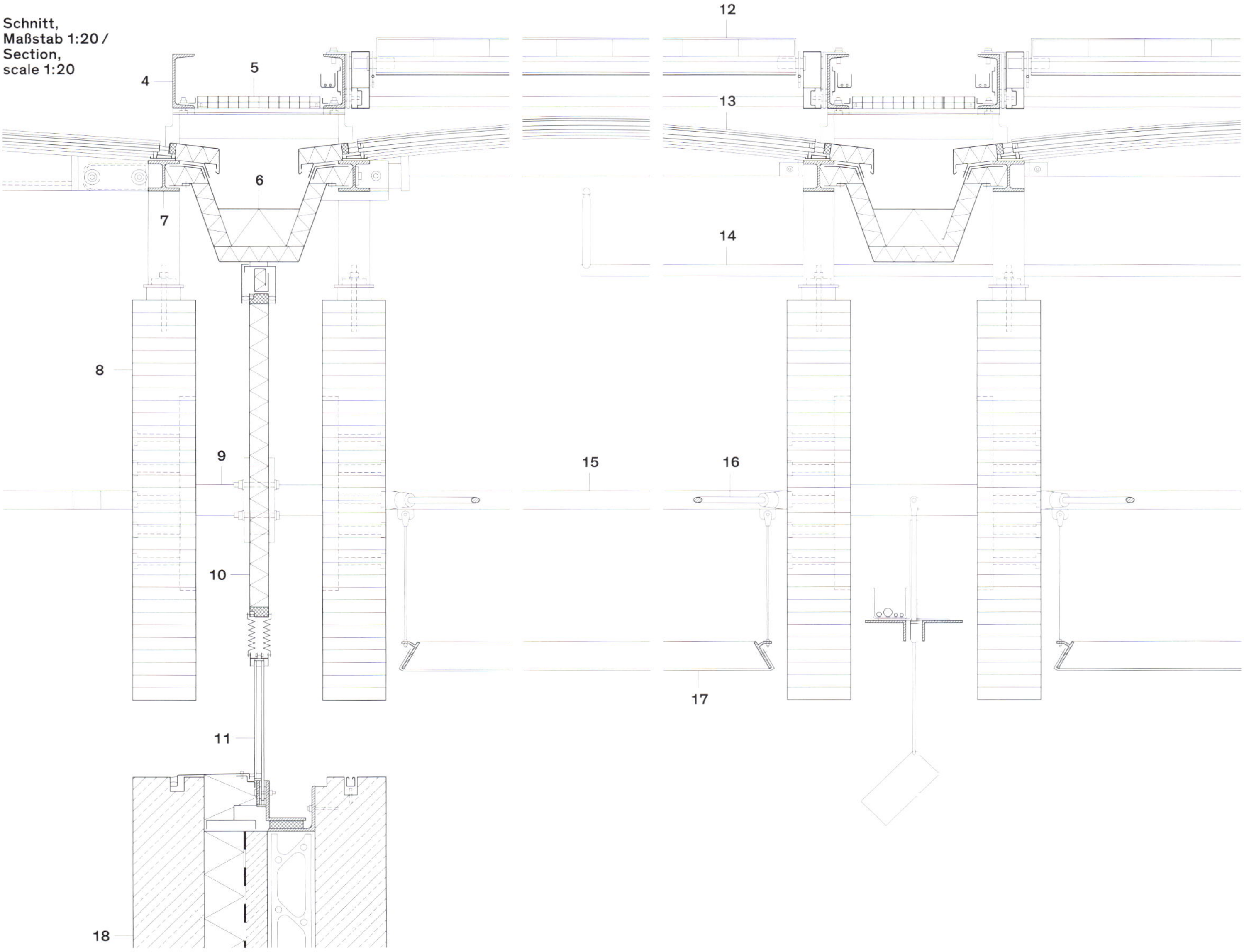

Die Axonometrie des Auflagerknotens für die Leimholzbinder-Zange zeigt das Verbindungselement aus massivem Aluminium und den Anschluss der Aussteifungselemente aus Stahl.

The axonometric of the point of support of glue-laminated paired beams shows the connection element of solid aluminium and the junction of the steel bracing members.

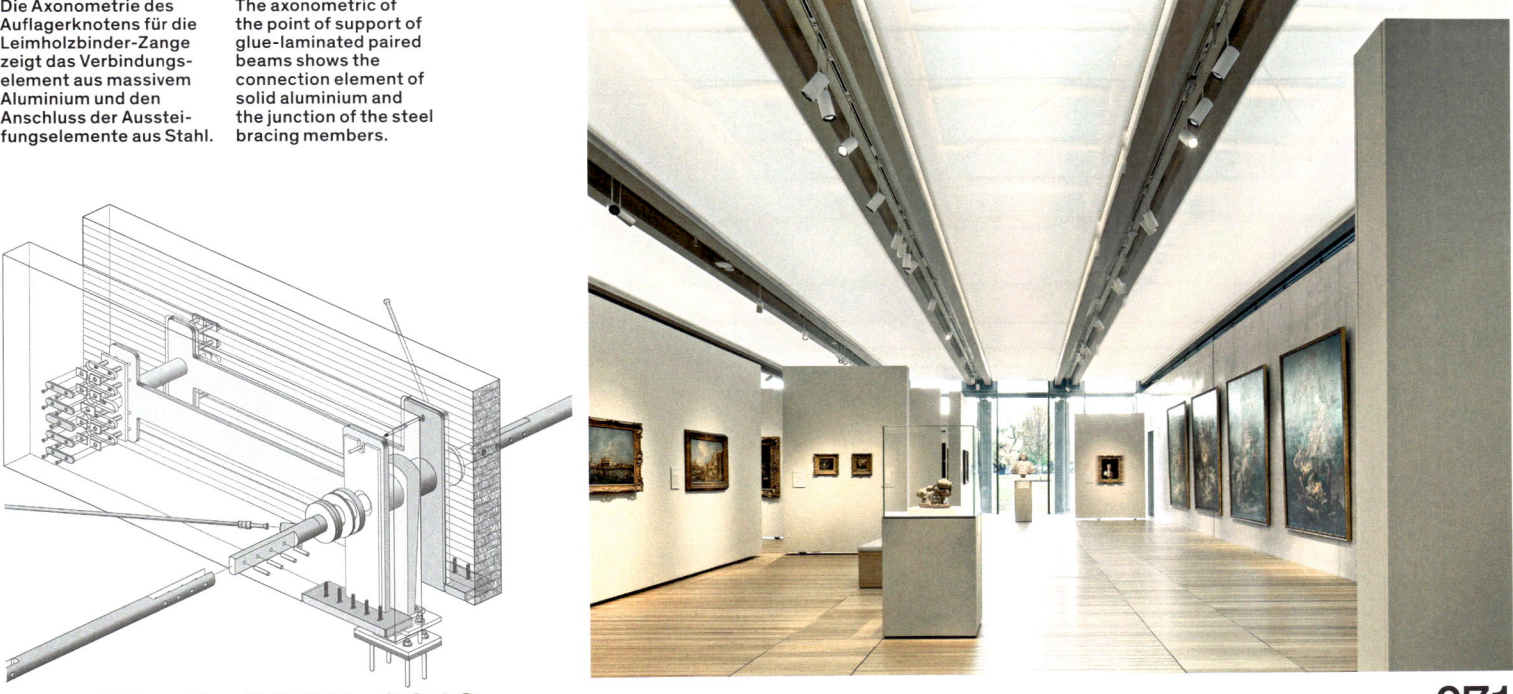

Fort Worth, 2007–2013

071

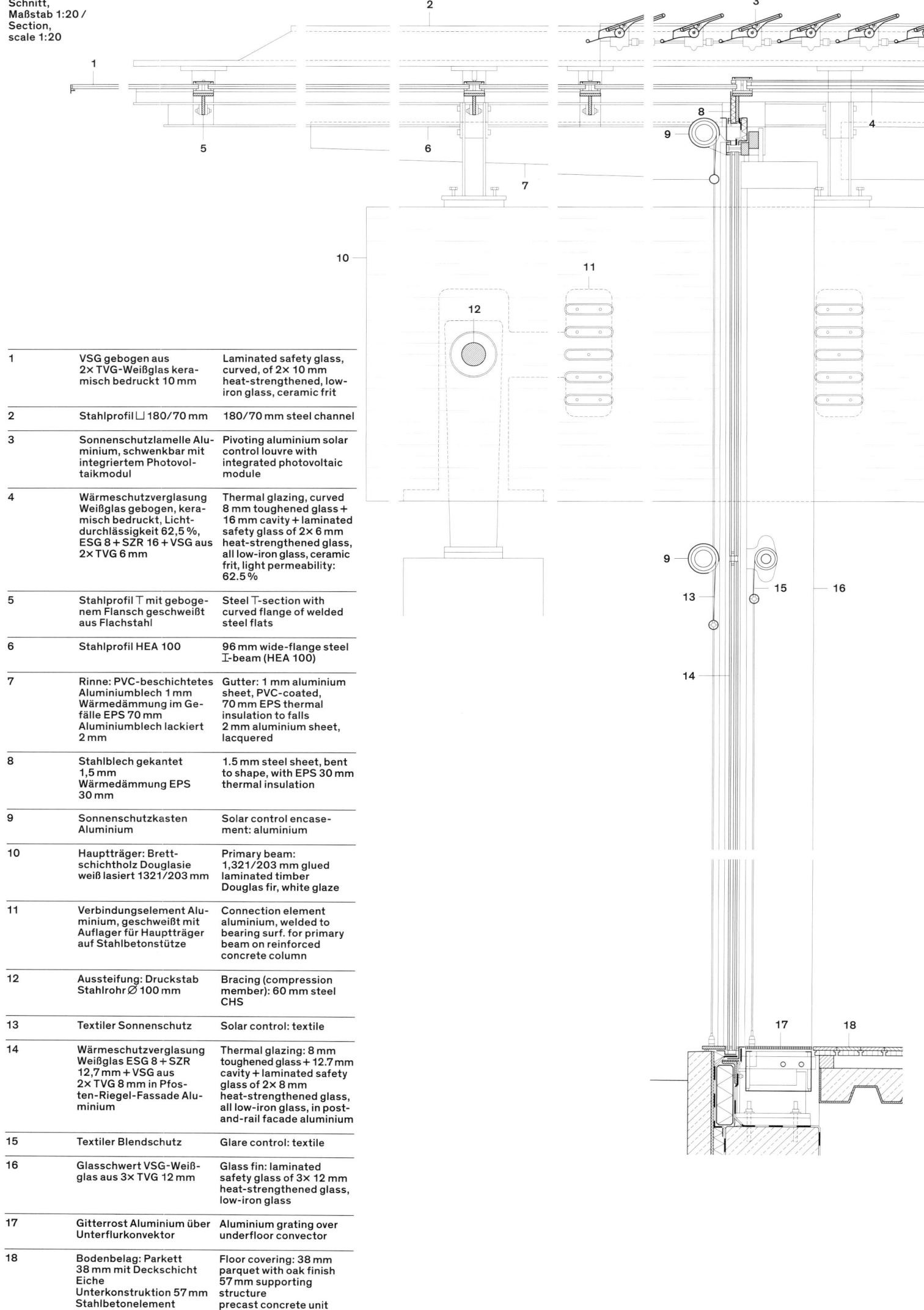

Schnitt, Maßstab 1:20 / Section, scale 1:20

1	VSG gebogen aus 2× TVG-Weißglas keramisch bedruckt 10 mm	Laminated safety glass, curved, of 2× 10 mm heat-strengthened, low-iron glass, ceramic frit
2	Stahlprofil ⌶ 180/70 mm	180/70 mm steel channel
3	Sonnenschutzlamelle Aluminium, schwenkbar mit integriertem Photovoltaikmodul	Pivoting aluminium solar control louvre with integrated photovoltaic module
4	Wärmeschutzverglasung Weißglas gebogen, keramisch bedruckt, Lichtdurchlässigkeit 62,5 %, ESG 8 + SZR 16 + VSG aus 2× TVG 6 mm	Thermal glazing, curved 8 mm toughened glass + 16 mm cavity + laminated safety glass of 2× 6 mm heat-strengthened glass, all low-iron glass, ceramic frit, light permeability: 62.5%
5	Stahlprofil T mit gebogenem Flansch geschweißt aus Flachstahl	Steel T-section with curved flange of welded steel flats
6	Stahlprofil HEA 100	96 mm wide-flange steel I-beam (HEA 100)
7	Rinne: PVC-beschichtetes Aluminiumblech 1 mm Wärmedämmung im Gefälle EPS 70 mm Aluminiumblech lackiert 2 mm	Gutter: 1 mm aluminium sheet, PVC-coated, 70 mm EPS thermal insulation to falls 2 mm aluminium sheet, lacquered
8	Stahlblech gekantet 1,5 mm Wärmedämmung EPS 30 mm	1.5 mm steel sheet, bent to shape, with EPS 30 mm thermal insulation
9	Sonnenschutzkasten Aluminium	Solar control encasement: aluminium
10	Hauptträger: Brettschichtholz Douglasie weiß lasiert 1321/203 mm	Primary beam: 1,321/203 mm glued laminated timber Douglas fir, white glaze
11	Verbindungselement Aluminium, geschweißt mit Auflager für Hauptträger auf Stahlbetonstütze	Connection element aluminium, welded to bearing surf. for primary beam on reinforced concrete column
12	Aussteifung: Druckstab Stahlrohr ⌀ 100 mm	Bracing (compression member): 60 mm steel CHS
13	Textiler Sonnenschutz	Solar control: textile
14	Wärmeschutzverglasung Weißglas ESG 8 + SZR 12,7 mm + VSG aus 2× TVG 8 mm in Pfosten-Riegel-Fassade Aluminium	Thermal glazing: 8 mm toughened glass + 12.7 mm cavity + laminated safety glass of 2× 8 mm heat-strengthened glass, all low-iron glass, in post-and-rail facade aluminium
15	Textiler Blendschutz	Glare control: textile
16	Glasschwert VSG-Weißglas aus 3× TVG 12 mm	Glass fin: laminated safety glass of 3× 12 mm heat-strengthened glass, low-iron glass
17	Gitterrost Aluminium über Unterflurkonvektor	Aluminium grating over underfloor convector
18	Bodenbelag: Parkett 38 mm mit Deckschicht Eiche Unterkonstruktion 57 mm Stahlbetonelement	Floor covering: 38 mm parquet with oak finish 57 mm supporting structure precast concrete unit

Kimbell Art Museum Expansion

Auditorium Del Parco, L'Aquila, IT

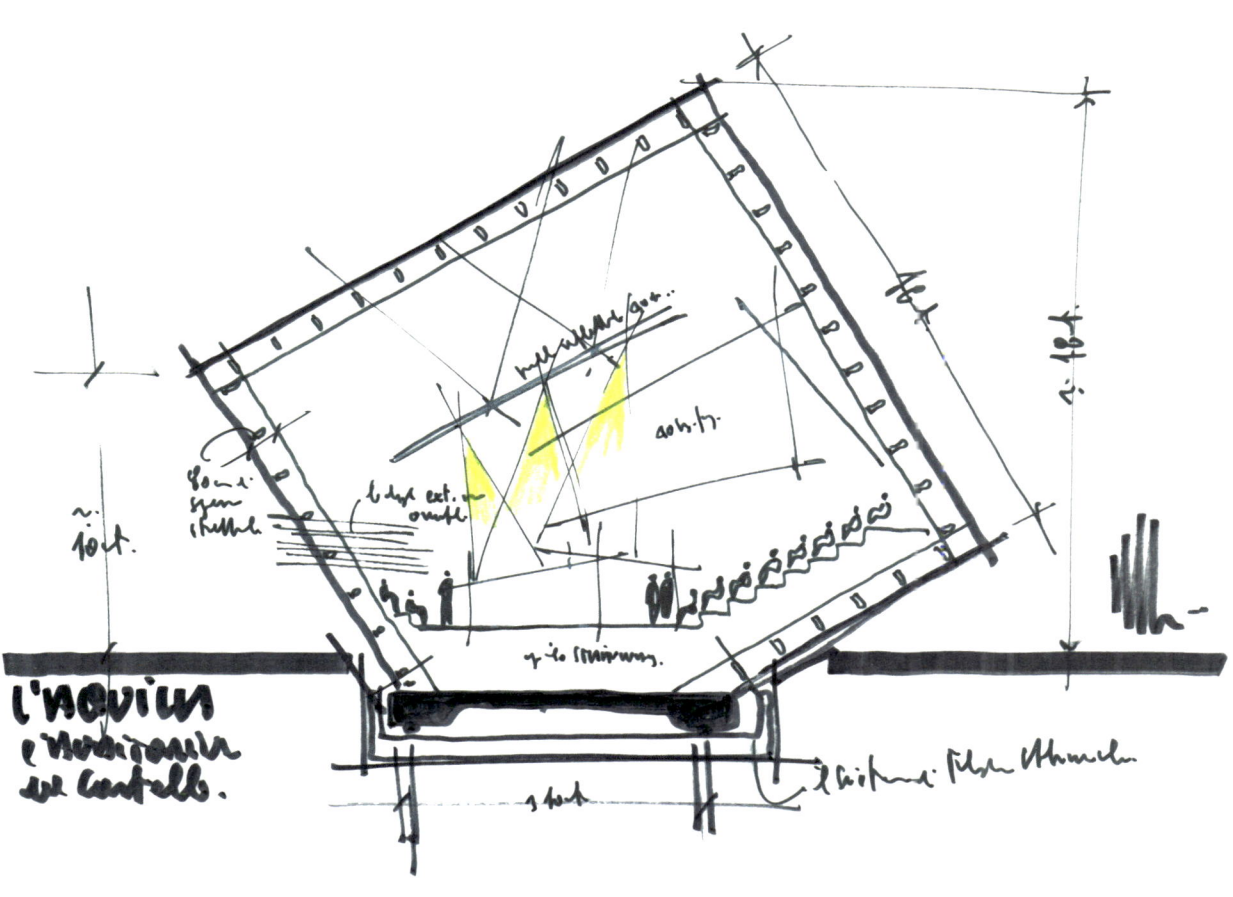

Entwurfsskizze von Renzo Piano / Design sketch by Renzo Piano

Konzertsaal in L'Aquila

Text: Claudia Fuchs
Detail 10/2013

Im April 2009 wurde L'Aquila, die Hauptstadt der Abruzzen, von einem Erdbeben schwer getroffen. Seither ist das erheblich beschädigte Stadtzentrum nur mit Genehmigung zugänglich, die Bewohner wurden umgesiedelt. Urbanes Leben und kulturelle Aktivitäten kamen zum Stillstand. Ein Zeichen des Aufbruchs setzt seit Herbst 2012 ein neues temporäres Konzerthaus, gestiftet von der Provinz Trento. Am Rand der Altstadt, im Park der historischen Festung, ziehen drei farbig gestreifte Holzkuben die Blicke auf sich. Dynamisch ragt der auf die Kante gestellte Konzertsaal hervor, flankiert von zwei kleineren Bauten. Der nördliche ist den Musikern vorbehalten, der westliche nimmt das Foyer, das öffentliche Café und Technikräume auf. Verglaste Verbindungsgänge führen in den Saal, der die Zuhörer mit warmen Rottönen empfängt.

    Der vollständig aus Holz gefertigte Kubus wirkt selbst wie ein Musikinstrument. Da die geneigten Wände jedoch den Schall direkt zur Quelle zurückwerfen, mussten für ein ausgewogenes Klangbild die Raumoberflächen entsprechend optimiert werden: Fräsungen in unterschiedlicher Breite und Tiefe an Wand- und Deckenelementen streuen den Schall, in die Decke sind Absorptionsflächen integriert. Zudem dienen abgehängte Akustiksegel aus gebogenen Holzplatten der Schalllenkung.

    Innerhalb von acht Monaten wurden die drei Kuben aus vorgefertigten Tannenholz-Bauteilen montiert. Das Tragwerk für Dach und Wände besteht aus einem Gitterrost aus Brettschichtholzträgern, der beidseitig mit Brettsperrholzplatten beplankt ist. 40 mm starke Lärchenholzbretter in 21 Farben bilden die Fassadenbekleidung. Als Interimsbau für die Dauer der Sanierung des bestehenden Konzertsaals in der nahen Festung bietet das »Auditorium del Parco« mit 240 Plätzen nicht nur ein außergewöhnliches Raum- und Klangerlebnis. Es hat sich darüber hinaus mit dem Café und Open-Air-Veranstaltungen zum beliebten Treffpunkt und zu einer öffentlichen Piazza entwickelt.

Concert Hall in L'Aquila

Text: Claudia Fuchs
Detail 10/2013

In April 2009, L'Aquila, the capital of the Abruzzi region in central Italy, was seriously hit by an earthquake. The city centre was heavily damaged, and urban life and cultural activities came to a standstill. The erection of a temporary concert hall in 2012, donated by the Province of Trento, was, therefore, a token of a new beginning. Three colourfully striped wooden cubes catch the eye in the park around the historic fort on the edge of the old city, with the volume containing the concert hall jutting out at an angle. Tilted and seemingly set on edge, it is flanked by two smaller structures. The northern one is reserved for musicians, while the western structure houses the foyer, a public café and spaces for mechanical services. Glazed corridors lead from these two ancillary volumes into the auditorium, where concertgoers are welcomed by the warm reddish tones of the interior.

    Built entirely of wood, this concert hall is not unlike a musical instrument in itself. Since the sloping walls reflect sound directly back to its source, however, the internal surfaces had to be treated in order to ensure balanced acoustics. These were achieved by milling the wall and soffit elements to different widths and depths. In addition, absorbent surfaces were integrated in the ceiling. Finally, the needs of sound diffusion are met by suspended acoustic sails, consisting of curved timber sheeting.

    The three cubes were assembled from prefabricated softwood elements within a period of eight months. The structure for the roof and walls consists of a grid of laminated-timber beams lined on both faces with laminated cross-boarded sheeting. For the facade cladding, 40 mm larch boarding in 21 different colours was used. Conceived as an interim solution to last for the duration of the rehabilitation of the existing concert hall in the nearby fortress, the Auditorium del Parco contains 240 seats and affords not just an exceptional spatial and auditory experience. With its café and open-air events, it has also become a popular meeting place with the features of a public piazza.

Schnitte, Grundrisse,
Maßstab 1:500 /
Sections, Floor plans,
scale 1:500

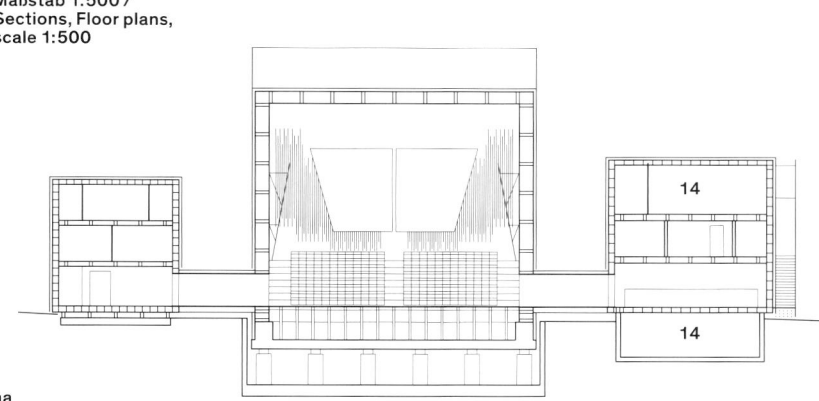

aa

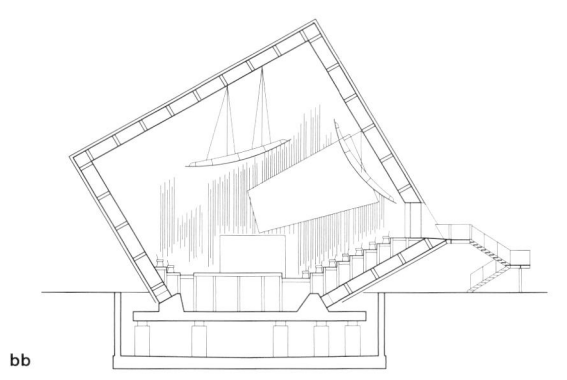

bb

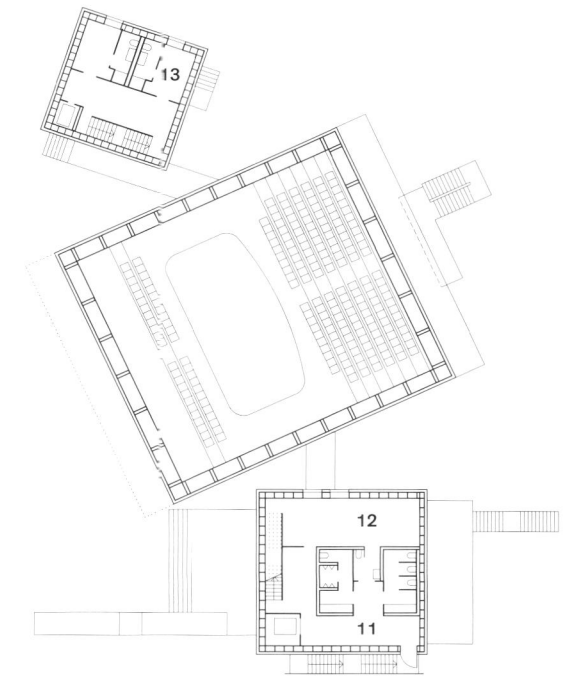

1. Obergeschoss /
First floor

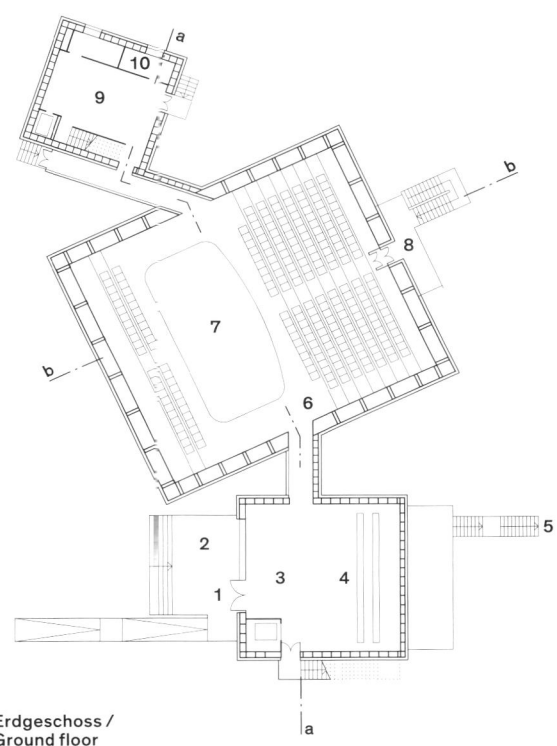

Erdgeschoss /
Ground floor

1	Haupteingang	Main entrance
2	Terrasse	Terrace
3	Foyer / Café	Foyer / Café
4	Ticketverkauf / Bar	Ticket desk / Bar
5	Zugang Untergeschoss	Access to basement
6	Konzertsaal	Concert hall
7	Bühne	Stage / Platform
8	Notausgang	Emergency exit
9	Künstlerbereich	Performers' realm
10	Direktion	Administration
11	Besuchertoiletten	Public toilets
12	Lager / Requisite	Store / Props
13	Künstlergarderoben	Performers' dressing rooms
14	Technik	Mechanical services

Lageplan,
Maßstab 1:5000 /
Site plan,
scale 1:5,000

L'Aquila, 2010–2012

077

Explosionsaxonometrie /
Exploded axonometric:

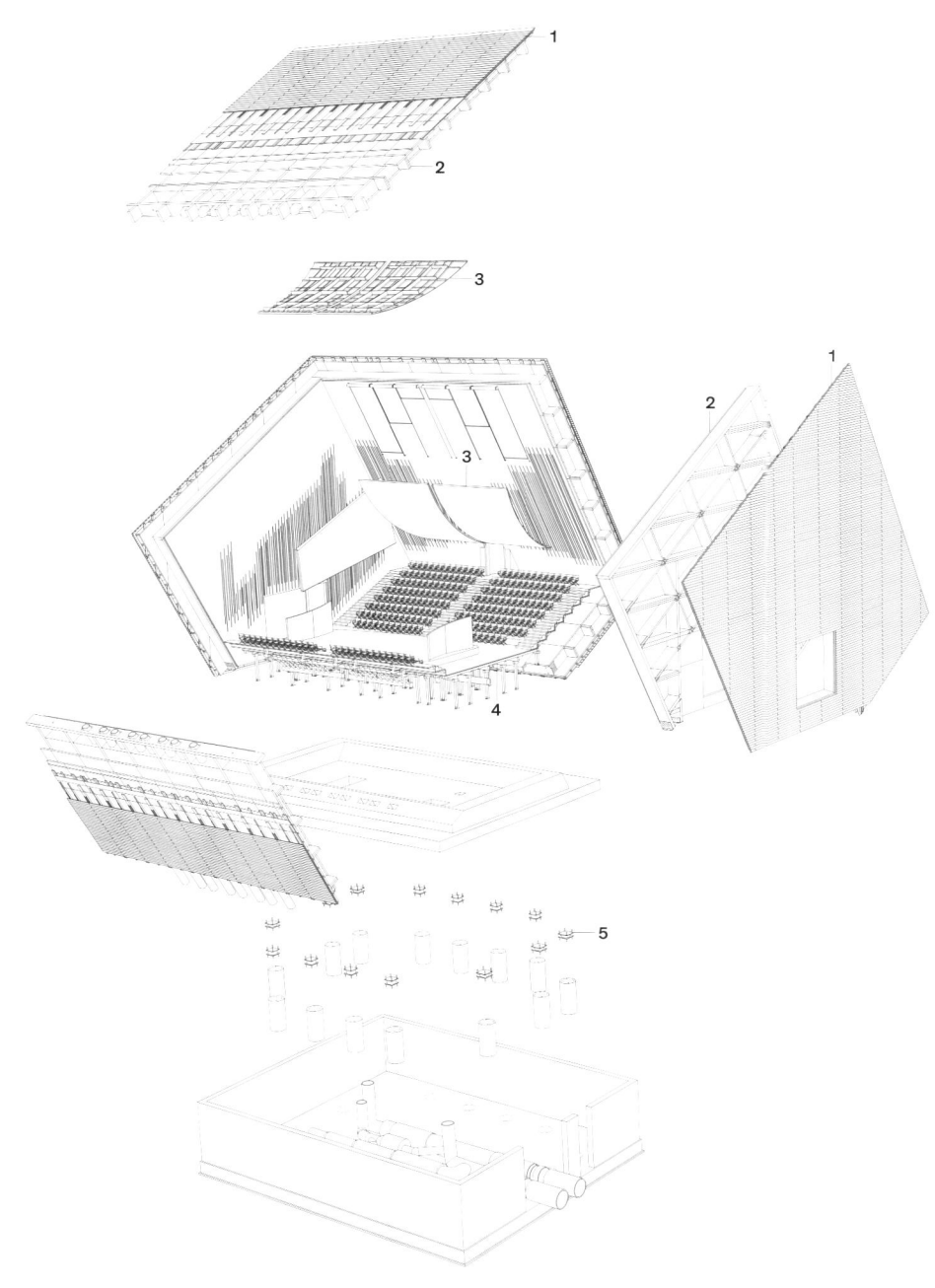

1	Lärchenschalung auf Unterkonstruktion	Larch boarding on supporting structure
2	Trägerrost BSH, beidseitig beplankt mit Brettsperrholzplatten	Grid of glued laminated timber beams with cross laminated timber panels
3	Akustiksegel	Acoustic sails
4	Bühne und Sitzreihen, Unterkonstruktion Holz	Platform and rows of seating on timber supporting structure
5	Elastomerlager als Dämpfer bei Erdstößen	Elastomer bearers as damper against earth tremors

L'Aquila, 2010–2012

Auditorium Del Parco

Auditorium Del Parco

Schnitt Konzertsaal, Maßstab 1:50 /
Section through concert hall, scale 1:50

1	Schalung Lärche, thermisch modifiziert, lasiert, ölimprägniert 40 mm Lattung Tanne 40/60 mm Abdichtung Bitumenbahn OSB-Platte 20 mm Hinterlüftung 20 mm Kantholz Tanne 80/100 mm, dazwischen Wärmedämmung 80 mm Brettsperrholzplatte Tanne dreilagig 96 mm Träger BSH Tanne 200/720 mm Brettsperrholzplatte siebenlagig, raumseitig mit Akustikfräsung, rot lasiert 202 mm	40 mm oil-impregnated larch boarding, thermally treated 40/60 mm s. w. battens bituminous sealing layer 20 mm oriented-strand board 20 mm rear-ventilated cavity 80/100 mm s. w. bearers with 80 mm thermal insulation 96 mm three-layer cross laminated timber s. w. panel 200/720 mm cross laminated timber s. w. beams 202 mm red-glazed seven-layer cross laminated timber panel with acoustic milling
2	Akustikpaneel Sperrholzplatte 30 mm mit Deckfurnier Fichte	30 mm plywood acoustic panel
3	Bodenaufbau Tribüne: Dielen Lärche 17 mm Furnierschichtholzplatte 39 mm	Floor construction to tier of seating: 17 mm larch boarding 39 mm laminated veneer lumber panel
4	Stahlplatte ∟ 700/510/10 mm	700/510/10 mm sheet-steel angle
5	Abluft	Air extract
6	Zuluft	Air intake

Auditorium Del Parco

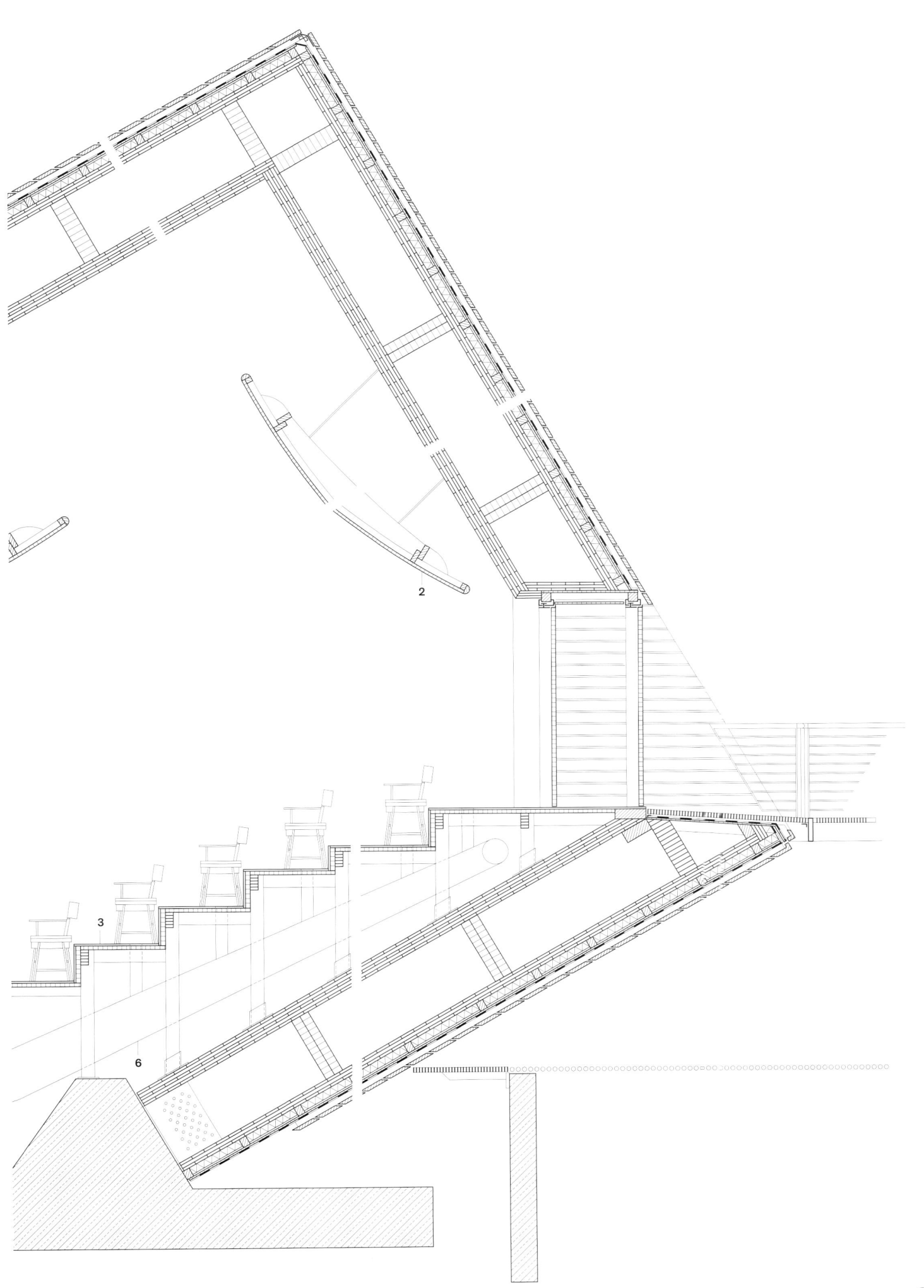

L'Aquila, 2010–2012

Chicago Art Institute – The Modern Wing, Chicago, IL, USA

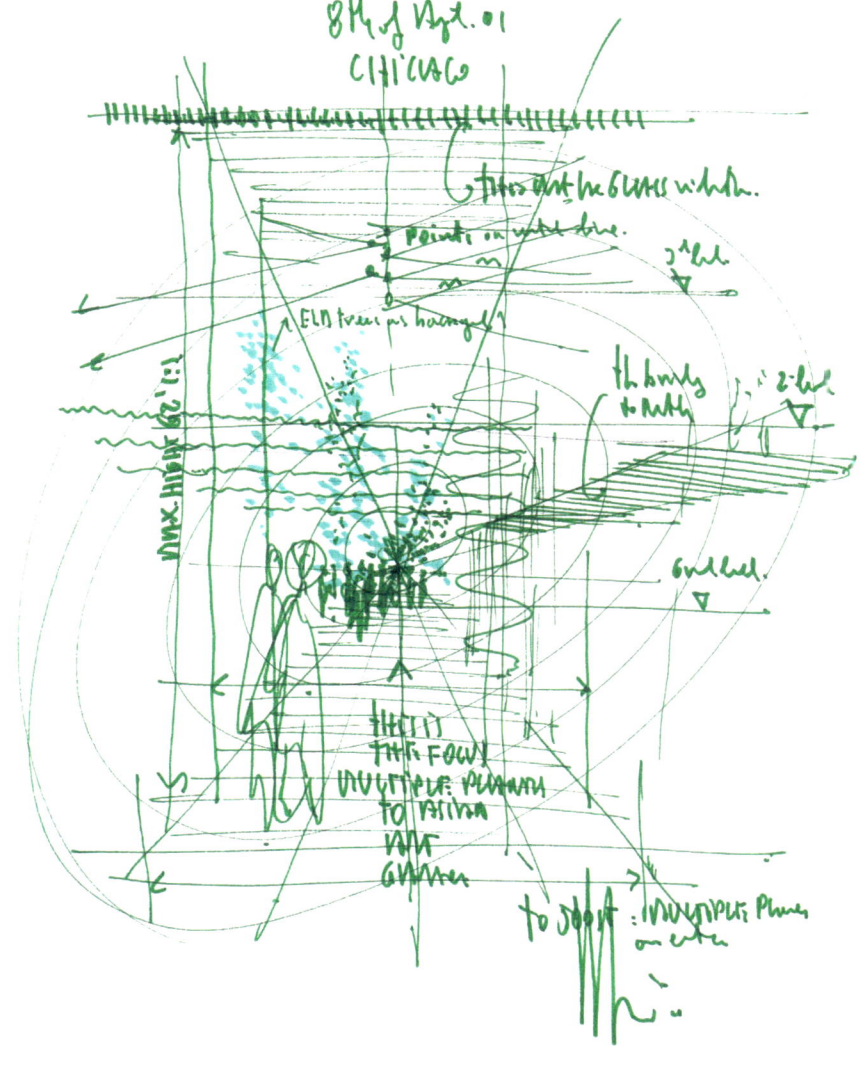

Entwurfsskizze von Renzo Piano / Design sketch by Renzo Piano

Das Lichtkonzept des Museums

Text: Andrew Sedgwick
Detail 4/2010

Als die beiden Museumsgebäude – der Modern Wing des Art Institute of Chicago und das Museum Brandhorst in München – kurz nacheinander im Mai 2009 eröffnet wurden, zeigten sich darin zwei Lichtkonzepte zur Präsentation der großen Kunstwerke des 20. Jahrhunderts mit kleinen, aber feinen Unterschieden. Beide Gebäude sind von europäischen Architekten entworfen, das Chicagoer Museum von Renzo Piano Building Workshop, das Münchner Museum von Sauerbruch Hutton. Die Lichtkonzepte stammen vom selben Lichtdesigner: Arup aus London. Die Hauptausstellungsräume in den Obergeschossen der beiden Gebäude weisen auf den ersten Blick eine ähnliche Beleuchtungslösung auf: Lichtdecken überspannen die Räume und lassen ein diffuses, gleichmäßiges Licht auf allen Flächen entstehen.

Beim Einsatz von künstlichem Licht dagegen beschreiten die beiden Institutionen ganz unterschiedliche Wege. Da in einem modernen Museum die auf die Exponate fallende Lichtmenge begrenzt werden muss, hatte dies Auswirkungen auf die Konzepte, wie der Eintritt und die Verteilung des direkten Sonnenlichts und des Tageslichts insgesamt reguliert wird. Hier folgt das Art Institute of Chicago dem Ansatz der meisten nordamerikanischen Museen: Im Vordergrund steht die Überzeugung, dass Kunstwerke in der Regel vom warmen Licht und der Fokussierung durch schienenmontierte Halogen-Punktstrahler profitieren. In direktem Gegensatz dazu steht die in München umgesetzte Haltung, wo so lange wie möglich versucht wird, die Zuschaltung von künstlichem Licht zu vermeiden.

Die beiden Entwürfe zeigen auch konträre Haltungen gegenüber dem Einsatz von Technik in einem modernen Gebäude: In München wurde eine Reihe von motorgesteuerten automatischen Lichtsteuerungssystemen installiert, um das vorrangige Ziel einer maximalen Nutzung von Tageslicht zu erreichen, während in Chicago Einfachheit durch möglichst wenige bewegliche Teile angestrebt wurde, um den Wartungsaufwand zu minimieren.

Lighting a Museum

Text: Andrew Sedgwick
Detail 4/2010

When two new museum buildings opened within days of each other in May 2009 – the Modern Wing of the Art Institute of Chicago, and the Brandhorst Museum in Munich – they demonstrated two subtly contrasted curatorial approaches to the lighting of great 20th-century art. Both are designed by European architects – Renzo Piano Building Workshop in Chicago, and Sauerbruch Hutton in Munich – and both share a common lighting designer: Arup, based in London. At first sight, the primary top-floor gallery spaces in both buildings also have similar lighting solutions: panelised luminous ceilings across the full extent of each room, which provide diffuse and uniform light over the surfaces.

It is in their attitude to electric lighting that the two institutions have taken substantially different paths; and because total light exposure in a modern museum has to be limited, this is reflected in the solutions found for controlling the entry and distribution of daylight from the sun and the sky. In this respect, the Art Institute of Chicago follows the approach of the majority of North American museums – based on a belief that most artworks benefit from the warmth and focus provided by track-mounted halogen spotlights. This is in direct contrast to the position taken in Munich, where one went to great lengths to avoid the use of electric light unless this was absolutely necessary.

The two designs also reveal different attitudes towards the use of technology in a modern building. In Munich, a number of motorised and automated light-control systems have been put into service with the primary goal of maximising the hours of natural lighting, whereas in Chicago there is a strong desire for simplicity and a minimum of moving parts in order to avoid future maintenance liabilities.

Chicago, 2000–2009

089

Effektive Beleuchtungskonzepte tragen wesentlich zum Erfolg von Ausstellungsräumen bei, und der Einsatz von Tageslicht kann den Genuss der Kunstwerke verstärken. Tageslicht wird häufig für Räume bevorzugt, in denen Gemälde und Skulpturen ausgestellt werden. Da die Lichtverhältnisse bei jedem Besuch etwas anders sind, macht die große Bandbreite von Tageslicht oft den Charme eines Ausstellungsraums aus.

Der richtige Einsatz von Tageslicht in einem Museum kann sowohl für den Betrieb als auch für das Renommee deutliche Vorteile bringen: Tageslicht ist umweltfreundlich und kostenlos; richtig reguliert eingesetzt, kann es eine wichtige Rolle innerhalb des Konzepts für ein Niedrigenergiegebäude spielen. Unzureichend kontrolliertes Sonnenlicht kann aber auch große Nachteile für Museen und Galerien bringen, z. B. Räume zu stark aufheizen oder für Kunstwerke zu intensiv sein. Diese gegensätzlichen Pole muss ein guter Entwurf berücksichtigen.

Bei der Entwicklung von Beleuchtungskonzepten für Museen und Galerien geht es um eine Balance zwischen den konservatorischen Notwendigkeiten für die Exponate und einer guten Ausleuchtung für die Betrachtung dieser Exponate. Zudem legen heute oft Leihverträge zwischen den Institutionen Beleuchtungsstärke und Belichtungsdauer genau fest. Daher bedarf es eines flexiblen und zugleich sehr professionellen Ansatzes, um sicherzustellen, dass Ausstellungsräume den internationalen Standards nachkommen, aber zugleich auch den ästhetischen Reiz für die Besucher bewahren. Die Sammlung moderner Kunst des Art Institute wird im dritten Stock des Modern Wing ausgestellt und befindet sich damit direkt unter dem markantesten architektonischen Element des Projekts – dem »fliegenden Teppich«. Das weit vorspringende Lamellendach schützt die von oben belichteten Ausstellungsräume ganzjährig vor direkter Sonneneinstrahlung. Eine filigrane Stahlkonstruktion trägt das gut 4300 m² große Dach aus speziell für dieses Museum angefertigten Aluminiumlamellen im Abstand von 4,5 m über dem Ostpavillon des neuen Gebäudes.

Das Ziel eines einfachen, passiven natürlichen Belichtungssystems wurde zu einem frühen Zeitpunkt des Projekts festgelegt. Analysen der Wetterdaten von Chicago hatten ergeben, dass der größte Anteil der natürlichen Schwankung in der Tageslichtstärke – je nach Bewölkung – durch den Wechsel von direktem und diffusem Sonnenlicht entsteht. Nordlicht ohne direkte Sonnenstrahlung bietet daher das konstanteste natürliche Licht. Ohne direkten Sonnenlichteinfall verhindert man zudem eine zu starke Erwärmung der Räume im Sommer.

Das Profil der Lamellen des »fliegenden Teppichs« soll daher ganzjährig eine direkte Sonneneinstrahlung verhindern, aber zugleich möglichst viel Nordlicht in die Räume holen. Als Farbe der Lamellen wurde ein sehr blasses, neutrales Grau gewählt, um eine genau begrenzte Menge interreflektierte und diffuse Sonnenstrahlung durch das Glasdach darunter eintreten zu lassen: Auf diese Weise nehmen die Besucher der Ausstellung immer noch ein wenig das Vorbeiziehen der Wolken am Himmel sowie das wechselnde Sonnenlicht wahr. Ein Dach mit Doppelverglasung unter dem »fliegenden Teppich« bietet Witterungsschutz und filtert einen großen Anteil der ultravioletten Strahlung heraus.

Die sichtbaren Decken der Ausstellungsräume für die Sammlung moderner Kunst bestehen aus einem gazeartigen Material aus Polyesterfasern, das auf 1,5 × 2,7 m große Aluminiumrahmen gespannt ist. Durch das Gewebe entsteht ein diffuses, schattenfreies und gleichmäßiges Licht auf den Wänden. Wie durch einen Schleier ist dennoch die gesamte Konstruktion wahrnehmbar. Für die elektrische Beleuchtung sorgen Wolfram-Halogenlampen, die an Schienen zwischen den mit Gewebe bespannten Rahmen hängen. Ein Teil dieser Lampen leuchtet während der gesamten Öffnungszeiten, aber die Mehrheit wird gedimmt und in der Lichtstärke der Helligkeit draußen angepasst. Da in diesem Beleuchtungssystem keine beweglichen Teile enthalten sind, musste über detaillierte Modellberechnungen sichergestellt werden, dass die Kunstwerke nur der vorgegebenen Lichtmenge ausgesetzt sind. Die Anteile von Tageslicht und künstlichem Licht wurden für jede Stunde eines Standardjahrs in Chicago bezogen auf jeden Raum ermittelt, um vorherzusagen, wie viel Licht an den einzelnen Standorten auf die Kunstwerke fällt.

Die Ausstellungsräume im zweiten und dritten Stock erhalten überwiegend Kunstlicht, profitieren jedoch von den vollständig verglasten Fassaden, die einen großartigen Blick auf den angrenzenden Millennium Park und die Skyline von Chicago bieten. Jalousien aus grobem Gewebe im Zwischenraum der Doppelfassade verhindern, dass die Kunstwerke zu viel Licht erhalten. Ein zweites System innen liegender Jalousien bietet an sehr hellen Tagen einen zusätzlichen Schutz.

Effective lighting is essential for the success of any display space, and the exploitation of natural light can add substantially to visitor enjoyment. Natural light is often the preferred option for rooms where paintings and sculpture are displayed. The variability of daylight can be an asset, altering the ambience of gallery interiors so that they differ subtly each time a visitor walks around them.

In today's world, the appropriate use of natural light in art museums can bring significant operational and reputational benefits: daylight is carbon-free and cost-free and, if properly harnessed, it can play an important part in creating a low-energy building. There are, however, downsides to the uncontrolled use of natural light in museums and galleries. Sunlight has the potential to overheat a space or flood it with illumination that is too intense for the artworks. These challenges must be addressed through careful design.

In planning lighting systems for museums and galleries, a balance must be struck between the conservation of the works on display and the strength and clarity of light required by the visitor. In addition, inter-gallery loan agreements increasingly include stringent requirements relating to levels of illumination and their duration. An imaginative and expert approach is therefore needed to ensure that galleries and museums meet international standards, while maintaining an aesthetic appeal to the visitor.
The modern collection of the Art Institute of Chicago is now displayed on the third floor of the new Modern Wing and sits immediately beneath one of the iconic architectural elements of the project – the "flying carpet". This prominent raft of shading louvres protects the top-lit galleries from direct sunlight throughout the year. The more than 4,300 m² array of custom-designed aluminium louvres is supported on a filigree structural steel system 4.50 metres above the east pavilion of the new building.

The objective of a simple and passive natural lighting system was established early in the project. Analysis of Chicago sky data showed that the largest part of the natural variation in daylight levels arises from the presence or absence of direct sunlight, as cloud cover varies; luminance is most constant from the northern part of the sky dome, where the sun is always absent. Preventing direct sunlight from entering the skylight system also helps to avoid excessive heat gains in the summer months.

The profile of the "blades" of the flying carpet was designed to prevent the entry of direct sunlight throughout the year, while maximising the ingress of light from the northern parts of the sky. The finish of the blades – in a very pale and colour-neutral grey – was chosen to allow a limited amount of inter-reflected and diffused sunlight to enter the skylights below: in this way, visitors to the galleries beneath are still mildly aware of passing clouds and the coming and going of the sun.

Double-glazed skylights beneath the flying carpet keep out the Chicago weather and incorporate a high-performance filter for ultraviolet radiation.

The visible ceilings of the galleries containing the modern collection are formed from gauze-like polyester fabric stretched horizontally in 1.50 × 2.70 m aluminium frames. The fabric diffuses the transmitted light to a certain degree, ensuring a shadow-free, even level of lighting along each gallery wall, while being sheer enough to permit veiled views through to the roof above, thus allowing visitors to sense the full volume of the construction. Electric lighting is provided by tungsten halogen fixtures mounted on tracks between the fabric panels. A number of these fixtures are fully energised during opening hours, but the majority are controlled by a dimming system that gradually supplies the fixtures with energy when daylight levels are falling. Since the lighting systems for the modern collection contained no moving parts, detailed modelling was carried out to ensure that annual degrees of exposure to illumination are within acceptable ranges. The lighting levels from the sun and sky, as well as from the supplementary electric lighting, were calculated for every hour of a typical year in Chicago and combined to predict the likely light exposures for various gallery locations.

The second and third-floor galleries also benefit from fully glazed north facades, which provide great views of the nearby Millennium Park and the Chicago skyline beyond. Open-weave fabric blinds within these cavity facades protect the art in the spaces behind from excessive exposure to light. A second set of internal blinds is also deployed under the brightest conditions.

Dachelement aus Aluminiumlamellen /
Roof element consisting of aluminium louvres or fins

Funktion / Lichttransmissionsgrad der Dachschichten:
a Lamellen: Schutz vor Direktstrahlung
  $t_1 = 17\%$
b Unterkonstruktion: tragende Struktur
  $t_2 = 82\%$
c Oberlicht: Wetterschutz + UV-Filter
  $t_3 = 34\%$
d Lichtdecke: Lichtstreuung + Sichtdecke
  $t_4 = 38\%$
  Rest-Beleuchtungsstärke an Wänden
  $E_{v6} = 1\% E_{h1}$

Function / Degree of light transmission of roof layers
a fins: protection against direct insolation
  $t_1 = 17\%$
b supporting structure / load-bearing structure
  $t_2 = 82\%$
c glazed roof: weather protection + UV filter
  $t_3 = 34\%$
d lighting ceiling: light diffusion / visible soffit
  $t_4 = 38\%$
  remaining lighting intensity on walls
  $E_{v6} = 1\% E_{h1}$

Tageslichtprognose Obergeschoss – typische Tagesverläufe der Beleuchtungsstärke 1,5 m über Fertigfußboden /
Daylighting estimates for upper floor – typical conditions during the course of the day for lighting intensity 1.50m above floor level

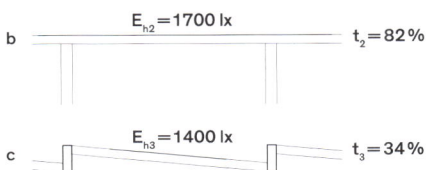

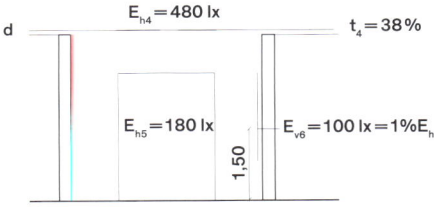

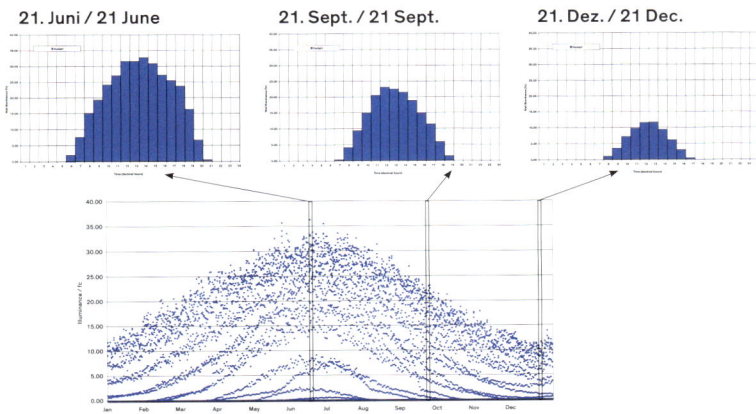

21. Juni / 21 June   21. Sept. / 21 Sept.   21. Dez. / 21 Dec.

$E_{h1} - E_{h5}$, E_{v6} exemplarische Horizontal- / Vertikalbeleuchtungsstärken [lx]
$E_{h1} - E_{h5}$, E_{v6} typical horizontal/vertical lighting intensities [lx]

$t_1 - t_4$ Lichttransmissionsgrade
$t_1 - t_4$ degrees of light transmission

Chicago, 2000–2009

The New York Times Building, New York, NY, USA

Entwurfsskizze von Renzo Piano /
Design sketch by Renzo Piano

New York Times Building

Text: Thomas Madlener
Detail 9/2007

Die 1851 gegründete New York Times, deren auffallend schmales, hohes Verlagshaus von 1904 dem Times Square zu seinem Namen verhalf, verließ nach einem knappen Jahrhundert ihren seit 1913 genutzten Sitz an der 43. Straße. Seit 2007 residieren Redaktion und Verwaltung der wohl wichtigsten Tageszeitung der USA in einem modernen Wolkenkratzer. Im Gegensatz zu vielen Bürotürmen, die in erster Linie der Demonstration von Macht und Geld dienen oder mit wilden Gesten um Aufmerksamkeit ringen, tritt der Times Tower eher bescheiden auf. Dafür überzeugen die sorgfältig ausgearbeiteten Details und die beispielhafte Offenheit. Gerade die erscheint beim ersten bedeutsamen Hochhaus Manhattans seit dem 11. September 2001 nicht selbstverständlich. Doch entschied man sich nach den Anschlägen, das Projekt im Sinne des Wettbewerbs von 2000 fortzuführen und keine bunkerartige Festung zu bauen. Die Gebäudestruktur wurde dennoch überarbeitet und in einigen Punkten verbessert.

Aufwendige Beleuchtungsstudien, Blockheizkraftwerk, Unterflurkühlsystem sowie die zweite Hülle demonstrieren ein Bemühen um Nachhaltigkeit – mit modernen »grünen« Gebäuden in Europa kann der Turm in energetischer Hinsicht allerdings nicht ganz konkurrieren. Doch die vorgehängten Keramikscreens sind vor allem auch als architektonisches Mittel konzipiert, das die Proportionen verschlankt und mit einer besonderen Mischung aus Reflexion und Transparenz wechselnde Licht- und Wetterstimmungen sanft abbildet.

New York Times Building

Text: Thomas Madlener
Detail 9/2007

Founded in 1851, the New York Times, whose strikingly narrow, high-profile publishing house gave Times Square its name and had been in use since 1913, left its seat on 43rd Street almost a century later. The editorial staff and administration of the most important US daily newspaper are now at home in a modern skyscraper. Unlike many office towers that are demonstrations of wealth and power or that try to catch the eye with wild gestures, the new Times Building appears rather modest. All the more convincing are its painstaking details and open quality – something not to be taken for granted in the aftermath of 11 September 2001. Although it is the first major high-rise block to be erected in Manhattan since that date, a decision was taken to uphold the spirit of the architectural competition held in 2000 and not to create a bunker-like stronghold. The building structure was, nevertheless, reworked and improved in certain respects.

Elaborate lighting studies, the installation of a cogenerating unit, an underfloor cooling system, and the addition of a second skin demonstrate a pursuit of sustainability, even if the tower cannot quite compete with modern "green" buildings in Europe in its energy balance. The outer screen of ceramic rods was also an architectural concept to achieve more slender proportions and – through a special mix of transparency and reflection – to gently depict changing weather and daylight conditions in the facade.

Schnitt, Grundrisse, Maßstab 1:1500 /
Section, Floor plans, scale 1:1,500

Die Geschosse unterhalb des mittleren Technikgeschosses werden von der New York Times genutzt (Regelgrundriss rechts, möblierter Grundriss 19. Obergeschoss, siehe S. 127), die Geschosse darüber (Regelgrundrisse Mitte und links) werden vermietet. / The floors below the middle services storey are used by the New York Times (standard floor plan on right; furnished floor plan of 19th floor, see p. 127). The floors above are leased out (standard floor plans left and middle).

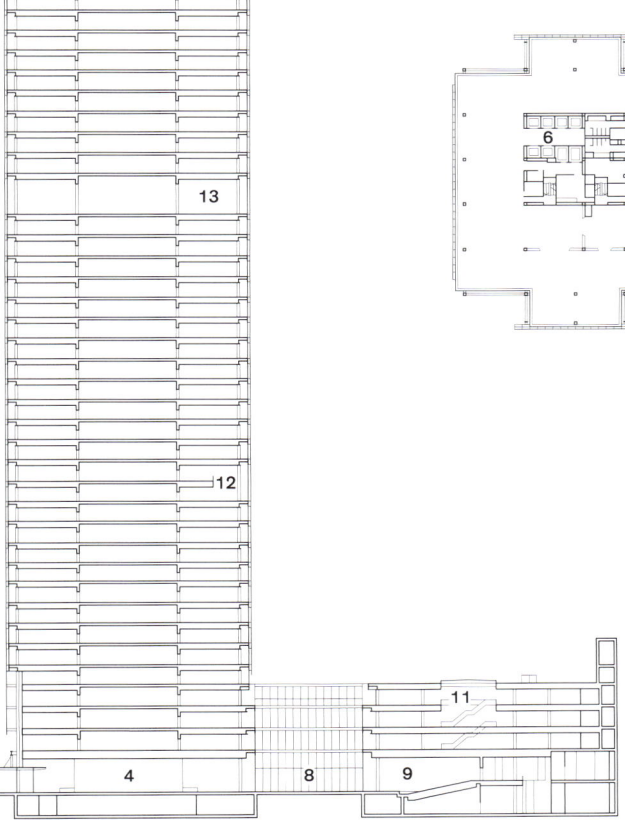

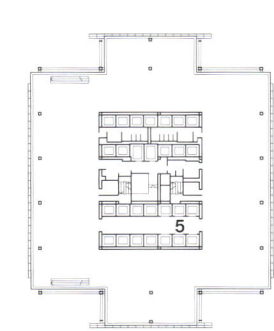 

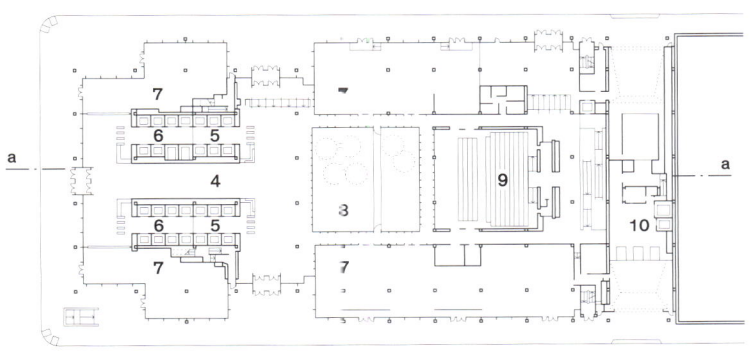

aa

1	NY Times Building	NY Times Building
2	Hearst Tower	Hearst Tower
3	Empire State Building	Empire State Building
4	Lobby	Lobby
5	Aufzüge NY Times	Lifts to NY Times
6	Aufzüge Mieter	Tenants' lifts
7	Laden	Shop
8	Garten	Garden
9	Auditorium	Auditorium
10	Ladezone	Loading area
11	Newsroom	Newsroom
12	Cafeteria	Cafeteria
13	Technikgeschoss	Services storey

Lageplan, Maßstab 1:10 000 / Site plan, scale 1:10,000

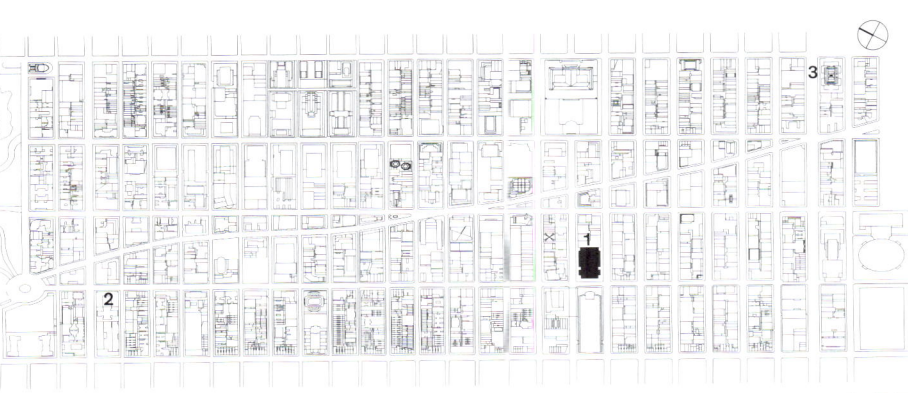

New York, 2000–2007

Entwurfsskizze zur Gebäudestruktur / Design sketch of building structure

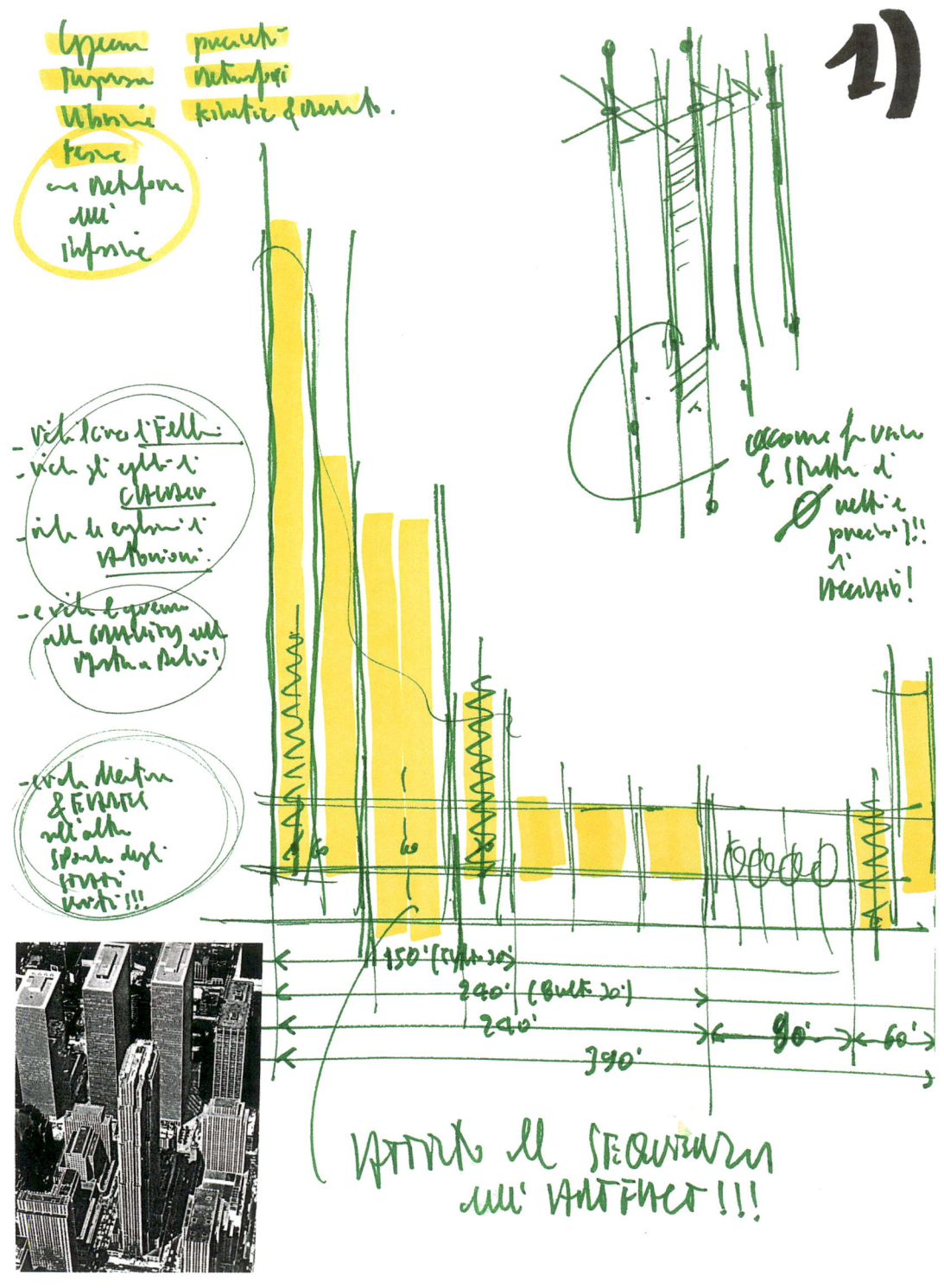

098 The New York Times Building

New York, 2000–2007

Reflexion, Schichtung, Leichtigkeit –
Ein Gespräch zum Entwurf mit dem Projektleiter Erik Volz

Interview:
Thomas Madlener
Detail 9/2007

Detail: Was sind Ihrer Meinung nach die wichtigsten Aspekte des Entwurfs?
Erik Volz: Wolkenkratzer sind oft Symbole von Arroganz und Macht, doch gerade bei der New York Times wollten wir dem etwas entgegensetzen, einen möglichst transparenten und leichten, bescheidenen und zugänglichen Turm schaffen.
Die Idee, das Gebäude in Scheiben aufzulösen, war wichtig – Reflexion, Leichtigkeit und Tiefe der Fassade – ebenso, wie der Turm den Boden berührt und oben endet; die generelle Transparenz und Offenheit.

Hatte die New York Times besondere Vorstellungen, eine besondere Beziehung zum Projekt?
Bei einem Wettbewerb wie diesem kann man normalerweise recht sicher sein, dass der Bauherr hinter dem Projekt steht, das ist immer ein guter Start. Von anfangs 128 Büros blieben nach mehreren Runden acht übrig, die intensiver besucht wurden, vier durften dann in New York präsentieren, am 11. September 2000. Dabei wurde betont, dass man kein fertiges Projekt suchte, sondern einen Architekten, der sich, seine Denkweisen und Entwurfsprozesse präsentieren sollte.
Der Grundgedanke, der damals schon bestand, war die Idee der Scheiben als vorgehängte Keramikscreens; auch der außen liegende Stahlbau war schon angedeutet. Die grundlegende Formfindung war im Falle dieses Hochhauses relativ evident; die Schwierigkeit, den Entwurf interessant zu machen, liegt eher in der Textur, im Detail.

Wie haben Sie den Entwurf entwickelt?
In der frühen Phase haben wir viel mit Papiermodellen gearbeitet, in kleinem Maßstab, ca. 20 mm hoch. Wir nennen sie »Origami«-Modelle. Es gab natürlich auch frühe Skizzen. Die Idee der Scheiben lässt sich gut zweidimensional darstellen, doch will man in

Reflection, Layering, Lightness –
An Interview with Project Architect Erik Volz on the Design

Interview:
Thomas Madlener
Detail 9/2007

Detail: Would you briefly describe the chief aspects of the design?
Erik Volz: Skyscrapers are often symbols of arrogance and power. With the New York Times, we wanted to oppose this approach and create a tower that was as transparent, light, modest and accessible as possible.
The idea of resolving the building into a number of layers was important; so too was reflection, lightness and the depth of the facade. The junction between the tower and the ground at its base, and its termination at the top, plus the general sense of transparency and openness were crucial.

Did the clients have their own ideas, a special relationship to the building?
In a competition like this you can usually be sure that the client is behind the project, that's always a good start. From initially 128 studios, after several stages eight were left that were scrutinised more closely, four of whom were then allowed to present their concepts in New York on 11 September 2000. It was emphasised that the brief did not call for a finished product but for architects who were to present themselves, their way of thinking and their design methods.
The basic concept, which already existed back then, was one of suspended ceramic screens as layers; the external steel structure was already hinted at, too. Designing the high-rise building's form was relatively self-evident in this case. Making that form interesting was more a matter of texture and detail.

How did you continue the development of the project in this early phase?
Small-scale paper models were very important for us, approximately 20 mm high – "origami" models, as we call them. There were, of course early sketches, too. The idea of slabs is well presented in two dimensions, but if you want to move on to the next phase,

The New York Times Building

die nächste Phase gehen, sind Modelle sehr hilfreich. Wir haben um die 50 »Origami«-Modelle gebaut, beim Wettbewerb stand eine ganze Reihe zur Präsentation auf dem Tisch. In der Regel bauen wir auch frühzeitig Modelle aus Holz, das hat eine besondere Haptik und ist Teil unserer Bürotradition.

Neben der besonderen Textur entscheidet sich die Qualität eines solchen Projekts vor allem an der Basis und an der Spitze. Bei beidem versuchen wir, eine gewisse Leichtigkeit zu erzielen. Der Mittelteil ist bis auf die Haustechnikgeschosse unvermeidlich repetitiv.

Oben sollte sich der Turm auf angenehme Weise mit dem Himmel verbinden. Die Screens schieben sich über das eigentliche Volumen hinaus, entmaterialisieren sich mit abnehmender Dichte der Röhren. Sie bilden eine Art Krone, in der ein Dachgarten sitzt, und aus deren Mitte ein gut 90 m hoher Mast aufragt. Ursprünglich sollte

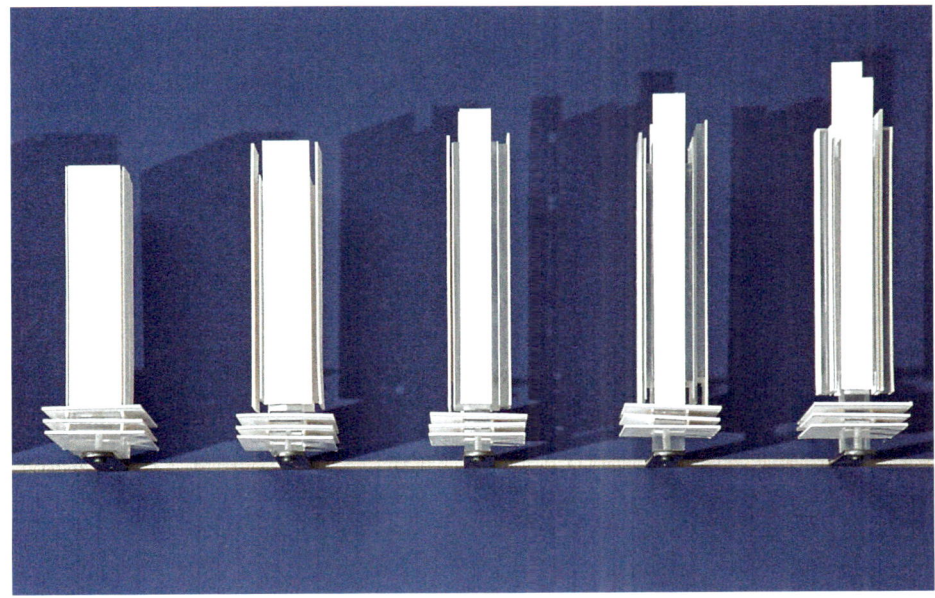

Evolution der Gebäudekubatur anhand von »Origami«-Modellen, (»von der Raupe zum Schmetterling«, Renzo Piano) / Development of building volume using origami models ("from worm to butterfly", Renzo Piano)

Wettbewerbsdarstellung zu Transparenz und Reflexion der Fassade / Depiction of facade transparency and reflection for the competition

New York, 2000–2007

er flexibel sein, eine Art Windmesser. So könnte die New York Times, die wichtigste Zeitung Amerikas, auch bildlich zeigen, woher der Wind weht. Doch mit heutigen Mitteln hätten wir nur eine polygonale Krümmung erzielt, mit deutlich sichtbaren Knicken und dicken, störenden Anschlüssen zwischen den Segmenten. Auf jeden Fall wäre es zu aufwendig und zu teuer geworden.

An der Basis, wo dieser Turm, dieses potenziell arrogante Geschöpf, auf den Boden trifft, war es besonders wichtig, Leichtigkeit und Offenheit zu demonstrieren, mit einer einladenden Erdgeschosszone.

Von der 8. Avenue sieht man zwischen den Aufzugskernen entlang der Hauptachse durch Lobby und Garten bis in das Auditorium. Auch zwischen der 40. und der 41. Straße, den beiden Seitenstraßen, bleibt das Sockelgeschoss transparent. Hier zeigt sich wieder die Idee der Schichtung, des Layerings: Es gibt diverse Glasfassaden, doch die Durchsicht ist komplett erhalten. Sämtliche Einbauten in den Läden müssen hier unter Augenhöhe bleiben. Außerdem ist das Erdgeschoss mit 6,5 m für New Yorker Verhältnisse relativ hoch und erscheint auch dadurch leicht und offen, ohne arrogant oder einschüchternd hoch zu wirken.

Zusätzlich gibt es an der 8. Avenue einen Rücksprung der inneren Glasfassade in den unteren vier Geschossen, über den sich von oben der Screen schiebt, sodass sich diese Schürze, dieser Rock, wie Renzo es nennt, noch einmal abhebt.
Grundsätzlich ist die Basis folgendermaßen organisiert: Durch die zwei »Parteien«, die Times und die Mieter in den oberen Etagen, gibt es zwei Lobbies, eine erschlossen von der 8. Avenue und eine Durchgangslobby zwischen den Seitenstraßen, die zusammen eine T-förmige Lobby ergeben. Die verbindende, etwa 9 m breite Passage zwischen den Aufzugskernen, entlang der eben erwähnten Hauptachse, wird links und rechts von einem Kunstobjekt aus kleinen Bildschirmen flankiert, die die Neuigkeiten aus dem Newsroom in verschiedenster Form abbilden. Um diese Mittelachse freizuhalten, mussten Gebäudetechnik und Fluchtwege in die Doppelwand der Aufzugschächte gelegt bzw. um sie herum umgeleitet werden.

models are very helpful. We built about 50 "origami" models, and there was a whole row of them on the presentation table at the competition. As a rule, we also build wooden models at an early stage, which has a special feel and is part of our office tradition.

Besides its special texture, the quality of a project like this is determined above all by the base and the tip of the tower. In both situations, we tried to achieve a sense of lightness. The middle part is inevitably repetitive except for the building engineering levels.

At the top, we wanted the tower to connect to the sky in a pleasant way. The screens extend above the actual volume and dematerialise with the decreasing density of the rods. They form a kind of crown in which a roof garden sits and from the centre of which a 90 m tall mast extends. Originally it was supposed to be flexible, a kind of anemometer. Thus, the New York Times as America's most important newspaper would have figuratively showed which way the wind was blowing. But with today's means we would have only achieved a polygonal curvature, with clearly visible kinks and thick, disruptive joints between the segments. In any case, it would have been too time-consuming and too expensive.

At the base, where this potentially arrogant creature of a tower hits the ground, it was also particularly important to show a quality of lightness and openness, with an inviting ground-floor area.

From 8th Avenue, one has a view through the lift cores along the main axis, through the lobby and the garden to the auditorium. Between 40th and 41st Streets, too, the plinth storey remains transparent. Here the idea of stratification or layering again becomes visible: there are various glass facades, but transparency is maintained. All fittings in the shops must remain below eye level here. The 6.50-metre-high ground floor is also relatively tall for New York, but it enhances this sense of openness without appearing arrogant or intimidating.

In addition, there is a recess in the inner glass facade of the lower four storeys on 8th Avenue, over which the screen is suspended from above, so that this "apron" or "skirt", as Renzo calls it, sets itself apart again.

Zwischen Lobby und Sockelbau liegt der Garten als eher kontemplatives Element, der den Arbeitplätzen in diesem »Podium« eine besondere Qualität gibt, auch als Ausgleich zu den Büros mit Aussicht weiter oben im Turm. Und er verbessert die Belichtung bei fast 15 m Gebäudetiefe erheblich.

Die New York Times wollte den Kern der Redaktion, den Bereich, in dem die Zeitung mit immerhin ein paar Hundert Journalisten zusammengestellt wird, auf maximal drei Etagen zusammenfassen. Die Ebenen im Turm sind dazu zu klein. Daher haben wir diesen »Newsroom« als dreistöckige Struktur interpretiert, die sich im Podium um ein zentrales, glasgedecktes Atrium legt. Renzo spricht von der »bakery«, weil hier nachts das Licht etwas länger brennt.

Um in den oberen Etagen die Transparenz zu wahren, wollten wir Zellenbüros an der Fassade unbedingt vermeiden. Rings um die Kerne gibt es gläserne Besprechungsboxen, doch die Peripherie bleibt offen. Der Großraum sollte auch nicht zu tief werden, um keine Mitarbeiter vom Tageslicht abzuschneiden.

Bevor wir mit dem Projekt begannen, lag das typische New Yorker Bürogeschoss bei etwa 3700 m², auch für uns galt diese Vorgabe. Der Wolkenkratzer wäre damit halb so hoch und von den Proportionen her weit weniger interessant. Wir mussten vermitteln, dass der Turm genauso gut und ähnlich effizient ist, wenn man die Geschossfläche auf ca. 2500 m² herunterschraubt. Inzwischen liegt auch der Standard in dieser Größenordnung, weil man verstanden hat, dass natürliche Belichtung die Qualität der Arbeit erheblich fördert.

Ein weiteres wichtiges Element der Büroetagen der Times sind die Verbindungstreppen an der Fassade, um Zirkulation und Kommunikation zwischen den Ebenen zu verbessern und die Nutzung der Aufzüge zu reduzieren. Sie gewähren nicht nur den Mitarbeitern Ausblicke und damit eine gewisse Nähe zur umgebenden Stadt, sie bilden auch zur Straße hin etwas vom Innenleben der Zeitung ab.

In der Cafeteria im 17. Stockwerk haben wir eine Ebene ausgelassen – der zweigeschossige Raum erzeugt eine wesentlich höhere Quertransparenz. Man sitzt

Principally, the base is organised as follows: thanks to the two parties, the New York Times and the tenants on the upper floors, there are two lobbies, one accessible from 8th Avenue and a through lobby between the side streets, which together form a T-shaped lobby. The connecting, approximately 9-metre-wide passage between the lift cores, along the main axis just mentioned, is flanked on the left and right by an art object of small screens that display the news from the newsroom in various forms. To keep this central axis free, mechanical services and escape routes were placed in the double walls of the lift shafts or diverted around them.

A garden between the lobby and the plinth structure is a more contemplative element, also giving the workplaces in this "podium" a special quality, to compensate in a way for the offices with a view further above in the tower. This greatly improves the daylighting of the building, which is almost 15 m deep.

The New York Times wanted to concentrate the main section of the editorial department, the area in which the newspaper is compiled by at least a few hundred journalists, on a maximum of three floors, but the levels in the tower are too small for that. We therefore interpreted the newsroom as a three-storey structure laid out around a glass-roofed atrium. Renzo speaks of the "bakery" because here the lights stay on a little longer at night.

To maintain the sense of transparency on the floors above, it was important to keep single office cells away from the facade. Glass discussion boxes were laid out around the cores, and the outer face remains free. The open space was also designed not to be so deep as to cut off staff from the daylight.

Before we began work on this project, a typical floor in a New York office block had an area of 3,700 m², and that was also our requirement. That would have meant a building only half as high as the present one and with far less interesting proportions. We had to convince the clients that an area of about 2,500 m² per storey would be just as good and similarly efficient. In the meantime, the standard has come down to roughly this size, since people have realised that proper daylighting is conducive to good work.

inmitten der Wolkenkratzer von Midtown Manhattan, die Keramikrohre an der Fassade laufen hier ununterbrochen durch, mit leicht reduzierter Dichte. Der Effekt erinnert an eine japanische Wand. Ursprünglich planten wir, diesen gleichmäßigen Rhythmus der Stäbe über das ganze Gebäude zu ziehen.

In der Cafeteria wie in der Lobby fällt die Wand in orangefarbenem venezianischen Stucco auf, kombiniert mit Rot- und Holztönen. Sämtliche Innenräume sind durch diese Farbigkeit aufgewertet, auch die Büros: mit Kirschholzeinbauten und roter Farbe am Kern und an den Verbindungstreppen. Von außen gut sichtbar, setzen diese einen farbigen Akzent in der relativ monochromen Außenhaut.

Wie entstanden die Fassadenecken?

Diese »corner notches« entsprangen der Idee, den Turm über Eck aufzulösen – die Diagonalansicht wird schmaler und der Turm schlanker in der Proportion. Auch die Screens treten zurück. Sie überschieben sich an den Schmalseiten und ziehen sich an den Längsseiten zurück, dadurch scheint das Gebäude aus vier Hauptscreens zusammengesetzt, die sich an der Ecke nicht berühren, sondern deutlich öffnen. So nimmt man in erster Linie die Breite des Screens war und nicht die Gesamtbreite des Gebäudes.

War es dem Bauherrn gegenüber schwierig zu begründen, dass man nicht das ganze mögliche Volumen ausfüllt?

Das war nicht einfach, doch eine Eigenheit des Immobilienmarkts hat uns geholfen: In den USA sind Eckbüros sehr begehrt. An einem Turm mit quadratischem Grundriss gibt es nur vier, durch die »notches« hat man acht. Die New York Times hat sich jedoch von uns überzeugen lassen, in diesen Ecken die Verbindungstreppen unterzubringen.

Die außen liegende Stahlkonstruktion ergab sich aus diesen »notches«?

Wenn man etwas aus dem Baukörper herausschneidet, sollte man auch etwas von dem, was normalerweise dahinterliegt, zeigen. Dadurch war das Freilegen der Konstruktion

The linking staircases next to the facade are another important element of the office storeys because they improve circulation and inter-level communication and reduce the use of lifts. They provide members of the staff with views of the city and thus create a certain proximity to the surroundings while also revealing something of the life of a newspaper to the world outside.

In the cafeteria on the 17th floor, we skipped one level – the two-storey space there has a much higher cross-transparency. You sit amid the skyscrapers of Midtown Manhattan, the ceramic rods on the facade are continuous here, at a slightly reduced density. The effect is reminiscent of a shoji screen. Originally, we planned to use this uniform rhythm of the rods all over the building.

In the cafeteria and in the lobby, a wall in orange Venetian stucco is combined with a red tone and the colours of wood. All interiors are enhanced by the use of colours, including the offices with their cherry-wood fittings and the red of the core and connecting staircases. Clearly visible from the outside, this forms a bright contrast to the relatively monochrome external skin.

How did you develop the recessed corners of the facade?

These "corner notches" came from the idea of dissolving the tower at its corners. The view on the diagonal is shortened, and the tower has more slender proportions. The ceramic screens also appear to be much narrower. They extend on the narrow sides and retract on the long sides, so the building seems to be composed of four main screens that do not touch each other at the corners but open clearly. In effect, you perceive mainly the width of the screens and not so much the overall width of the building.

Was it difficult to convince the client to accept a reduction of the full volume?

It wasn't easy, but a peculiarity of the real estate market helped us: in the US, corner offices are much sought after. In a square tower, there are only four of them; but as a

Schnittansicht und Detail
Gebäudeecke /
Section and elevation,
with details of corner

Modell Gebäudeecke /
Model of corner of
building

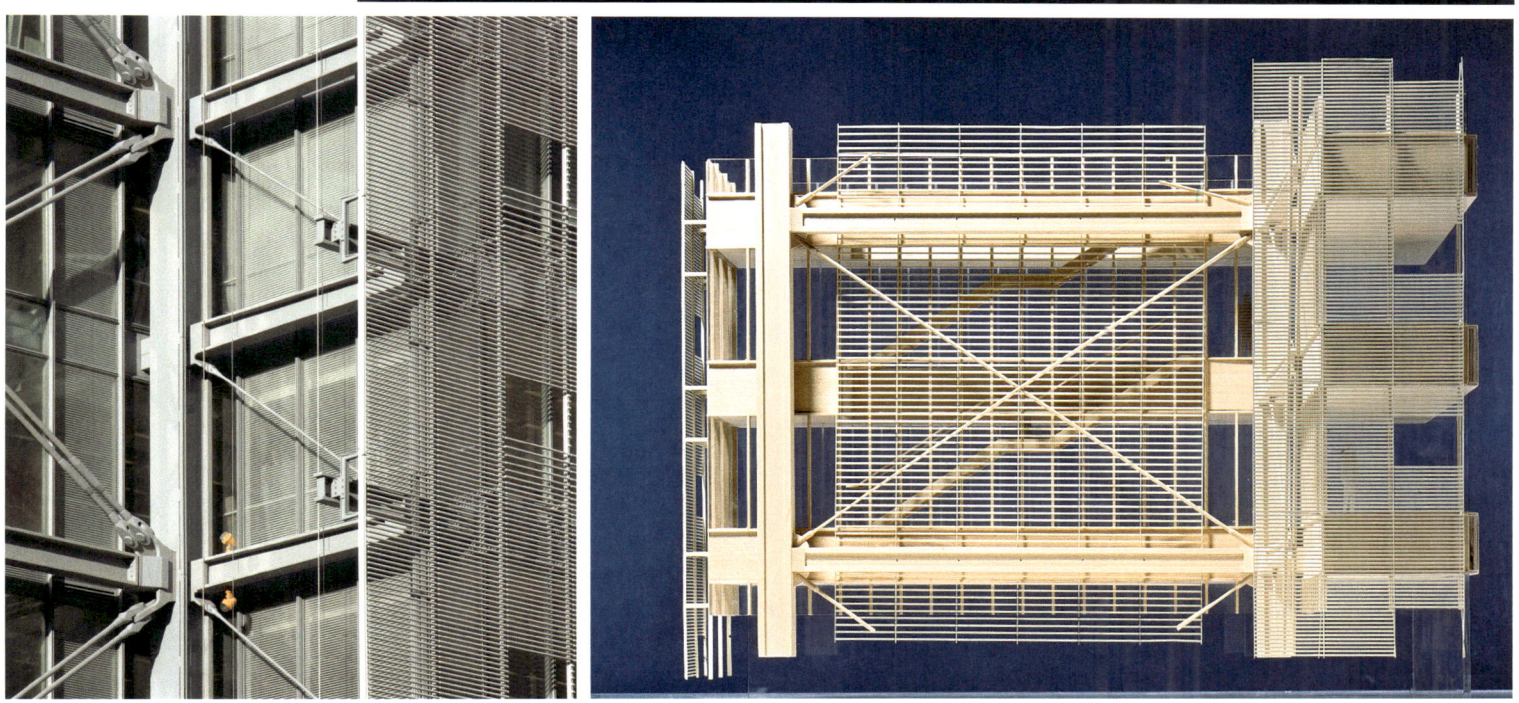

New York, 2000–2007

»Krone« und Basis des Turms, dazwischen die repetitiven Regelgeschosse / "Crown" and base of tower with repeating standard floors between

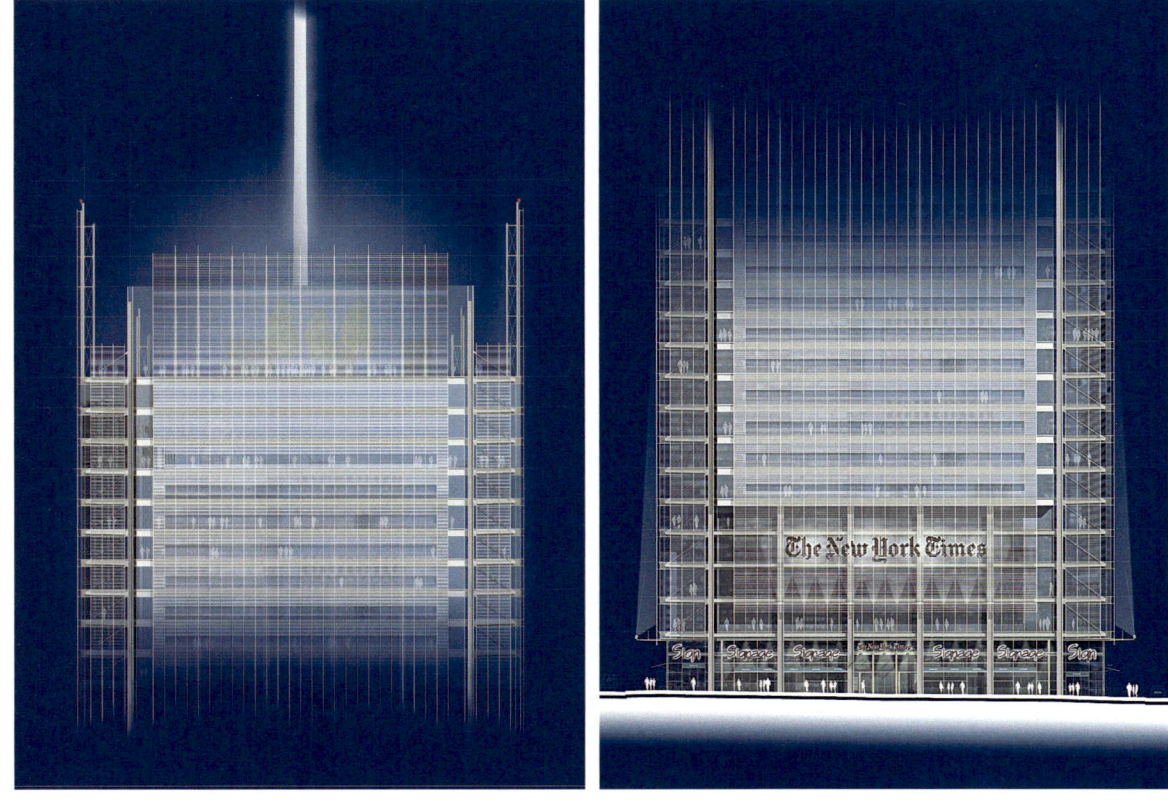

Detailliertes Präsentationsmodell inmitten abstrahierter Landmarks Manhattans, u. a. McGraw-Hill, Chrysler und Empire State Building / Detailed presentation model amid abstract landmarks of Manhattan, including McGraw-Hill, Chrysler and Empire State Buildings

106

The New York Times Building

logisch. Der Stahlbau sieht innen allerdings nicht genau so aus. Die außen liegende Tragstruktur ist maßgefertigt, so konnten wir die Knoten klar ausformulieren, die Kraft der Konstruktion zeigen und besonders an den Proportionen von Stützen, Trägern und Spannseilen arbeiten. Die Flansche werden nach oben immer dünner, entsprechen so in idealisierter Weise dem Kräfteverlauf. Das Gebäude wird dadurch nach oben leichter.

Zudem ergeben sich Einsparungen von ein paar Hundert Tonnen Stahl, das macht etwa 2 bis 3 Millionen US-Dollar. Auch das war nicht unwichtig, die Kosten wurden regelmäßig kontrolliert. In New York verkleidet man den Stahlbau in der Regel; wenn man ihn sichtbar belassen will, muss man gehörig Überzeugungsarbeit leisten.

Wurden bis in die Details Modelle angefertigt?

Wir machen nicht für jeden Knoten ein Modell, aber für die repetitiven Knoten, die wichtigen Details schon. Für die Anschlüsse der außen liegenden Stahlstruktur haben wir vier bis fünf große Modelle gebaut, teils aus Holz, teils aus Schaumstoff. Hier kommen viele Elemente zusammen. Das ist vom Design her schon aufwendig, darüber hinaus werden sehr große Kräfte übertragen. Es gibt z. B. einige relativ dicke Bleche mit langen Kanten, um die Länge der Schweißnähte zu maximieren, da die Lasten über Kontaktflächen übertragen werden. Bei diesem über 250 m hohen Stahlbau gibt es natürlich auch viele Toleranzen zu berücksichtigen, man benötigt variable Fugen, in die sich dünne Ausgleichsbleche drücken lassen. Auch hierfür konnten wir am Modell relativ zurückhaltende Schattenfugen definieren.

Wir zeichnen solche Details in der Regel 2D am Computer und gehen dann ins Modell. Wenn nötig, setzen wir das danach in 3D am Rechner um, doch wir versuchen den 3D-Prozess eher im Modell durchzuspielen. Renzo mag es lieber am Modell, das ist einfacher zu kontrollieren, man kann es drehen, wie man will – der Zugang ist viel direkter als am Bildschirm. Außerdem haben wir eine gut ausgestattete Modellbauwerkstatt.

result of the notches here, there are eight. Having said that, we managed to persuade the New York Times to place connecting staircases at these points.

Was the external steel structure the outcome of these notches?

If you cut away part of the building volume, it makes sense to show what lies behind. The exposure of the structure was also a logical outcome of this. However, the steelwork doesn't look the same on the inside. The external structure is tailor-made. We were able to formulate the nodes clearly, to show the strength of the construction and to work particularly on the proportions of the supports, beams and tension cables. The flanges become thinner and thinner, thus optimally corresponding to the flow of forces. As a result, the building seems to become lighter with increasing height.

This also helped to save a few hundred tonnes of steel, $2–3 million worth, in fact. Which wasn't trivial, the costs were checked regularly. Steelwork is usually clad in New York. If you want to leave it exposed, it takes quite a lot of persuasion.

Were models built for the details?

We don't make models for every node, but we do for repetitive nodes and important details. For the connections of the external steel structure we built four or five large models, partly in wood, partly in foamed plastic. This is where many elements come together, it is complex in terms of design and, in addition, very large forces are transferred here. There are, for example, some relatively thick sheets with long edges to maximise the length of the welds, as the loads are transferred via contact surfaces. Over a height of 250 m there are a lot of tolerances to be taken into account in the steel structure. You need variable joints into which thin shimming plates can be pressed. In the model, we were able to define relatively restrained shadow joints.

We normally draw details of this kind two-dimensionally on the computer and then proceed to the model. If necessary, we translate this into a 3D computer depiction, but we prefer to work three-dimensionally on a model. Renzo prefers the model, it's easier

Wie gestaltete sich die Entwicklung der Fassade?

Zum einen war die Schichtung für uns ein Thema, vor allem aber bestimmte die Idee der Reflexion unser Bild von der Fassade – ohne dabei eine gewisse Transparenz aufzugeben.

Bei den ehemaligen Twin Towers des World Trade Centers – man kann sich über deren Architektur sicher streiten – hat der Edelstahl die Umgebung schön reflektiert. Einen ähnlichen Effekt versprachen wir uns, in verfeinerter Form mit linear fragmentierten Reflexionen von glasierten Keramikrohren, den »Baguettes«, wie wir sie inzwischen nennen, in einem gewissen Abstand vor einer Klarglasfassade. Dies ergibt nicht die harte Reflexion eines Spiegels, sondern eine durch das Weiß der Keramik etwas gediegenere, angenehmere.

War Keramik von Beginn an als Material für die äußere Fassadenschicht vorgesehen?

Keramik hat eine gewisse Tradition in unserem Büro, denken Sie z. B. an die Gebäude am Potsdamer Platz. Und das Bild, diese gebrannte Erde in den Himmel zu hängen, gefiel Renzo sehr gut. Keramik ist zudem ein Material, das über Tausende von Jahren seine Qualität behält. Auch das war spannend, ein Material für die Ewigkeit auf ein doch eher vergängliches Gebäude zu setzen.

Und Keramik ist etwas unregelmäßig, wirkt dadurch interessant und lebendig. Natürlich gab es einen gewissen Druck, die äußere Schicht etwa in Aluminium auszuführen. Es hieß, Keramik kostet doppelt so viel, ist schwer und bricht, und man könne doch mit Aluminium und einer Glasur fast denselben Effekt erzielen. Doch es ist nicht das Gleiche. Spätestens die Mischung aus besonderer Reflexion und Unregelmäßigkeit an der Fassade hat visuell überzeugt – auch den Bauherrn.

Wenn die Sonne auf- oder untergeht, ist das Gebäude rot, an einem schönen Tag ist es hell und freundlich, nach einem Schauer eher bläulich, und an einem trüben Tag ist es leider etwas traurig, aber das hat ja auch einen gewissen Reiz. Die frühe Morgensonne lässt das Gebäude hell erscheinen, da das Licht dann von der Seite kommt

to control, you can look at it whichever way you want and access is much more direct than on the screen. We also have a well-equipped model workshop.

Can you describe the process of developing the facade?

On the one hand, the idea of layering was important to us; but our vision of the facade was determined above all by a concept of reflection – without abandoning a certain transparency.

At the former Twin Towers of the World Trade Center – you can certainly argue about their architecture – the stainless steel beautifully reflected the surroundings. We hoped to achieve a similar effect, in a refined form with linearly fragmented reflections of glazed ceramic rods – the "baguettes", as we call them – which are set at a distance from the clear-glass facade. They don't produce a hard mirror-like reflection, but something more pleasant and tasteful, resulting from the white of the ceramic.

Was ceramic intended as a material for the outer facade layer from the outset?

The use of ceramic has a certain tradition in our office, take the buildings at Potsdamer Platz, for example. And Renzo liked the metaphor of fired earth hanging in the sky.

Ceramic is also a very durable material, it retains its quality over thousands of years. That, too, was exciting, putting a material for eternity on a rather transient building.

Ceramic is also slightly irregular, which lends it an interesting and lively appearance. Of course, there was a certain pressure to use aluminium for the exterior, for example, but it's not the same. In the end, the combination of the special reflecting quality and the irregular finish of the facade convinced the clients too.

When the sun rises or sinks, the building glows red, and on a fine day, it's bright and friendly. After rainfall, it is rather bluish, and on a dull day, it is a little sad, but there is a certain charm to that too. The early morning sun makes the building appear bright,

Schriftzug an der Fassade: auf die Keramikrohre geschobene schwarze Aluminiumprofile (eine frühere Variante sah ein reines Relief vor, ohne Farbunterschiede) / Masthead on the facade: black aluminium sections pushed over the ceramic tubes (an earlier version proposed a simple relief without colour contrast)

New York, 2000–2007

und man von unten nicht nur die Schattenseite der Rohre sieht. Betrachtet man das Gebäude von weiter oben, wirkt es daher auch heller, eher weiß, von der Straße eher gräulich. Je nach Standpunkt und Lichteinfall verändert sich auch die wahrgenommene Dichte des Screens. Von Weitem erscheint er relativ dicht, doch bei gewissem Lichteinfall, vor allem nachts, tritt er stark zurück. Ebenso nimmt zur Turmspitze hin die Dichte des Screens ab, von einer Regeldichte von 50 % (Abstand zwischen den Rohren entspricht deren Durchmesser) bis zu 12,5 % an der oberen Kante. Von der Straße aus gesehen lässt dies die Fassade beinahe homogen in den Himmel übergehen. Aus größerer Entfernung oder von einem erhöhten Standpunkt aus erkennt man über dem obersten Geschoss, wo der Screen keinen Gebäudehintergrund mehr hat, schon einen gewissen Bruch. Ca. 8,5 m hohe, mit nach oben abnehmender Dichte bedruckte Glasscheiben mildern diesen Übergang ab.

Auch über die gesamte Höhe der Fassade variiert die Dichte des Screens: Unterhalb der Geschossdecken schützen dichter gesetzte Rohre vor zu hoher Sonneneinstrahlung, im Brüstungsbereich erleichtern größere Abstände Blicke hinunter auf die Straße.

Um den Effekt des Ablösens vom Gebäude zu verstärken, ist der Screen zudem farblich abgesetzt: Die Baguettes samt der Kammprofile dazwischen sind in gebrochenem Weiß gehalten, die darunterliegende Tragkonstruktion in Grau.

Wir wollten auch nachts die Präsenz der hellen Keramikfassade bewahren, mit nach oben abnehmendem Weißglimmer – kein harter Schwarz-Weiß-Schatten, eher grau-weiß mit den Reflexen der Stäbe. Wir planten außerdem die Beleuchtung der Screens vom Podium aus, ebenso vom Vordach und vom gegenüberliegenden Bus-Terminal. In den »notches« soll ähnlich wie beim Centre Pompidou die Stahlstruktur sanft beleuchtet werden. Die hier angebrachten Leuchten verfolgen die Diagonalen der Auskreuzungen. Sie sind im typischen Gelb der New Yorker Taxis gefärbt, als Symbol der Bewegung der Stadt, die sich punktförmig nach oben hangelt.

---

as the light comes from the side and, when looking from below, you don't see only the shadow side of the rods. If you look at the building from above, it also looks brighter, more white, while it appears more grey from the street. Depending on the point of view and the incidence of light, the perceived density of the screens also changes. From a distance, it appears relatively dense, but at a certain incidence of light, especially at night, it retreats noticeably. The density of the screens also decreases towards the top of the tower, from a normal density of 50 % (distance between the rods corresponds to their diameter) down to 12.5 % at the upper end. Viewed from the street, this makes the facade merge with the sky almost homogeneously. From a greater distance or from an elevated position, you can already see a certain break above the top floor where the screens no longer have a building background. Approximately 8.50-metre-high glass panels, printed with decreasing density towards the top, mitigate this transition.
Over the entire height of the facade, the density of the screens also varies. Below the floor levels, the rods are set closer together to protect against excessive insolation. In the balustrade areas, greater spacings allow a clearer view from the building down to the street.

To heighten the effect of detachment from the building, the screens also contrast in colour. The "baguettes" and the comb-like sections between them are off-white, while the load-bearing structure to the rear is grey.

We wanted the tower to retain something of its white quality even at night, so we used a white glimmering tone that diminishes in intensity with increasing height – no hard black-and-white shadows, more like a greyish white with the reflections of the rods. We also plan to illuminate the screens from the podium, as well as from the canopy and opposite bus terminal. Similar to the Centre Pompidou, the "notches" are intended to gently illuminate the steel structure. The lamps attached here follow the diagonals of the outcrossings. They are coloured in the typical yellow of the New York taxis, as a symbol of the movement of the city, and progress upward point by point.

1:1-Modell Fassadenaufhängung /
Full-scale model of facade suspension

Mock-up Fassade /
Mock-up of facade

Mock-up eines Viertelgeschosses /
Mock-up of a quarter of a storey

New York, 2000–2007

Die »Baguettes« gab es wohl nicht als fertiges Bauprodukt?
Von anderen Projekten kannten wir Firmen, die ähnliche Produkte herstellen, aber nirgendwo gab es ein rundes, weißes Rohr, das die technischen Anforderungen erfüllte.
Zuerst wollten wir weiße Terrakotta, doch bestand sie nicht unsere aufwendigen Tests. Es gab physische Tests, Widerstandstests, statische Tests, aber auch Wasseraufnahmetests und Frosttests. Das Material musste absolut geschlossen sein, nicht porös, damit kein Wasser eintritt und gefriert. Aufgrund des New Yorker Klimas, mit seinen hohen Temperaturschwankungen über das Jahr, mussten wir eine hochtechnische Keramik auswählen.
Es gab kein geeignetes Bauprodukt, doch das in den Bereichen Hochöfen, Isolatoren und Motorenteile verwendete Aluminiumsilikat erfüllte unsere Anforderungen. Und für Fließbänder in Schmelzöfen und als Elektroisolator gab es ein geeignetes Rohr, das wir in punkto Gewicht und Durchmesser anpassen konnten.
Als zusätzliche Sicherung sahen wir ein in der Röhre durchlaufendes Aluminiumprofil vor, das im Schadensfall größere Bruchstücke und vor allem das ganze Rohr in seiner Lage hält – nur kleinste Splitter fallen nach unten. Dies mussten wir insbesondere für den Bauprozess einkalkulieren, aber auch für unvorhersehbare Einwirkungen wie etwa ein großer Vogel oder Schäden bei der Reinigung, die von außen über abgehängte Körbe erfolgt. Die offenen Bänder im Screen sind hoch genug, dass man mit passendem Werkzeug die innere Glasfassade komplett erreicht.

Wirkung und Funktion haben Sie sicher an Mock-ups überprüft?
Der Mock-up-Prozess war relativ aufwendig. Wir mussten klären, ob sich der Aufwand lohnt: visuell, aber auch technisch und funktional. Deshalb gab es drei Phasen. Zuerst ein Mock-up aus Holz, an dem wir vor allem die Gestaltung prüften – gebaut von einer italienischen Firma, mit der wir öfter zusammenarbeiten. Die zweite Mock-up-Phase war Teil eines kleinen Fassadenwettbewerbs. Dabei ging es um die Herangehensweisen

The "baguettes" presumably didn't exist as a finished product.
From other projects we knew firms that manufacture similar products, but nowhere could we obtain a round white rod that would meet the technical requirements.
At first we wanted white terracotta, but it didn't pass our elaborate tests. Physical tests were carried out, tests for resistance, structural tests, as well as tests for water absorption and frost resistance. The material had to be absolutely non-porous, otherwise water could penetrate it and freeze. In view of the great range of temperatures in New York over the year, we had to select a high-grade ceramic.
Although no suitable building product was available, the aluminium silicate used in the field of blast furnaces, and for insulators and motor parts met our needs. Taking a rod used for conveyor belts in smelting furnaces and for electrical insulators, we adapted it in terms of weight and diameter.
As an additional safety measure, we inserted a continuous aluminium section in the rod, which in case of damage holds larger fragments and, above all, the entire rod in its position – only tiniest fragments can fall. We had to take this into account in particular for the construction process but also to cover all eventualities, such as a large bird flying into the facade or damage caused during cleaning, which is carried out from cradles suspended on the outside. The open bands on the screens are high enough that you can completely reach the inner glass facade with an appropriate tool.

You certainly tested the effect and function with mock-ups.
The mock-up process was relatively elaborate. We had to see whether the whole outlay was worthwhile – not just visually, but technically and functionally as well. That's why there were three mock-up phases. The first one – in wood – served mainly to test the design. It was built by an Italian company with which we often collaborate. The second mock-up phase formed part of a small facade competition. This involved the companies' methods of implementation, as well as detailed aspects relating to

der Firmen an die Umsetzung, um Funktion und Qualität bis ins Detail, aber natürlich auch um den Preis.

Eine weitere Herausforderung bei der Umsetzung lag darin, dass es beim Bauen in New York City keinen Platz gibt, entsprechend teuer ist die Arbeit vor Ort – man muss die Zeit auf der Baustelle möglichst reduzieren. Das führte dazu, nicht nur den Screen, sondern die ganze zweischichtige Fassade als Elementfassade zu bauen. Eine Einheit ist ein Geschoss hoch und ein Modul breit, etwa 4,2 m × 1,5 m, und wird komplett als zweischichtiges Element eingehängt. Die Toleranzen zwischen den Elementen sind zwar bei zweischichtigen Bauteilen etwas größer, was zu etwas dickeren Profilen führt, andererseits ist die Konstruktion dadurch einigermaßen fehlerverzeihend. Für europäische Ansprüche könnte das Profil noch etwas schlanker sein, eingebaut in so eine zweischichtige Struktur ist es aber in Ordnung.

In der dritten Mock-up-Phase wurde auf Wunsch der New York Times ein Viertel eines Geschosses gebaut, komplett mit Verbindungstreppe, Fassade, dem richtigen Glas und allen Workstations. So konnten wir die Wirkung von innen sowie die Lichtverhältnisse und Arbeitsbedingungen prüfen. Die richtige Belichtung für Computerarbeitsplätze bei dem hohen Tageslichtanteil zu ermitteln, war dabei relativ komplex. Zudem ist die New York Times extrem demokratisch – und schlimme Gerüchte verbreiten sich besonders schnell: Man sprach von Heizkörpern vor den Fenstern und dass man nicht nach außen sieht. Das dritte Mock-up half, solche Gerüchte schnell einzufangen.

Zusätzlich zur zweischichtigen Elementfassade der Büroebenen gibt es noch die Erdgeschossfassade unterhalb des Screens, die sehr schön geworden ist und auch entscheidend zu Transparenz und Offenheit der Turmbasis beiträgt.

function and quality. The price was also an important consideration, of course. Another challenge in realising the scheme was that there's simply no space to work on site in New York City, which makes construction expensive. On-site work has to be reduced as far as possible. That led to a decision to construct not just the screens, but the entire double-skin facade as a prefabricated system. The units are one storey high and one module wide (approx. 4.20 × 1.50 m) and are fixed in position as entire two-layer elements. Tolerances between double-skin units need to be a little larger, which means the use of somewhat thicker sections. On the other hand, the construction is relatively tolerant towards errors. For European tastes, the section might be a little more slender, but built into a two-layer structure like this, it's fine.

In the third mock-up phase, the New York Times commissioned an entire quarter of a storey, including the stairs, the facade, the right glass and all workplaces. This helped us to test the effect from the inside as well as the lighting and working conditions. Determining the appropriate daylighting for computer workplaces with such a high daylight factor was a relatively complex process. In a democratic organisation like the New York Times, bad rumours spread like wildfire: people were talking of radiators in front of the windows and of not being able to see out of the building. This third mock-up also helped to dispel such rumours quickly.

In addition to the facade to the office storeys, there's a ground-floor facade to the storefront below the screens. It has turned out very well and makes a decisive contribution to the sense of transparency and openness at the base of the tower.

Vertikalschnitt,
Horizontalschnitt,
Maßstab 1:100 /
Vertical and horizontal
sections through facade,
scale 1:100

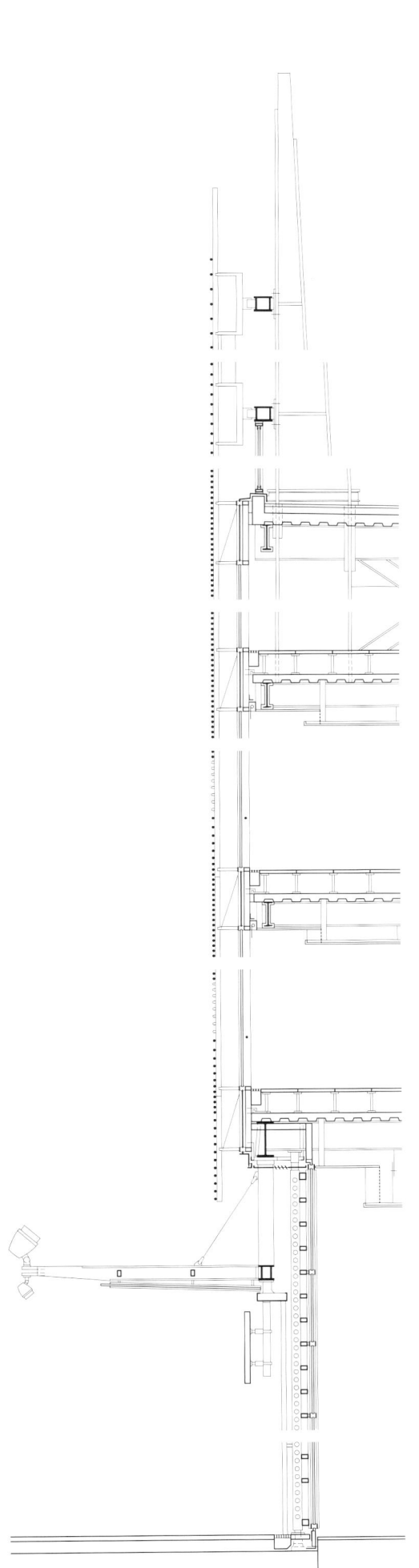

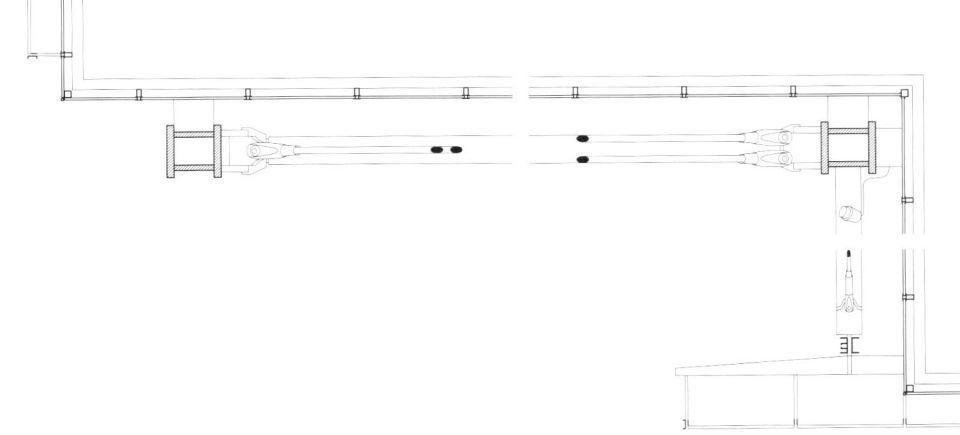

New York, 2000–2007

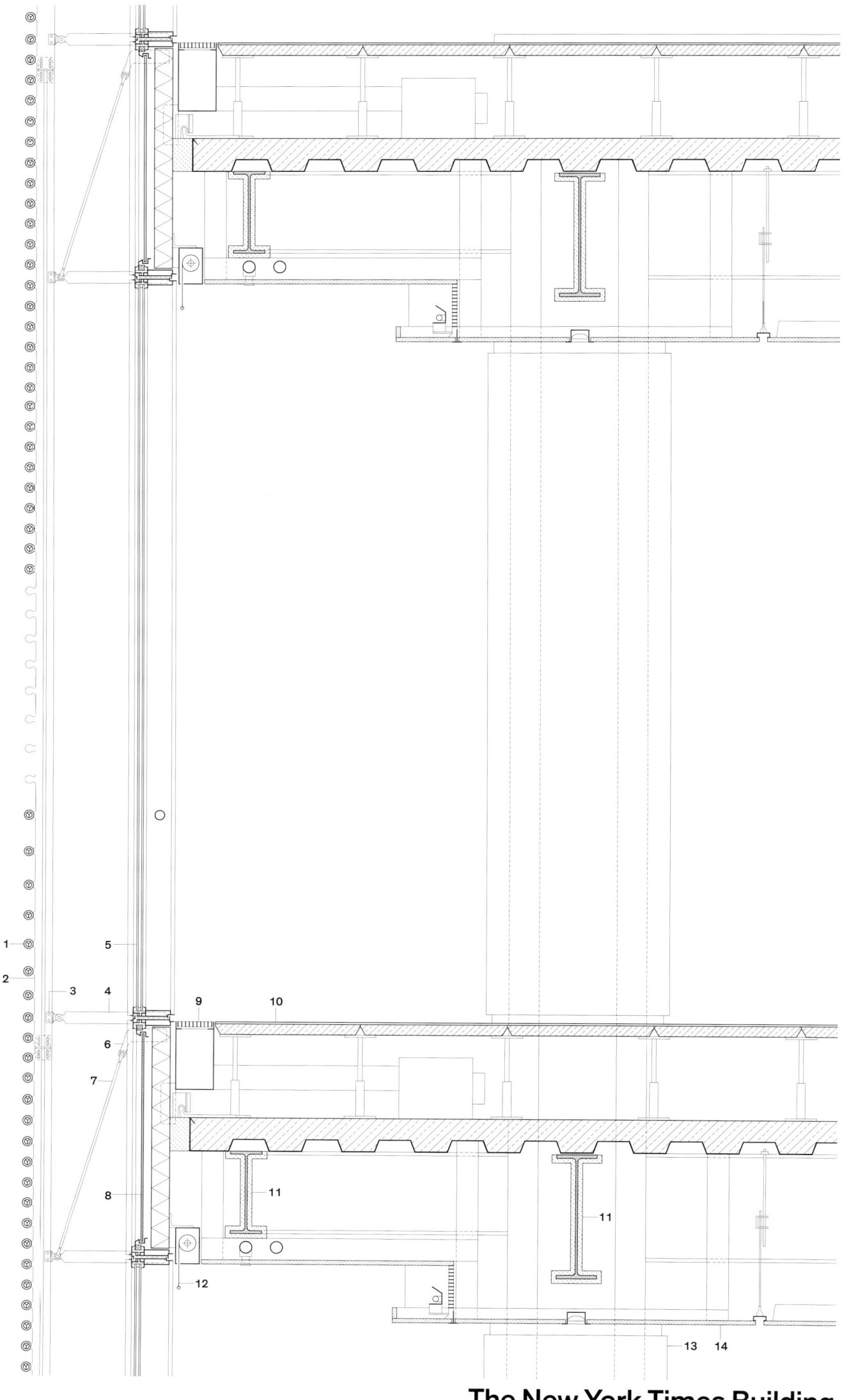

Detailschnitt Fassade,
Maßstab 1:20 /
Sectional details of facade,
scale 1:20

1	Keramikrohr (Aluminiumsilikat) glasiert Ø 16 mm auf Aluminiumprofil extrudiert, Abstände unterhalb der Decke dichter (Sonnenschutz) als im Brüstungsbereich	Ø 16 mm glazed ceramic tube (aluminium silicate) fixed to extruded aluminium section; more closely spaced below floor (as sunscreen) than at balustrade level
2	Kammprofil Aluminium lackiert	Aluminium comb section, painted
3	Befestigungsprofil Aluminium gefräst lackiert	Aluminium fixing piece, milled and painted
4	Aluminiumstrebe gefräst lackiert 51 mm/9,5 mm	51/9.5 mm aluminium strut, milled and painted
5	Isolierverglasung Float 6 + SZR 13,2 + TVG (untere Geschosse VSG) 6 mm	Double glazing: 6 mm float glass + 13.2 mm cavity + 6 mm partially toughened glass (lower floors in lam. safety glass)
6	Verbindungsplatte Aluminium lackiert	Aluminium connecting plate, painted
7	Rundrohr justierbar lackiert Ø 9,5 mm	Ø 9.5 mm adjustable tube, painted
8	Verkleidung Deckenstirn: steifes Aluminiumblech lackiert (in Fassadenecken ohne vorgehängte Keramikrohre: Glas bedruckt)	Cladding to edge of floor: rigid sheet aluminium, painted (printed glass in recessed facade corners where no ceramic tubes outside)
9	Auslass Zuluft gewärmt/gekühlt	Heated-/cooled-air inlet
10	Doppelboden Teppich auf Faserplatten	Hollow-floor construction: carpet on fibreboard
11	Deckenträger Stahlprofil I brandschutzummantelt	Steel I-beam with fire-resisting sheathing
12	Automatischer Sonnenschutz innen liegend	Automatic sunblind internally
13	Stahlstütze I mit Brandschutzverkleidung	Steel I-column with fire-resisting cladding
14	Akustik-Elementdecke abgehängt	Prefabricated suspended acoustic soffit

New York, 2000–2007

Die Tragstruktur des New York Times Building

Text: Tom Scarangello
Detail 9/2007

Die Primärtragstruktur des New York Times Building besteht aus einem ausgesteiften Stahlkern mit zwei geschosshohen Auskragungen bis zur Außenfassade (in den beiden Technikebenen auf halber Höhe und an der Spitze des Turms). Mit deren Stahlfachwerk gelingt es, die gesamte Gebäudetiefe zur Abtragung horizontaler Windlasten heranzuziehen.

Ein Aspekt, der dieses Gebäude aber in vielerlei Hinsicht einzigartig macht, ist die außen liegende Stahlstruktur in den Gebäudeecken. Einerseits ist diese integraler Bestandteil der architektonischen Gestaltung, andererseits spielt sie aber auch eine wesentliche Rolle im Tragwerk des Gebäudes. Renzo Piano und FXFowle wollten an dieser Stelle die Konstruktion sichtbar machen, sie aber nicht als Ornament behandeln, sondern aufzeigen, wie die Tragstruktur des Gebäudes funktioniert. Die außen liegenden Auskreuzungen konnten dabei ohne Brandschutzmaßnahmen konzipiert werden, da sie zur vertikalen Lastabtragung nicht zwingend notwendig sind, sondern vor allem zur Minimierung von Gebäudebewegungen beitragen. Im Prinzip könnte man auf diese sogar ganz verzichten – das Hochhaus würde auch dann noch sämtliche Sicherheitsvorschriften erfüllen, bei starkem Wind aber unangenehme Schwankungen aufweisen. Dem Nutzerkomfort auf herkömmliche Weise gerecht zu werden, hätte aufgrund größerer Profilquerschnitte entweder zu einem weitaus höheren Stahlverbrauch oder zu anderen aufwendigen konstruktiven Maßnahmen wie etwa Massedämpfern geführt. Da die außen liegenden Zugstäbe normalerweise keine Druckkräfte aufnehmen können, sind sie beim New York Times Building vorgespannt – mit dem Maximum der Kraft, die sie während der Lebensdauer des Gebäudes jemals zu erwarten haben. Die aus verschiedenen Richtungen auftretenden Windlasten führen somit entweder zu noch mehr oder eben zu weniger hohen Zugkräften – nicht aber zu Druckkräften, die ein Durchhängen der Zugstäbe zur Folge haben könnten. Letztlich führt die Vorspannung zu einem insgesamt sehr steifen Gebäude mit minimierten Gebäudebewegungen sowie einer effektiven Konstruktion.

The Load-Bearing Structure of the New York Times Building

Text: Tom Scarangello
Detail 9/2007

The primary lateral load-resisting structure consists of a braced steel core with outrigger levels that extend to the outer columns on the two mechanical services levels half way up and at the top of the tower. With this steel-grid construction, it was possible to exploit the full depth of the building to transmit lateral loads.

A unique aspect of this building's design is the exposed steel at its north and south faces. This serves both aesthetic and functional purposes, as it is integral to the architectural design and also bears a major part of the load. The architect's vision was to make the structure visible, not only for ornamental purposes, but also to express how it functions. This was achieved in part by designing the external bracing without fire protection, since they do not serve primarily to transmit vertical loads, but to control movement of the building. The building would still have complied with all safety regulations without them, but under strong wind conditions, users would have experienced an unpleasant swaying. Ensuring greater comfort by conventional means would have meant larger structural cross sections and thus use of more steel or the incorporation of more elaborate – and expensive – systems, such as a tuned mass damper. We paid special attention to the external tension bars in the steel structure. Slender tension rods cannot normally bear significant compression loading. They would sag or buckle. For this building, therefore, we created an X-brace system and prestressed the bars so that they would be able to resist the anticipated maximum forces. This means the bracing members always remain in tension regardless of which way the wind blows: the prestressed forces are merely increased or reduced. Fully activating the rods this way allowed us to efficiently meet the building's comfort criteria.

Herausforderung Temperaturschwankungen
Eine der größten Herausforderungen resultiert jedoch aus den Temperaturschwankungen, die unterschiedliches Dehn- und Schwindverhalten der inneren und äußeren Stahlelemente hervorrufen. Diese Materialbewegungen können bei einer immerhin 250 m hohen Stahlkonstruktion, Oberflächentemperaturen zwischen ca. -20 °C und +50 °C und dem Temperaturunterschied zur im klimatisierten Gebäudeinneren liegenden Stahlkonstruktion (bei rund 21 °C) erheblich sein. Wären die außen liegenden Fassadenstützen nur über die Geschossdecken an den Gebäudekern angebunden, müsste man Längenveränderungen von mindestens 10 cm erwarten – und das bei Außen- bzw. Innenstützen, die nur knapp 10 m auseinanderliegen. Um dies zu vermeiden, werden die Außenstützen über das aussteifende Stahlfachwerk der auskragenden Technikgeschosse in Position gehalten. Wenn sich die äußeren Stahlstützen nun – je nach Temperatur – ausdehnen oder verkürzen, werden sie immer auch versuchen, die inneren Stützen mit zu verändern. Durch das enge statische Zusammenspiel zwischen Kern, aussteifenden Auskragungen und außen liegender Stahlkonstruktion wird dies jedoch effektiv verhindert, sodass die Außenstützen selbst unter den ungünstigsten Bedingungen nur eine Längenveränderung von unter 3 cm aufweisen. Auf diese Weise hat die außen liegende Stahlkonstruktion ganz wesentlich dazu beigetragen, das Gebäude robuster und wirtschaftlicher zu machen – obwohl sie zunächst eher im Hinblick auf einen bestimmten architektonischen Eindruck entworfen wurde.

Challenging temperature fluctuations
One of the biggest challenges we faced was posed by temperature differences and the differential expansion and contraction between the inner and outer steel elements. With a 250-meter-high exposed steel structure, fluctuations of this kind can be considerable, with the exposed steel temperature ranging from -25 °C to +55 °C. This is in contrast to the temperature of the steel members inside the building, which is a relatively constant 20 °C to 22 °C, insulated from the outside extremes of summer heat and winter cold. If the external facade columns were tied to the core of the building solely via the floor beams, this could result in changes in elevation of 10 cm or more on upper floors, with external and internal columns only 10 m apart. To mitigate this, the outer exposed columns are linked to the inner ones by outriggers at the mechanical services storeys. Once they were linked, when the outer steel columns expand or contract, the internal columns were also forced to move as well, introducing compatibility between the elements. The tight structural links between the core, the bracing outrigger construction and the exposed steel effectively mitigate this potential for excessive differential movement. Under the most unfavorable conditions, the differential movement between internal and external columns remains smaller than 3 cm. The outer steel structure thus makes a major contribution to achieving a more robust and economical building – even though this structure was designed in the first instance for its architectural character.

Slender in optics and statics
Another important aspect was that Renzo Piano

New York, 2000–2007

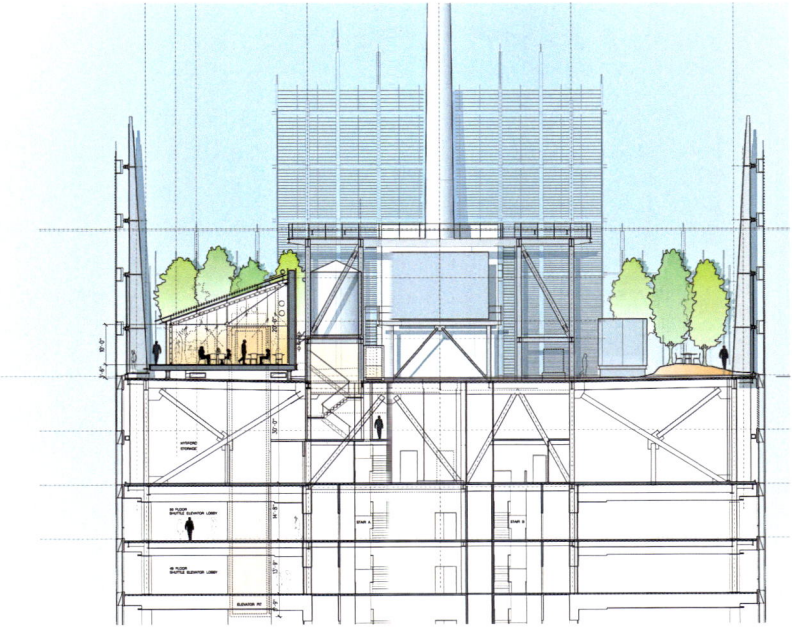

Schnitt durch die Turmspitze mit geschosshohen Auskragungen im Technikgeschoss / Section through top of tower with outriggers on services level

Verschlankung nach Optik und Statik

Wichtig in diesem Zusammenhang war, dass Renzo Piano die Konstruktion auf subtile Art und Weise mit zunehmender Höhe immer leichter und filigraner wirken lassen wollte. Die sichtbaren Profile der Außenstützen sollten nach oben stetig schlanker werden, was allerdings nicht ganz mit dem tatsächlichen, wegen der Windkräfte eher parabolischen Kräfteverlauf übereinstimmt. Um nun aber diese idealisierte, lineare Verschlankung zu ermöglichen, wurden kastenförmige Außenstützen konzipiert, die jeweils aus vier zusammengesetzten Stahlplatten bestehen. Diese wurden so angeordnet, dass die Plattenstärke nur an den beiden äußeren, gegenüberliegenden Platten ablesbar ist und deren Dicke nach oben tatsächlich linear abnimmt – von ca. 10 auf 7,5 auf 5 bis hin zu 2,5 cm. Die beiden inneren Stahlplatten hingegen, deren Seitenansichten von außen nicht sichtbar sind, weisen je nach statischer Erfordernis abnehmende Plattenstärken auf, springen von ca. 20 zu 15 zu 13 cm. Durch dieses Kaschieren der Materialstärken gelang es, die Konstruktion optisch nach oben stetig leichter erscheinen zu lassen und sie dennoch statisch effizient zu dimensionieren.

So konnten wir sowohl dem Wunsch der Architekten nach sich linear verjüngenden Stützen als auch unserem Bemühen nach einer sinnvollen und wirtschaftlichen Konstruktion entsprechen.

Was die Entwicklung der konstruktiven Details angeht, so glich das Projekt letztlich mehr einer künstlerischen als einer Ingenieursarbeit. Bei den von uns sonst bearbeiteten Projekten verschwindet die gesamte Konstruktion meist hinter Gipskarton, Mauerwerk oder sonstigen Verkleidungen, stehen Aspekte der Funktionalität und Wirtschaftlichkeit im Vordergrund. In diesem Fall hingegen wurde jede einzelne Verbindung mit unglaublich hohem Aufwand entwickelt. Teilweise wurden 1:1-Modelle gebaut, um die Detailpunkte genau betrachten und den Stahlbaufirmen das geforderte qualitative und gestalterische Niveau demonstrieren zu können. Nicht zuletzt aufgrund seiner sichtbar inszenierten und doch nach statischen und wirtschaftlichen Gesichtspunkten sinnvoll konzipierten Tragstruktur handelt es sich beim New York Times Building um eine großartige Bereicherung der New Yorker Skyline.

wanted to make the construction appear progressively lighter and more transparent with height. The columns that are visible externally were to become increasingly slender towards the top – which does not entirely reflect the impact of the generally parabolic lateral force distribution resulting from wind. Nevertheless, to implement this ideal solution, box-sections of four steel plates were used. Two of these are visible in their thickness, and we reduced this thickness uniformly from about 10 cm to 2.5 cm in stages of roughly 2.5 cm. The dimensions of the two plates where the thickness is not visible were determined according to structural requirements. These also diminish from 20 cm to 13 cm approximately, but not linearly. By concealing the thickness of the steel this way, it was possible to create a sense of increasing lightness without compromising structural efficiency. We were able to reconcile both the architects' wish for tapering columns and our obligation to engineer a sound and efficient load-bearing structure.

In its details, the project is ultimately more of an artistic than an engineering object. In most of the projects in which we participate, the structure disappears behind plasterboard, cladding or brick walls, and functional, economic factors are primary. In the New York Times Building, every connection and junction was developed in incredible detail. In some cases, full-size models were built to assess the design and to demonstrate it to steel construction contractors. Not least because of the visually fascinating load-bearing structure – conceived according to sound engineering and economic principles – this development has proved to be a great addition to the New York skyline.

Die Planung aus Sicht des Bauherrn – ein Interview mit Hussain Ali-Khan von der New York Times

Detail: Welche Umstände haben zur Planung des Neubaus für die New York Times geführt und welche Visionen wurden damit verfolgt?

Hussain Ali-Khan: 1997 zog unsere Druckerei aus dem alten Stammgebäude in der 43. Straße in einen Neubau von James Stuart Polshek in Queens. Dadurch eröffnete sich die Chance auf eine vollständige Neustrukturierung des 1913 errichteten Verlagshauses. Eine Sanierung bei laufendem Betrieb erwies sich allerdings schon organisatorisch als schwierig; ein Umzug in temporäre Ersatzräumlichkeiten wäre nicht zu vermeiden gewesen. Zusätzlich prognostizierten erste Kalkulationen immens hohe Renovierungs- bzw. Umbaukosten. So kam die Frage auf, ob es nicht möglich wäre, für die gleiche Summe einen Neubau zu errichten, maßgeschneidert auf die Bedürfnisse der New York Times im 21. Jahrhundert. Mit diesem Ziel vor Augen wurden schließlich die Eckpunkte für ein Auswahlverfahren formuliert, mit Renzo Piano, Lord Norman Foster, Cesar Pelli und David Childs (SOM) mit Frank Gehry in der letzten Runde. Die Times war mit einem Team von Mitarbeitern äußerst intensiv an allen Entwurfs- und Planungsprozessen beteiligt. Dies hatte schließlich auch einige kleine Veränderungen am Gebäude zur Folge, um den wirtschaftlichen Zielen unseres Partners Forest City Ratner besser gerecht zu werden ...

... der Bauträger Forest City Ratner vermietet die obere Hälfte des Gebäudes ...

Das ist richtig. Es zeichnete sich ab, dass das Gebäude für uns allein zu groß werden würde. Also suchten wir nach einem Partner. Allerdings hatten wir – mehr vielleicht als andere Eigentümer – sehr präzise Vorstellungen vom Gebäude, um Redakteuren und Verwaltung eine optimale Arbeitsumgebung zu ermöglichen. Darüber hinaus sollte ein Bauwerk entstehen, das unsere Stellung in der Gesellschaft widerspiegelt, einen echten Beitrag zur Stadtgestaltung leistet und unseren innerbetrieblichen Bedürfnissen

The Planning from the Client's Point of View – Interview with Hussain Ali-Khan of The New York Times

Detail: What factors determined the planning of The New York Times Building, and what was the underlying vision?

Hussain Ali-Khan: We had just completed the production plant at Queens in 1997 designed by James Stuart Polshek, a beautiful new factory, and we transitioned our printing out of the West 43rd Street building. This presented an opportunity to upgrade our infrastructure and to do some renovations. We started to do some estimating on what it will take to design a big renovation, and it was very demanding and expensive. So we said, for that kind of money, maybe we can build a new building that is purpose-designed for a 21st-century media company; that would embody the "Rules of the Road" – our business and ethical guide for employees to be able to do their best work at The New York Times. At the end of the selection process – we didn't call it a design competition – we had settled on four teams of architects to present models and concepts: Renzo Piano, Lord Foster, Cesar Pelli and the team of David Childs (SOM) and Frank Gehry. The architect who was selected to actually do the building was Renzo Piano.

How was the collaboration with the architects, the developer and the engineers?

The Times was very deeply involved in every aspect of the design and the detailing of the building. The building changed a bit from the original design submission to become a better reflection of the brief and a better commercial venture for our partner, Forest City Ratner. They were an important part of the development team.

They are also renting the upper half of the building.

The building was going to be too big for the Times, so we needed a partner. It was a fairly traditional process, but we had very strong ideas in terms of how this building should

entspricht. Gemeinsam mit dem Wunsch nach niedrigen Betriebskosten führte dies zum Einsatz zahlreicher »grüner« Technologien. So zeigt sich das Gebäude durch seine allseitige Verglasung sehr transparent. Wie lässt sich aber daraus die größte Tageslichtausnutzung für die Innenräume ziehen, ohne die Menschen direktem Sonnenlicht auszusetzen? Um solche Fragen zu beantworten, wurden die Tageslichtexperten der Lawrence Berkeley National Labs hinzugezogen. Sie haben uns geholfen, ein Mock-up eines ganzen Geschossbereichs im Maßstab 1:1 zu bauen und damit zu experimentieren – ungefähr ein Viertel der Grundrissfläche über Eck inklusive Fassade und Möblierung. Dabei wurde eine ganze Reihe von Tageslichttechnologien getestet, was schließlich zu den verwendeten automatisierten Verschattungs- und Lichtsteuerungssystemen geführt hat. Die Entwicklungsarbeit verursachte zwar einige Mehrkosten, dafür ist das heutige Energieeinsparungspotenzial enorm – die Kostenersparnis bei der künstlichen Beleuchtung beträgt 30 bis 50 %.

Gab es eine Gegenüberstellung der reinen Baukosten und der späteren Betriebskosten? Wie schwierig war es, solche Technologien im Budget unterzubringen?
    Das Budget wurde im Jahr 2000 festgelegt und später nicht mehr korrigiert. Also mussten Wege gefunden werden, um neue Technologien in den Kostenrahmen zu integrieren. Im Vergleich zu herkömmlichen Systemen hat dies jedoch letztlich stets nur zu geringfügigen Verteuerungen geführt. So hätten wir Verschattungen und Leuchten ohnehin eingebaut – neu hinzugekommen sind lediglich entsprechende Steuerungseinheiten. Auch der Doppelboden war von Anfang an vorgesehen, neu ist die Lüftungsanlage darin. Doch selbst diese führte nicht wirklich zu Mehrkosten, denn sie wäre sonst in der Decke untergebracht worden. Stets wurden Mittel und Wege gefunden, um Kosten umzuverteilen oder nur geringfügig ansteigen zu lassen. Ein gutes Beispiel hierfür ist das Blockheizkraftwerk. Als wir einen Blick auf die Preise der für uns unentbehrlichen Notstromaggregate geworfen hatten, stellte sich die Frage, welchen Sinn es macht, viel Geld für Geräte auszugeben, die womöglich niemals zum Einsatz kommen würden. Im

serve as a place for employees to do their best work, a place that would reflect our standing in the community, that would make a real contribution to the city, and finally that would serve our long-term operational needs. That was what drove a lot of the really green technology in the building. Here was our opportunity to build into it some of the best energy- and money-saving technologies we could think of. So the building is transparent. But how do you get value from the beautiful clear glass and maximise daylight savings and actually protect people from the sun that's going to come through those windows? We engaged Lawrence Berkeley National Labs – the world experts on daylighting – to help us design a system. We did an experiment that involved building a replica of parts of one floor of the building. We tested a bunch of systems that allowed us to create a system that includes these automatic shades and dimmable lights. While this was a bit more expensive from a capital perspective, it should save us enormous amounts of money on operations – 30 to 50 percent of our energy from lighting, using this technology.

Was a comparison made between pure construction costs and long-term operating costs? How difficult was it to incorporate technology of this kind in the budget?
    The budget was fixed in 2000 or something like that. It hasn't changed. So we had to find ways to fit this technology into the budget. Now, it's a little more expensive than normative systems, but we were going to have to install shades anyway, so the parts that are extra are the motor units and controls. We were going to have to install a raised floor anyway, so the only part that's extra is a bit of the underfloor air-distribution system, and even that might not be considered extra, because we didn't have to put in an overhead air-distribution system. So we found ways to bring these things into the budget in a way that was kind of a replacement. A good example is our cogeneration system. When we looked at the budget for emergency generators, which is something we need – to protect our business from power outages – it was so expensive that we said: "Are we going to spend a lot of money on emergency generators that we might

alten Gebäude haben wir sie nur ein einziges Mal gebraucht. Um dieses Geld auf eine sinnvollere Weise anzulegen, haben wir uns für ein Aggregat entschlossen, das nicht nur im Notfall, sondern ständig Strom für den Eigenverbrauch liefert – z. B. für unsere Computerzentrale oder unseren Newsroom – und mit dessen Abwärme sich das Gebäude im Winter heizen und im Sommer teilweise kühlen lässt. Daraus ergibt sich ein Wirkungsgrad der Aggregate von 90 %. Im Unterschied zu den meisten Developern, die im Hinblick auf unterschiedlichste Nutzer möglichst variable Gebäude planen, haben wir als Eigennutzer die Gelegenheit ergriffen, ein für unsere Bedürfnisse tatsächlich maßgeschneidertes Gebäude zu entwickeln.

Der Erfolg eines derartigen Entwurfs- und Bauprozesses hängt immer auch von der richtigen Auswahl der ausführenden Firmen und der Koordination aller Beteiligten ab. Wie aktiv hat die New York Times diesen Prozess unterstützt? Hatten die Architekten mehr oder weniger freie Hand?

Nein. Es ist richtig, dass es ein großes Team zu steuern galt. Und manchmal lagen die Ziele der einzelnen Beteiligten nicht immer auf derselben Linie. Da wollte der Bauleiter schon mal die Bauarbeiten so schnell wie möglich abschließen, während die Architekten ihren Entwurf noch bis zur letzten Sekunde ausfeilten. Doch das ist bei allen Gebäuden so, die bis ins Detail mit aller Sorgfalt durchdacht werden. Während der Planungs- und Bauphase haben unser Partner Forest City Ratner und wir sehr auf die Einhaltung von Terminen, die Vollständigkeit der Planung sowie deren Realisier- und Bezahlbarkeit geachtet, beispielsweise bei der Prüfung der Angebote für die vorgehängte Außenfassade. Ursprünglich hatten wir diese lediglich mit Plänen ausgeschrieben, zurück kamen jedoch nur absolut unakzeptable Preise. Die Firmen hatten über die Risiken bei der Realisierung der Fassade spekuliert und diese eingepreist. Also haben wir vier potenzielle Hersteller beauftragt, ein 1:1-Modell zu planen und zu realisieren. Im Endergebnis stellte diese Vorgehensweise für die Firmen eine große Hilfe dar, machte das Modell doch deutlich, dass die Fassade weit weniger kompliziert war als befürchtet. Im

Vorgängerbau der New York Times an der 43. Straße, genutzt von 1913–2007 /
Previous New York Times Building on 43rd Street, in use from 1913 to 2007

New York, 2000–2007

Grundrisse Cafeteria (Plan RPBW) / Floor plan with cafeteria (plan by RPBW)

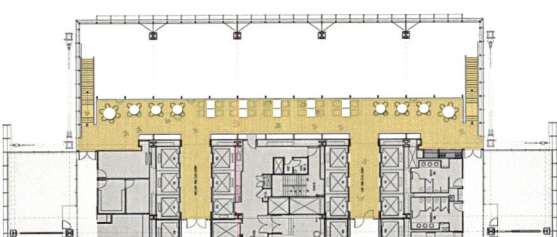
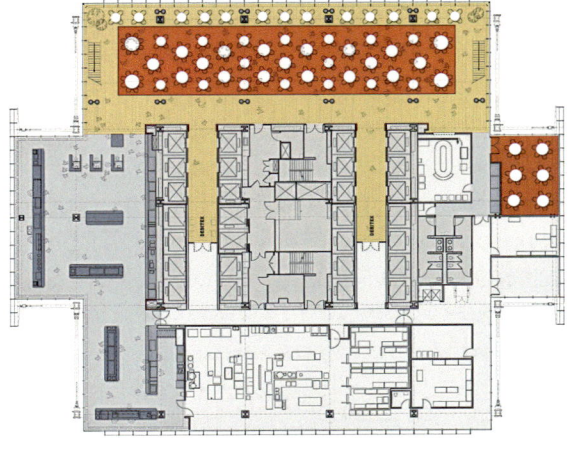

Lobby (Gensler, nach Leitlinien RPBW) / Lobby by Gensler, based on guidelines by RPBW

Cafeteria (Gensler, nach Leitlinien RPBW) / Cafeteria by Gensler, based on guidelines by RPBW

Wesentlichen besteht sie aus modularen Elementen aus Aluminium, Glas, einem Rahmen für die Keramikröhren und schließlich den Keramikröhren selbst. Die Röhren wurden übrigens in Deutschland hergestellt. Auf der Suche nach einer geeigneten Keramik hatten wir ein Werk für große Keramik-Abwasserrohre in Leipzig besucht. Diese wurden gerade in einen 1650 °C heißen Brennofen gerollt, als uns plötzlich auffiel, dass die kleinen Rollen darunter ebenfalls aus Keramik sein mussten – Stahl- oder Aluminiumrollen würden bei diesen Temperaturen schmelzen. So erfuhren wir von den feuerbeständigen, üblicherweise im Inneren eines Brennofens eingesetzten Keramikröhren der Firma Haldenwanger, die schließlich auch unsere 196 000 Röhren fertigte. Letztlich haben wir den Fassadenfirmen die Keramikröhren zur Verfügung gestellt. Erst an diesem Punkt war klar, dass Renzo Pianos Vision einer Keramikfassade überhaupt bezahlbar sein würde. Hätten wir die Auswahl geeigneter Keramikröhren den anbietenden Firmen überlassen, hätte das Ergebnis weit weniger unseren Vorstellungen entsprochen. Im Hinblick auf die Realisierung dieses wunderbaren Gebäudes haben wir den Firmen aufgezeigt, wo die Risiken der Herstellung liegen, aber auch welchen Leistungsumfang sie tatsächlich zu erbringen haben.

Wie wichtig war es, die Mitarbeiter, aber auch die Geschäftsführung der Times in diesen Planungsprozess einzubinden?
> Sie waren sehr eng eingebunden. Es wurden interne Gestaltungsteams aufgebaut. Der Art Director der Zeitung und der Senior Vice President Marketing etwa haben uns geholfen aufzuzeigen, wie Architektur und Innenraumgestaltung unsere Marke widerspiegeln.

Im Vergleich zum alten Verlagshaus hat sich das Arbeitsumfeld stark verändert …
> Das alte Gebäude war ja eigentlich eine Druckerei. Die unteren fünf Geschosse dienten der Zeitungsproduktion. Die Büroräume waren ziemlich dunkel und über die Jahre in kleine Einheiten unterteilt worden, weite, offene Bereiche suchte man vergeblich.

> never use?" So we built a cogenerator, which allows us to generate power continually for our own use, for our data center and our newsroom, and to use the heat from that generator to heat the building in the wintertime and cool a part of it in summertime. That allows us to get around 90 percent efficiency on the cogenerator. That's a really good example of how, instead of buying emergency generators just to sit around and collect dust, we have a system now that's going to be able to supply power in a much more efficient way. And it was a substitution of one system for another without changing the budget.

The success of such a design and construction process depends on the choice of people and firms involved. Did you give the architects a free hand in that respect?
> Oh, no! A very large team has to be managed, and sometimes the goals of the teams aren't always in perfect alignment. We were very active, along with our partner, Forest City Ratner, in managing the process. An example of this is the selection of the curtain-wall supply. We had originally just gone out with drawings, and the prices came back at an insupportable level. The reason for this was that the people were speculating on how much risk they would have to take in building this curtain wall. We paid four curtain-wall manufacturers to do engineering, to build a full-scale mock-up. This helped the companies to understand that it was not that complicated a curtain-wall. It's basically a unitised panel. It's aluminium extrusions, glass, a frame for ceramic rods, and the rods themselves. The rods the owners actually found during a tour of Germany. We watched sewer pipes rolling into a kiln with a temperature of 1,650 °C, and all of a sudden we realised that to withstand 1,650 °C, the rollers must be ceramic, because steel and aluminium will melt at those temperatures. Eventually, the company producing these rollers helped develop a process to make 196,000 ceramic rods. So we supplied the rods, and the curtain-wall manufacturers did everything else. This allowed us to realise Renzo Piano's vision in an affordable way.

New York, 2000–2007

Obwohl die Räume im Neubau nur halb so groß sind, hat man hier das Gefühl von räumlicher Großzügigkeit – die Mitarbeiter können das ganze Geschoss und selbst die Umgebung überblicken.

Ähnlich wie bei den Treppen an der Fassade – kaum ein Developer würde dafür teuer vermietbare Eckbüros opfern.
    Die Treppen gehen auf einen Vorschlag von Renzo Piano zurück. Eine gute Idee, weil in den Gebäudeecken eine großartige Verknüpfung der einzelnen Geschosse möglich ist. Darüber hinaus haben wir deutlich gemacht, dass wir mehr an Mobilität und Komfort der Mitarbeiter denken als an repräsentative Eckbüros. Ich glaube aber auch, dass man insgesamt flexibel sein muss, wenn man mit einem Architekten von der Größe Renzo Pianos zusammenarbeitet. Und dass man Freiräume schaffen muss, die es ermöglichen, den Entwurf zu verfeinern. In der Architektur gibt es keinen schnellen Weg zum Ziel. Vielmehr geht es um einen sich ständig verändernden Prozess. Dabei kommt es immer wieder vor, dass einzelne Details nicht perfekt sind. Doch wenn wir die Zeit und auch die Ressourcen haben, sollten wir versuchen, das Ergebnis so gut wie irgend möglich zu gestalten – ohne Zeitplan und Kostenrahmen aus den Augen zu verlieren, die bei dieser Arbeitsweise manchmal etwas aus dem Ruder laufen können. Letztlich muss man abwägen, was wirklich wichtig ist und was nicht.

Hussain Ali-Khan ist Vizepräsident der Immobilienentwicklung der New York Times Company.

This must be a completely new working environment after the old building of 1913.
    The old building was a printing factory, so the bottom five floors were all production-related. There was no wide-open space. Even though our floors are smaller here, they feel larger because of the expansiveness of the space. People can see outside, too. That gives you a greater expanse.

The stairs next to the facade are astonishing in this respect, too.
    The stairs were originally proposed by Renzo Piano, and we thought it was a great idea, because here they were an utterly great way to get from floor to floor. By putting them into the corner office location, it suggests that we were more interested in the mobility, comfort and convenience of employees, before putting offices in those positions. It's a really democratic decision to put those stairs on the window wall. But I think you have to remain flexible. In the end, you have to be able to decide what is really important in the planning of a building and in the perception of those people who come into contact with it.

Hussain Ali-Khan is Vice-President of Real-Estate Development for The New York Times Company.

Atrium mit Newsroom im Podium /
Atrium with newsroom in plinth structure

Grundriss 19. Obergeschoss mit Möblierung, Maßstab 1:800

Die Bereiche entlang der Fassade sind als Großraum organisiert, Einzelbüros sind um den Kern angeordnet und orientieren sich mit Glaswänden zum Großraum (Innenausbau Gensler nach Leitlinien RPBW), an den Ecken entlang der 8. Avenue sind Verbindungstreppen angeordnet.

Layout of 19th floor with furnishings, scale 1:800

The areas along the facades are used as open-plan offices. Single-office spaces are laid out around the core and are oriented to the open-plan areas, with dividing glass walls between the two. (Interior design by Gensler based on guidelines by RPBW.) At the corners along 8th Avenue are linking staircases.

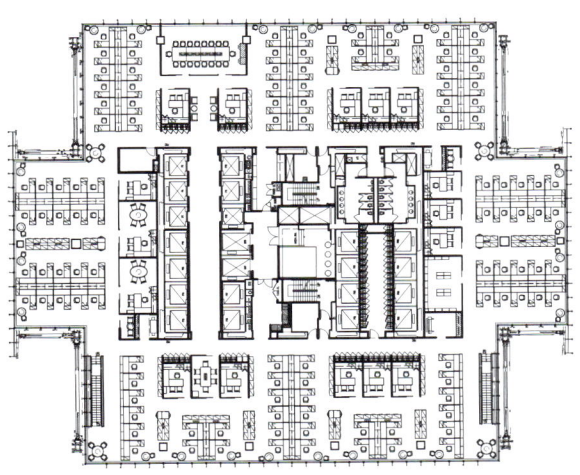

New York, 2000–2007

127

Maison Hermès, Tokio / Tokyo, JP

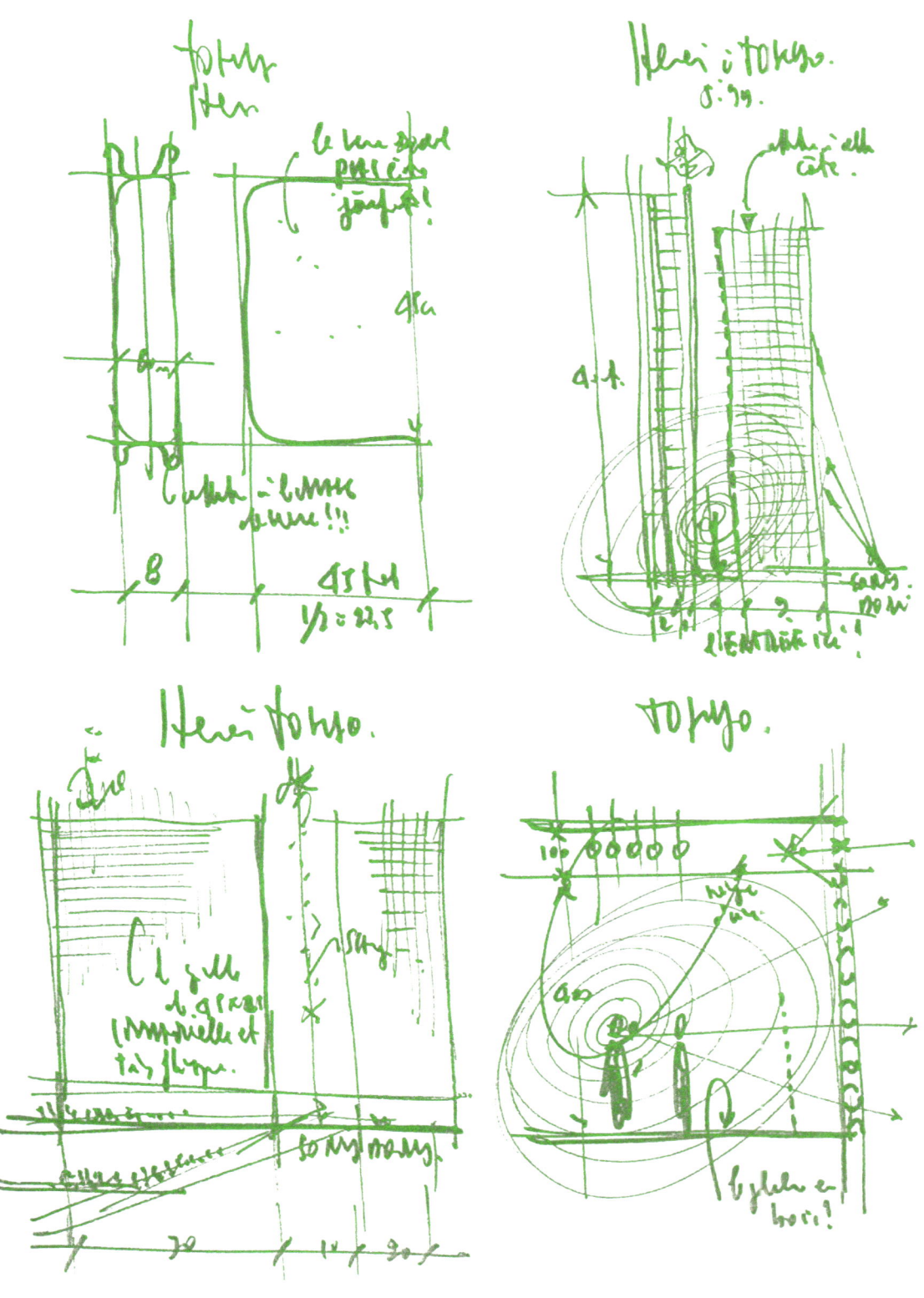

Entwurfsskizze von Renzo Piano / Design sketch by Renzo Piano

Kaufhaus in Tokio

Text: Andreas Gabriel
Detail 7/2001

Die japanische Hauptniederlassung von Hermès im Ginza-Distrikt mitten in Tokio fällt innerhalb des heterogenen Umfelds durch ihre großzügige Fassade aus Glasbausteinen auf. Bei Dunkelheit wirkt das Gebäude wie eine riesige schimmernde Laterne. Über einer Grundfläche von 45 × 11 m befinden sich auf insgesamt ca. 6000 m² Fläche in 15 Geschossen Verkaufs- und Ausstellungsräume, Büros, Werkstätten, ein Filmvorführraum, ein kleines Museum sowie ein Dachgarten. An der Längsseite bildet ein Gebäuderücksprung einen kleinen Hof von ca. 6 × 8 m. Vom Hof aus erreicht man die um zwei Ebenen tiefer gelegene Untergrundbahn über den hauseigenen Lift oder die Rolltreppe.

Die vorgehängte Fassade aus 45 × 45 mm großen, eigens für das Gebäude gefertigten Glassteinen reicht vollständig über die Geschosse und ist bei Räumen mit doppelter Höhe zusätzlich an einer Stahlsubkonstruktion rückverankert. Für die gerundeten Gebäudekanten wurden kleinere Formate eingesetzt. Wie ein gläsernes Gewebe legt sich die Hülle um das Gebäude, schirmt es gegen die hektische Stadt ab und erzeugt eine ruhige, gelassene Atmosphäre im Inneren. Sensibel reagiert die Fassade auf den Wechsel verschiedener Lichtstimmungen. Herstellungsbedingte Unregelmäßigkeiten der Glassteinoberflächen beleben das Zusammenspiel von Transparenz, Spiegelung, Textur und Schattenwurf. Bei deutlichen Bezügen zu Pierre Chareaus »Maison de Verre« in Paris wurde das Material hier auf einen großen Maßstab übertragen und in seinen Möglichkeiten durch eine technisch innovative Fugenausbildung erweitert. Die hohen Anforderungen an die Erdbebensicherheit erfüllt das Gebäude in Anlehnung an traditionelle japanische Tempelbauten durch ein elastisches Tragsystem. An bestimmten Punkten des Stahltragwerks wurden viskoelastische Dämpfungselemente eingesetzt. Die Verformungsmöglichkeit wurde gleichmäßig über die gesamte Struktur verteilt, jedes Element nimmt seinen Teil an Toleranz auf. So können sich die Fugen zwischen den Glassteinen jeweils um 4 mm verformen. Auf diese Weise bleiben bei Erdbeben sowohl Tragstruktur und Versorgungsleitungen unversehrt als auch die Wind- und Wasserdichtigkeit erhalten.

Department Store in Tokyo

Text: Andreas Gabriel
Detail 7/2001

Located in a heterogeneous area of the city, the new Japanese headquarters of Hermès in Tokyo is remarkable for its extensive glass-block facade. At night, the building resembles a huge, shimmering lantern. The 15-storey structure has a footprint 45 × 11 m in size and a total floor area of roughly 6,000 m². It houses sales and exhibition spaces, offices, workshops, film-showing facilities, a small museum and a roof garden. A recess in the long face of the building forms a small forecourt of approx. 6 × 8 m, from where there is access via the house's lift or escalator to the underground railway two levels below.

The curtain-wall extending across the whole facade consists of 45 × 45 mm glass blocks specially manufactured for this building, with smaller blocks around the curved corners. Where multistorey spaces occur, the facade is additionally anchored to the steel supporting structure. The envelope wraps around the building like a glass fabric, shielding it from the hectic city and creating a calm, serene atmosphere inside. The facade reacts sensitively to changing light conditions. Production-related irregularities in the glass surface enliven the interplay of transparency, reflection, texture and shadow. Clearly referring to Chareau's Maison de Verre in Paris, the material was applied to a larger scale here and expanded in its possibilities by a technically innovative joint geometry. The design was able to meet the high requirements for seismic safety with an elastic support system modelled on the principles of traditional temple construction. Viscoelastic dampers were inserted at strategic points of the steel load-bearing structure. Any deformation is spread evenly over the entire structure, each element taking its share of tolerance. The joints between the glass blocks, for example, can absorb deformation of up to 4 mm. In this way, both the support structure and the supply lines remain intact during earthquakes and the wind and water resistance is maintained.

Schnitt, Grundrisse,
Maßstab 1:400 /
Section, Layout plans,
scale 1:400

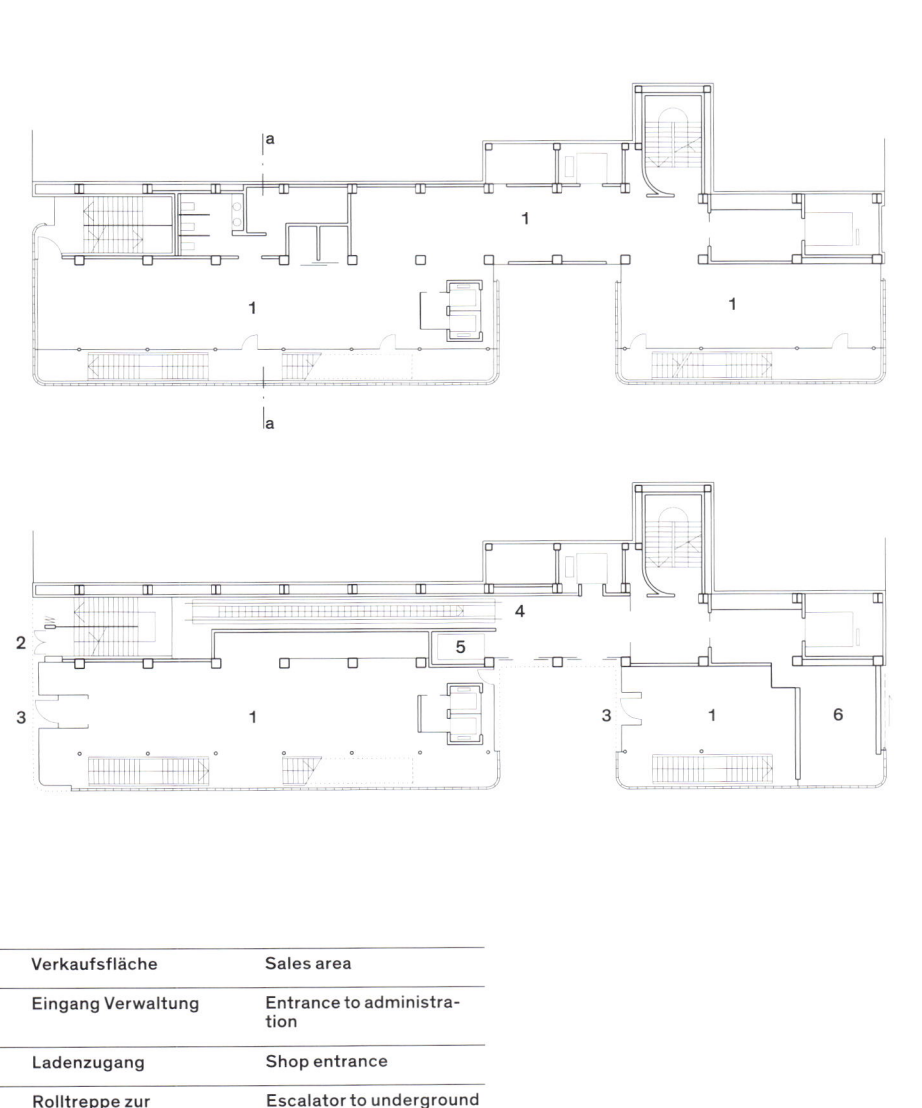
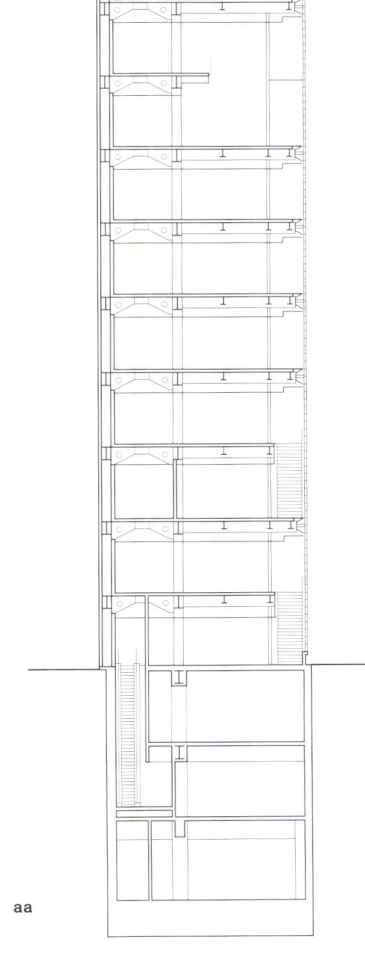

1	Verkaufsfläche	Sales area
2	Eingang Verwaltung	Entrance to administration
3	Ladenzugang	Shop entrance
4	Rolltreppe zur Untergrundbahn	Escalator to underground railway
5	Lift zur Untergrundbahn	Lift to underground railway
6	Garage	Garage

aa

Tokio / Tokyo, 1998–2006

131

Schnitt Fassade, Maßstab 1:20 /
Section through facade, scale 1:20

1	Glasstein 430/430/120 mm	430/430/120 mm glass blocks
2	Doppelboden mit Parkettoberfläche	Hollow floor construction with parquet finish
3	Stahlbetondecke auf verlorener Schalung aus Trapezblech 150 mm	150 mm reinforced concrete floor on ribbed metal sheeting as permanent formwork
4	Stahlblechpaneel gedämmt 50 mm	50 mm insulated sheet-steel panel
5	Stahlprofil I 375/300 mm mit Brandschutzbeschichtung 25 mm	300/375 mm steel I-beam with 25 mm fire-protective coating
6	Stahlprofil I HEA 200	Steel I-beam 200 mm deep
7	Stahlstab mit Gewindeenden Ø 16 mm mit Brandschutzanstrich	Ø 16 mm steel rod with threaded ends, with fire-resisting paint
8	Revisionsklappe	Inspection flap
9	Stahlprofil I 250/125 mm mit Brandschutzbeschichtung 25 mm	125/250 mm steel I-beam with 25 mm fire-protective coating
10	Gelenklager mit Kugelkopf aus feuerbeständigem Stahl Ø 140 mm	Ø 140 mm fire-resisting steel hinged bearing with ball and socket joint
11	abgehängte Decke Gipskarton 12,5 mm	12.5 mm plasterboard suspended soffit
12	Stütze Stahlrohr Ø 180/40 mm mit Brandschutzbeschichtung 10 mm	Ø 180/40 mm tubular steel column with 10 mm fire-protective coating
13	Stahlrohr Ø 50 mm mit Brandschutzanstrich	Ø 50 mm steel tube with fire-resisting paint
14	Flachstahl 170/20 mm	170/20 mm steel plate
15	Sonnenschutzrollo	Sunblind
16	Stahlrohr ⌷ 100/50/5 mm	100/50/5 mm steel RHS
17	Stahlwinkel L 140/135/15 mm	140/135/15 mm steel angle
18	Stahlprofil 80/53/3 mm	80/53/3 mm steel section
19	Silikonversiegelung dauerelastisch	Elastic silicone seal
20	EPDM-Profil	EPDM section
21	Kantenelement Glasstein	Glass-block edge element

Maison Hermès

Detailschnitte Fassade:
Anschluss an Stahlstütze
Regelanschluss /
Kantenausbildung,
Maßstab 1:5 /
Sectional details through
facade: connection to
steel column standard
connection / edge detail,
scale 1:5

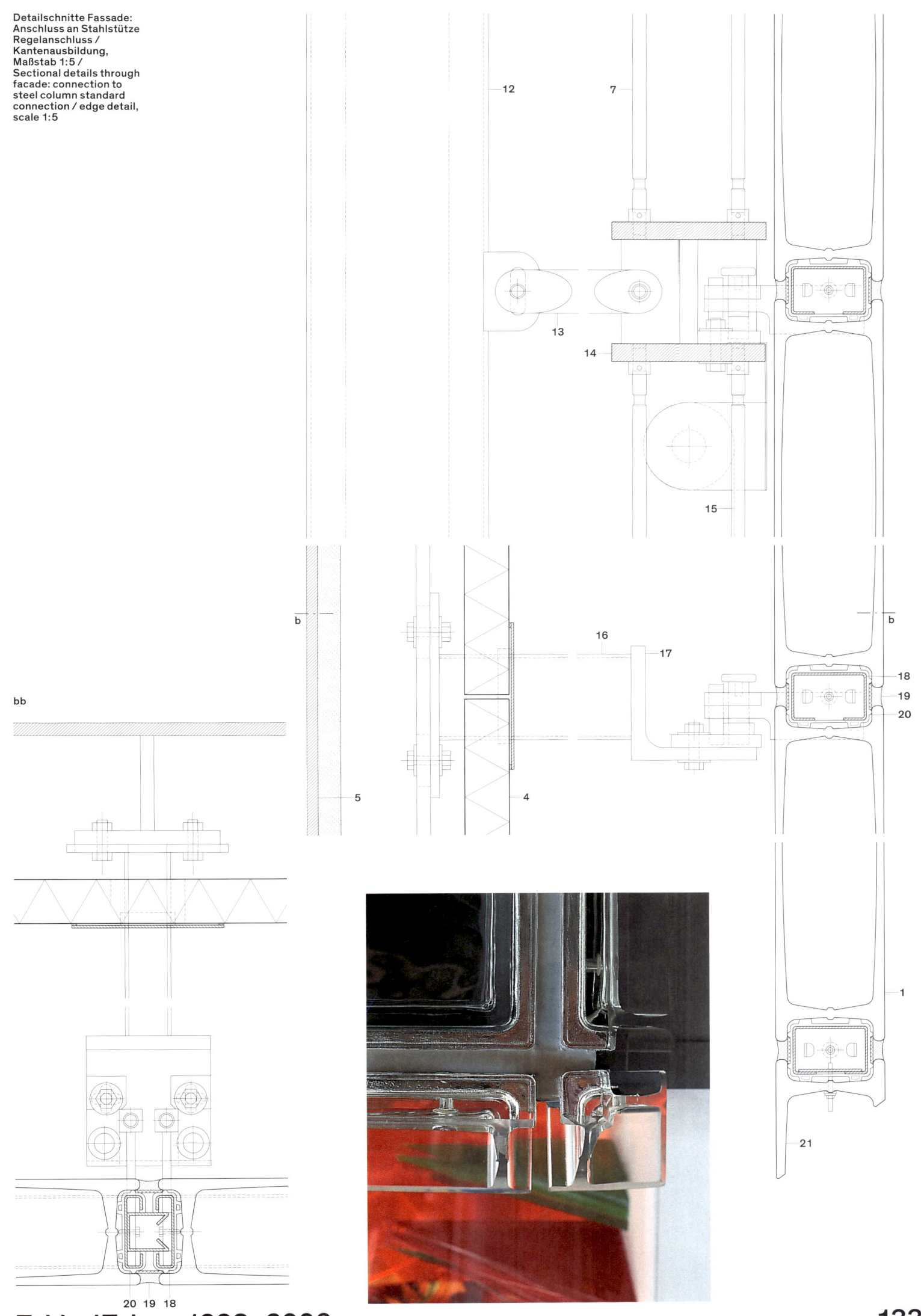

Tokio / Tokyo, 1998–2006

Zentrum Paul Klee, Bern, CH

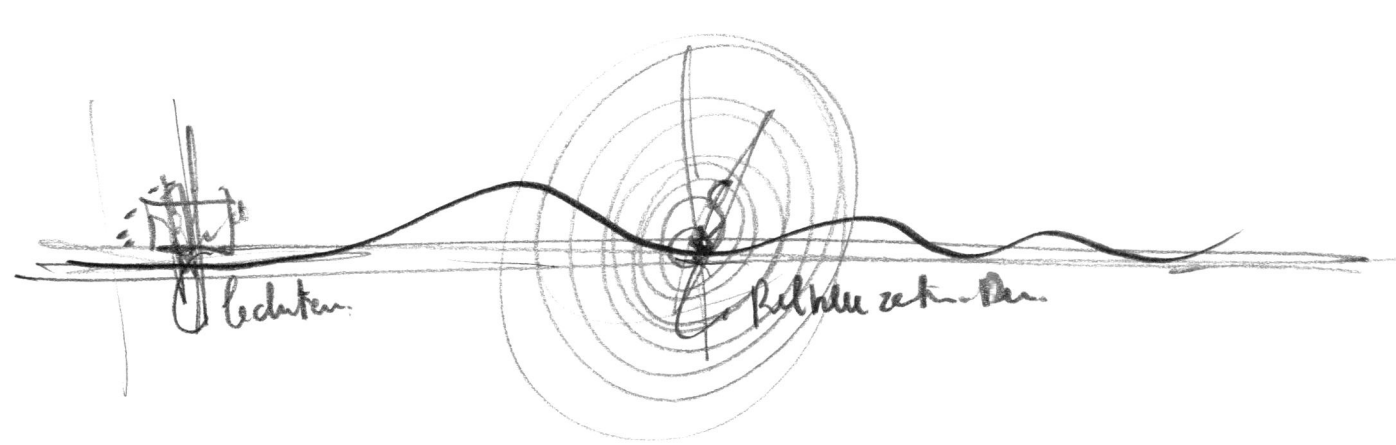

Entwurfsskizze von Renzo Piano / Design sketch by Renzo Piano

Schnitte,
Maßstab 1:1000 /
Sections,
scale 1:1,000

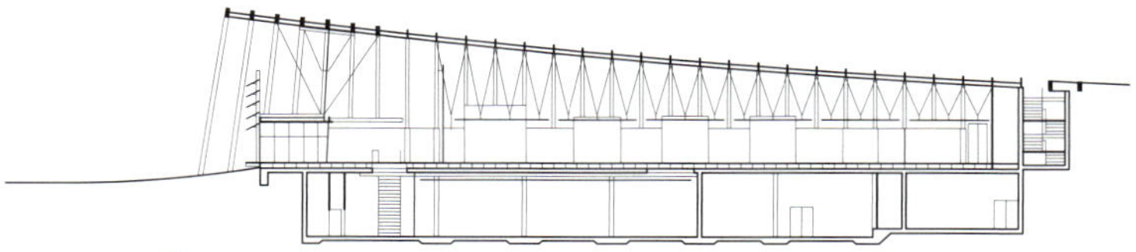

cc

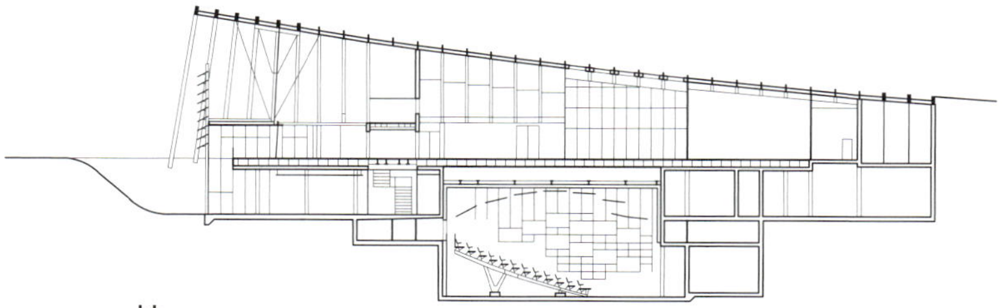

bb

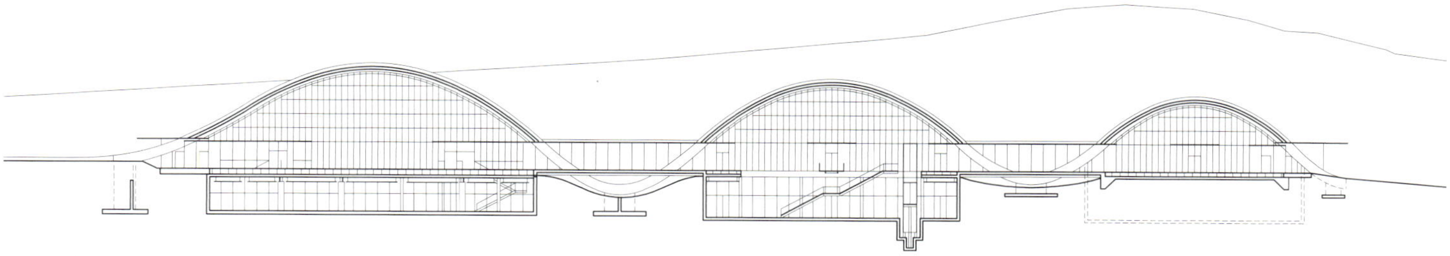

aa

Zentrum Paul Klee

Bern, 1999–2005

Zentrum Paul Klee in Bern

Text: Sabine Drey
Detail 7–8/2005

»Die zart geschwungene Linie des Hügels macht den ganzen Charme des Ortes aus.« Dieser erste Eindruck des Architekten führte zur Landschaftsskulptur des neuen »Zentrum Paul Klee« am Stadtrand von Bern: Drei Wellen schwingen sich über ein Getreidefeld und öffnen sich im Westen zum Tal. Ausgangspunkt für das Projekt war das Angebot der Schwiegertochter Paul Klees, der Stadt Bern 690 Gemälde zu schenken, wenn diese bis Ende 2006 ein Museum für rund 4000 Werke realisierte. Dank der Spenden des Chirurgen Maurice Müller konnte dieser Wunsch umgesetzt und das Raumprogramm sogar um ein Auditorium und ein Kindermuseum erweitert werden. Eine »Museumsstraße« im Erdgeschoss verbindet alle Nutzungen. Die Geometrie des Gebäudes besteht aus einer dreifach gekrümmten Fläche: Sie beschreibt sowohl im Grundriss als auch in beiden Aufrissen Kreissegmente. Man entschied sich für ein Tragwerk aus Stahlrippen, die mit computergesteuerten Brennschneidemaschinen in den vielen unterschiedlichen Formen ausgeschnitten und dann per Hand verschweißt wurden. Die Höhe der Träger differiert zwischen 800 und 1200 mm. Dazwischen sind Roste aus Rundrohren eingebracht, die in den Randbereichen in Bodennähe von erdgefüllten Blechschalen abgelöst werden, um einen sanften Übergang in die Landschaft zu erreichen. Auch die Auflagersituationen sind komplex: Während die Welle vorne in den Gegenschwung übergeht und an der niedrigsten Stelle punktgelagert ist, mündet sie weiter hinten im Erdreich. Dort nehmen die Stahlbetonwände der darunterliegenden Räume die Lasten auf. An allen Stellen sind die Bögen mit Zugseilen in den Deckenplatten verspannt. Am höchsten Punkt im Westen übernimmt das Dach zusätzlich die Lasten der abgehängten Fassade. Um diese möglichst flächig zu übertragen, verteilt ein v-förmiges System aus Stahlseilen und -rohren die Lasten auf jeweils fünf Rippen. Natürliches Licht war allerdings weder für das Auditorium noch für das Museum erwünscht – die Ausstellung ist in gedämpftes, kontemplatives Licht getaucht.

Paul Klee Centre in Bern

Text: Sabine Drey
Detail 7–8/2005

"The whole attraction of the place lies in the gentle curve of the hill." The architect's first impression of the site on the outskirts of Bern led to the design of the new Paul Klee Centre in the form of a landscape sculpture. Three waves rise and fall over a cornfield and open towards the valley in the west. The starting point for the project was the offer by Paul Klee's daughter-in-law to donate 690 paintings to the city of Bern, on condition that it build a museum for approximately 4,000 works by the end of 2006. Thanks to donations by surgeon Maurice Müller, it was possible not only to comply with this stipulation, but to extend the spatial programme with an auditorium, a children's museum and an administrative zone. All functions are linked with each other by a ground-floor "museum street".

The geometry of the building comprises a three-dimensionally curved surface based on segments of circles on plan and in both elevations. The load-bearing structure consists of steel ribs cut by computer-controlled oxyacetylene equipment in the many different forms required and then welded together by hand. The height of these beams varies from 800 to 1,200 mm. Between them is a tubular grille which, in order to achieve a gradual transition to the landscape, gives way at the edges near the ground to sheet-metal trays filled with earth. The support details vary, too. At the front, the wave swings from curve to counter-curve, with point bearings at the base. Further back, the curved geometry continues underground, where the reinforced concrete walls of the lower-floor spaces bear the loads. The curved arches are tied with tension cables to the floors. At the highest point, to the west, the roof also bears the loads of the suspended facade. To transmit these over as large an area as possible, a rocker-type system, consisting of steel cables and tubes, distributes the loads over groups of five ribs. Natural light was required neither for the auditorium nor for the museum. The exhibition is bathed in subdued, contemplative light.

Grundrisse,
Maßstab 1:3000 /
Floor plans,
scale 1:3,000

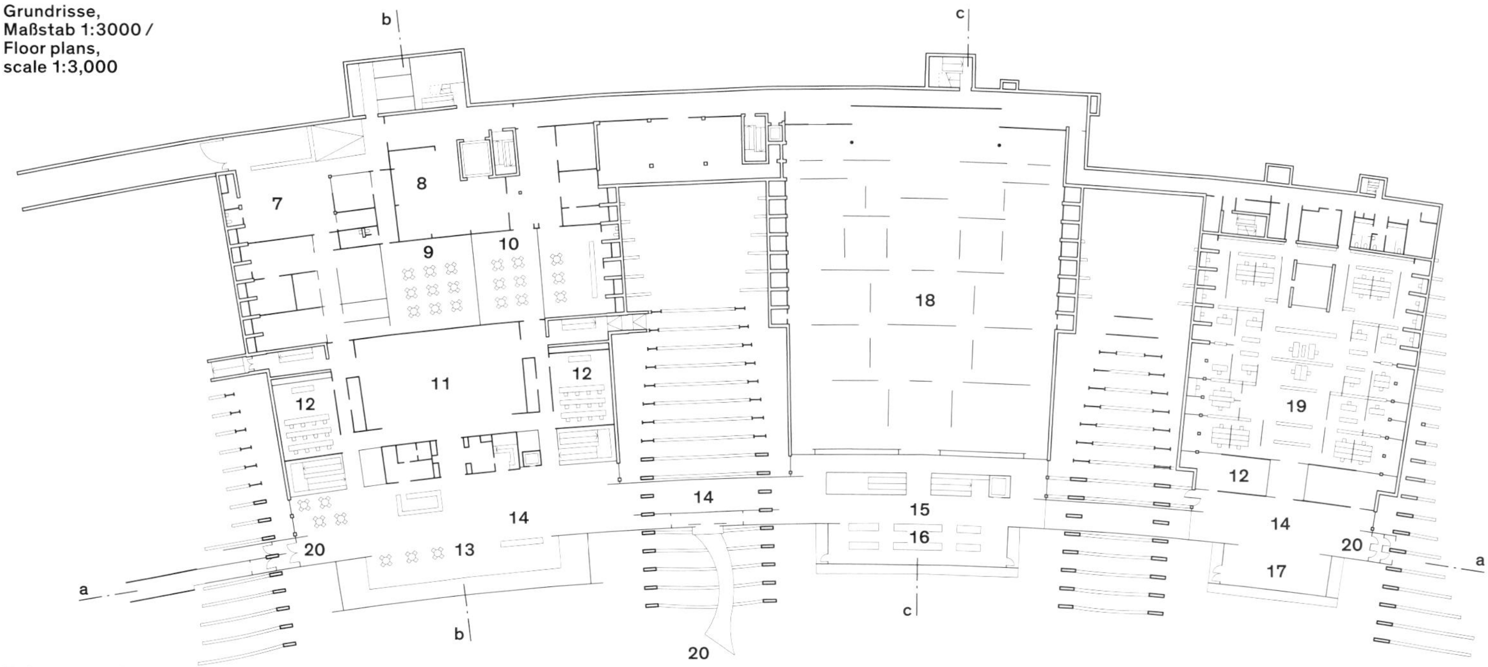

Erdgeschoss /
Ground floor

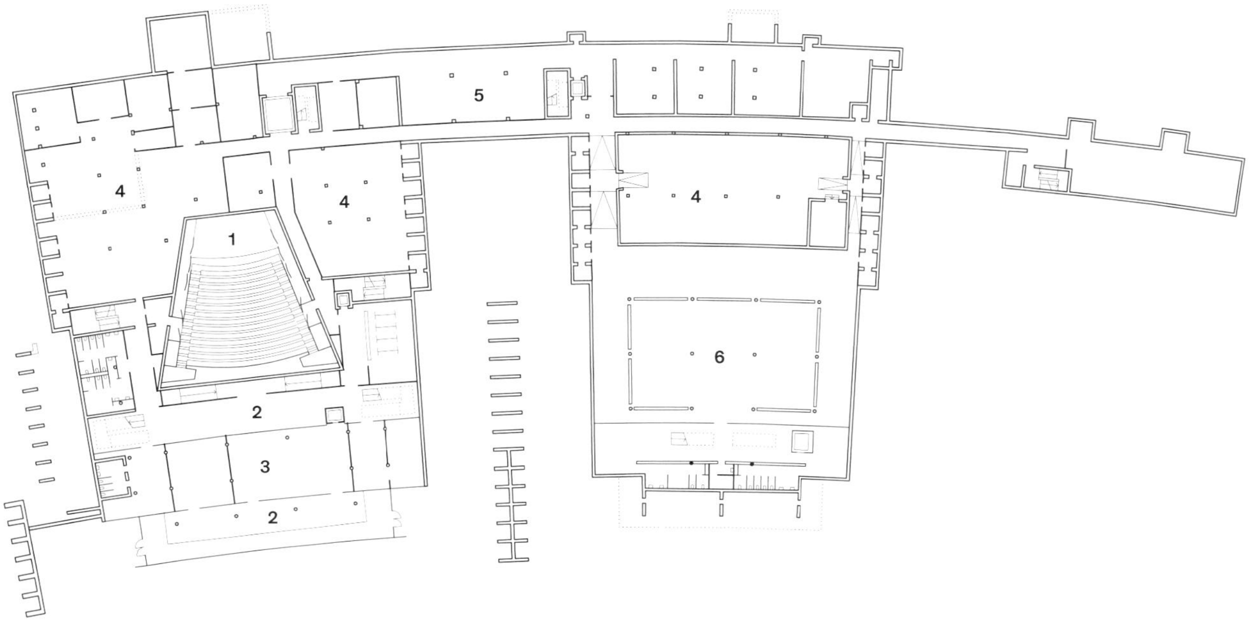

Untergeschoss /
Lower floor

1	Auditorium	Auditorium
2	Foyer	Foyer
3	Kindermuseum	Children's museum
4	Technik	Mechanical services
5	Lager	Store
6	Wechselausstellung	Temporary exhibitions
7	Anlieferung LKW	Lorry deliveries
8	Packraum	Packing room
9	Atrium	Atrium
10	Restaurant	Restaurant
11	Multifunktionsraum	Multifunctional space
12	Seminarraum	Seminar room
13	Besucherkommunikation	Visitors' lounge
14	Museumsstraße öffentlich zugänglich	Museum street, accessible to public
15	Kasse	Ticket office
16	Museumsshop	Museum shop
17	Digitales Archiv, Internetcafé	Digital archive, Internet café
18	Ausstellung Paul Klee	Paul Klee exhibition
19	Verwaltung	Administration
20	Besuchereingang	Visitor's entrance

Lageplan,
Maßstab 1:6000 /
Site plan,
scale 1:6,000

Bern, 1999–2005

A
Eingangspassarelle /
Pedestrian entrance
bridge
B
Ausstellungsbereich /
Exhibition area
C
Verwaltungsbereich /
Administration area

Zentrum Paul Klee

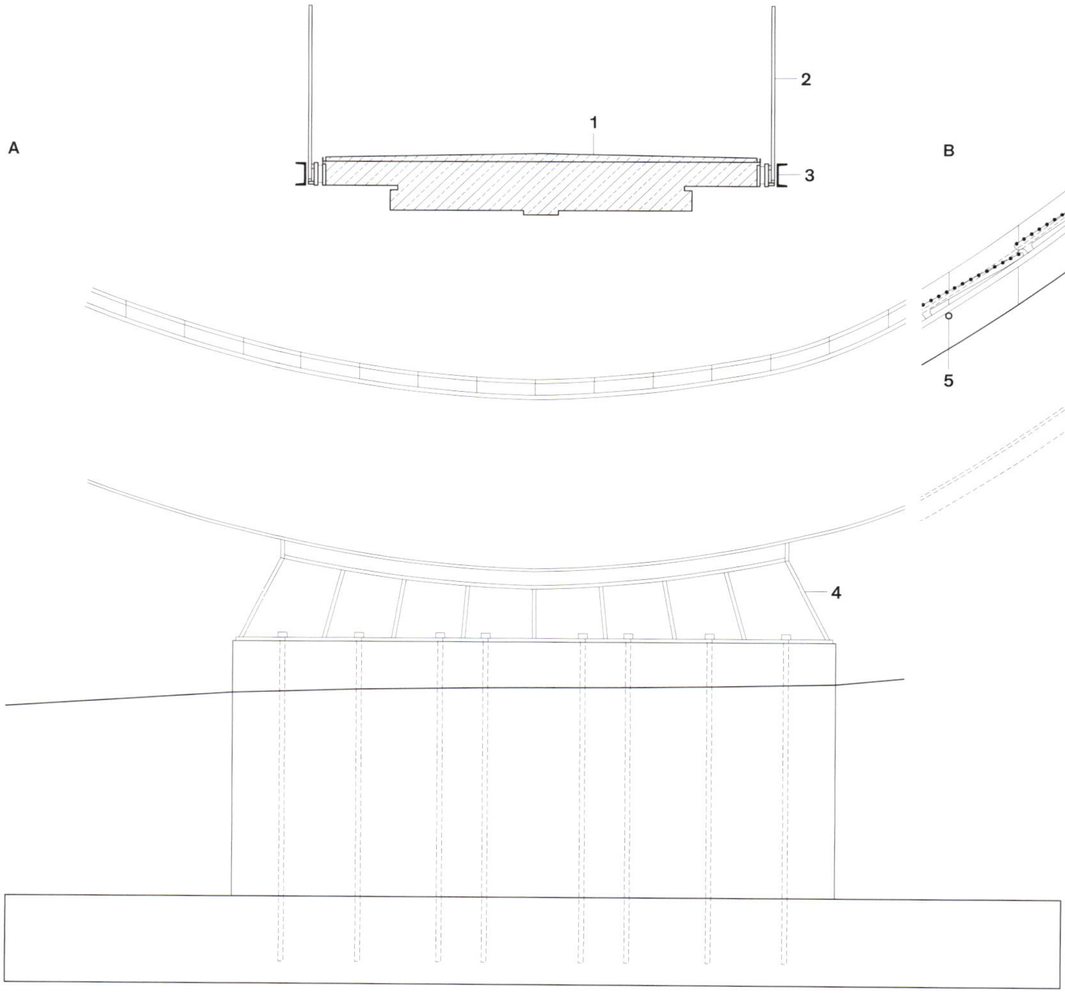

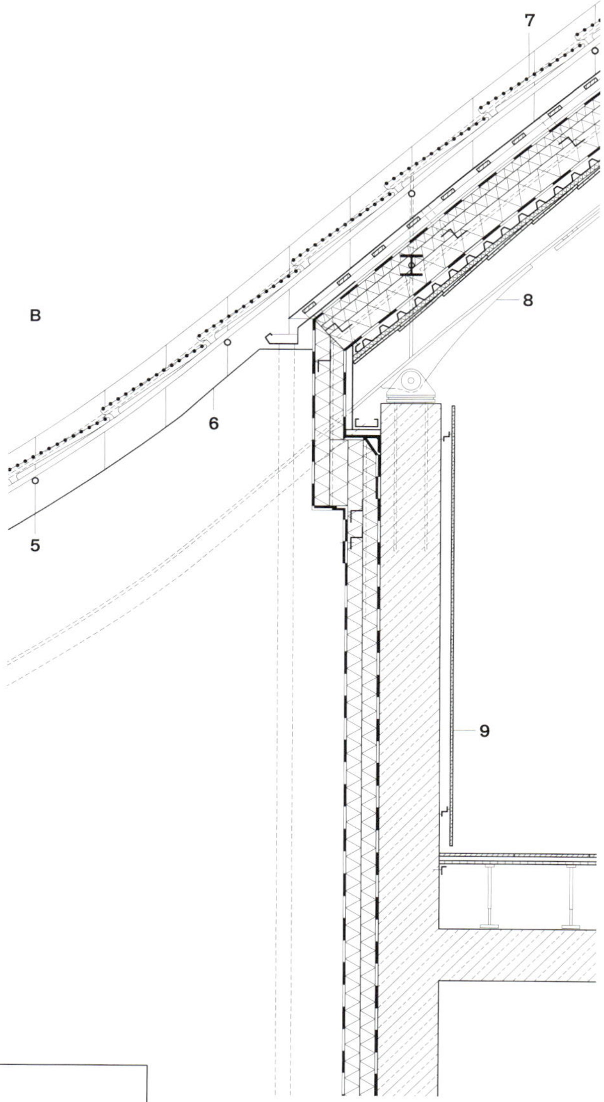

Vertikalschnitte, Maßstab 1:50 /
Vertical sections, scale 1:50

1	Hartbetonauflage 30–60 mm Stahlbeton 340 mm	30–60 mm granolithic paving to falls on 340 mm reinforced concrete slab
2	Brüstung VSG 2× 10 mm	Balustrade: lam. safety glass (2× 10 mm)
3	Stahlprofil ⌐ 160 mm, Elastomerstreifen Flachstahl 160/20 mm und 150/15 mm	160 mm steel channel; elastomer strip 160/20 and 150/15 mm steel flats
4	Auflager Stahlprofile verschweißt, auf Stahlbetonfundament, mit Stahlseilen horizontal verspannt	Welded steel support on reinforced concrete foundation with horizontal steel tensioning cables
5	Stahlrohr ⌀ 40 mm	⌀ 40 mm steel tube
6	Erdreich	Subsoil
7	Rost aus Aluminiumrohren ⌀ 16 mm Edelstahlblech 0,4 mm Lattung 24/100 mm Konterlattung 50/70 mm auf Distanzprofil Unterdachfolie geschweißt Wärmedämmung Glaswolle 280 mm Elastomer-Bitumenbahn kaltselbstklebend Trapezblech verzinkt 40 mm Lattung mit Akustikdämmplatte 30 mm Holzwerkstoffplatte 16 mm	⌀ 16 mm tabular aluminium grille 0.4 mm stainless-steel sheeting 24/100 mm wood battens 50/70 mm counterbattens on raising pieces foil roof lining with welded joints 280 mm glass-wool thermal insulation elastomer-bitumen layer, cold self-bonding galvanised steel ribbed sheeting 40 mm deep 30 mm acoustic insulation on battens 16 mm composite wood board
8	Auflager gelenkig: Flachstahl 2× 120/20 mm mit Stahlrohr ⌀ 110 mm	Hinged bearing: 2× 120/20 mm steel flats with ⌀ 110 mm steel tube
9	Gipsplatte glasfaserverstärkt 12,5 mm Aluminiumprofil 35 mm Stahlbeton 400 mm Anstrich bituminös Wärmedämmung Polystyrol 200 mm Drainageplatte 20 mm	12.5 mm glass-fibre-reinforced plasterboard 35 mm aluminium bearers 400 mm reinf. conc. wall with bituminous coating 200 mm polystyrene thermal insulation 20 mm drainage sheet
10	Stufenisolierglas Weißglas ESG 8 + SZR Argon 16 + VSG 21 mm mit Aluminiumdeckleisten Stahlrohr ⌐ 60/60 mm und ⌀ 159 mm	Offset double glazing with alum. cover strips: 8 mm toughened flint glass + 16 mm argon-filled cavity + 21 mm lam. safety glass 60/60 mm steel SHSs and ⌀ 159 mm steel tubes

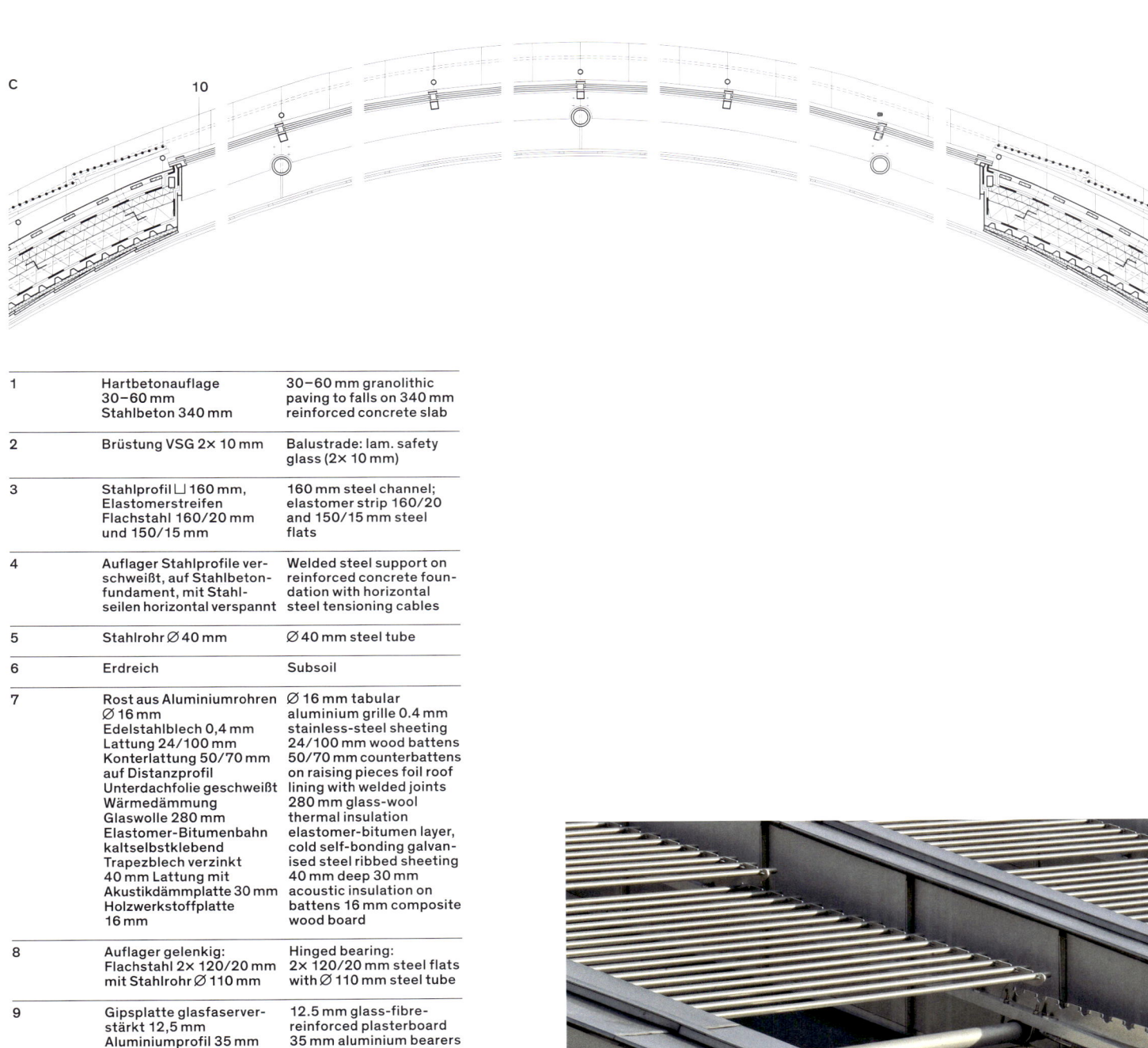

Bern, 1999–2005

Fassade Verwaltung,
Vertikalschnitt,
Maßstab 1:50 /
Facade administration
area, Vertical section,
scale 1:50

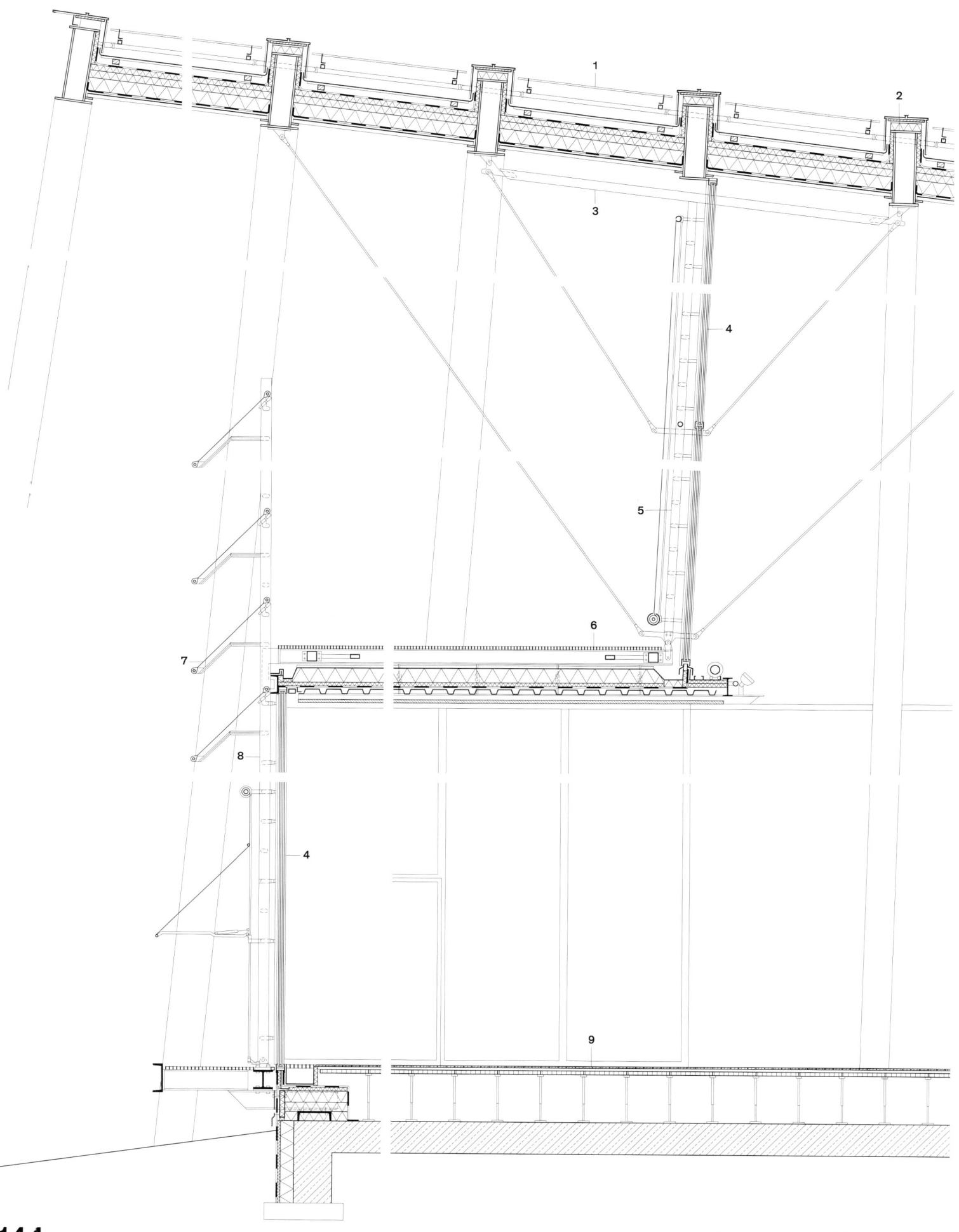

Zentrum Paul Klee

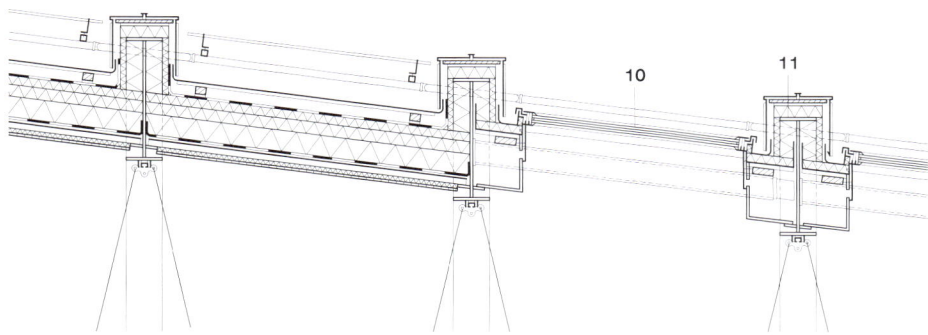

1	Rost aus Aluminiumrohren Ø 16 mm Stahlrohr Ø 40 mm Edelstahlblech 0,4 mm Lattung 24/100 mm Konterlattung 50/70 mm auf Distanzprofil Unterdachfolie geschweißt Wärmedämmung Glaswolle 280 mm Elastomer-Bitumenbahn kaltselbstklebend Trapezblech verzinkt 40 mm	Ø 16 mm tubular aluminium grille Ø 40 mm steel tubes 0.4 mm stainless-steel sheeting 24/100 mm wood battens 50/70 mm counterbattens on raising pieces foil roof lining with welded joints 280 mm glass-wool thermal insulation elastomer-bitumen layer, cold self-bonding galvanised steel ribbed sheeting 40 mm deep
2	Kastenträger geschweißt 300/800–1200/20 mm	Welded steel box girder 300/800–1,200/20 mm
3	Lastverteilung Stahlrohr ☐ 120/120/8 mm	120/120/8 mm load-distributing steel SHS
4	Isolierverglasung Weißglas ESG 8 + SZR Argon 16 + Float 2× 5 mm	Double glazing: 8 mm toughened flint glass + 16 mm argon-filled cavity + 2× 5 mm flint glass
5	Stütze Flachstahl 2× 90/10 mm	2× 90/10 mm steel flat post
6	Gitterrost 20 mm Stahlprofil HEB 160 mm Edelstahlblech 0,4 mm Wärmedämmung PU-Schaum 180 mm Elastomer-Bitumenbahn kaltselbstklebend Trapezblech verzinkt 40 mm Aluprofil 60/100 mm Gipskartonplatte 2× 12,5 mm	20 mm metal grating on steel I-beams 160 mm deep 0.4 mm stainless-steel sheeting 180 mm polyurethane-foam thermal insulation elastomer-bitumen layer, cold self-bonding galvanised steel ribbed sheeting 40 mm deep on 60/100 mm aluminium sections 2× 12.5 mm plasterboard
7	Sonnenschutz textil auf Stahlprofil ∟ 2× 30/30 mm	Fabric sunblind on 2× 30/30 mm steel angles
8	Stütze Flachstahl 2× 110/15 mm auf Ankerplatte	2× 110/15 mm steel flat post on anchor plate
9	Eichenparkett 16 mm Lattung 30 mm Holzwerkstoffplatte 40 mm Ständerboden	16 mm oak parquet flooring on 30 mm battens 40 mm composite wood boarding raised floor construction
10	Stufenisolierglas Weißglas ESG 8 + SZR Argon 16 + VSG 21 mm mit Aluminiumdeckleisten Stahlrohr ☐ 60/60 mm Stahlrohr Ø 159 mm	Offset double glazing with alum. cover strips: 8 mm toughened flint glass + 16 mm argon-filled cavity + 21 mm lam. safety glass 60/60 mm steel SHS Ø 159 mm steel tube
11	Stahlprofil geschweißt I 320/800–1200/20 mm	Welded-steel I-section 320/800–1,200/20 mm

High Museum Expansion, Atlanta, GA, USA

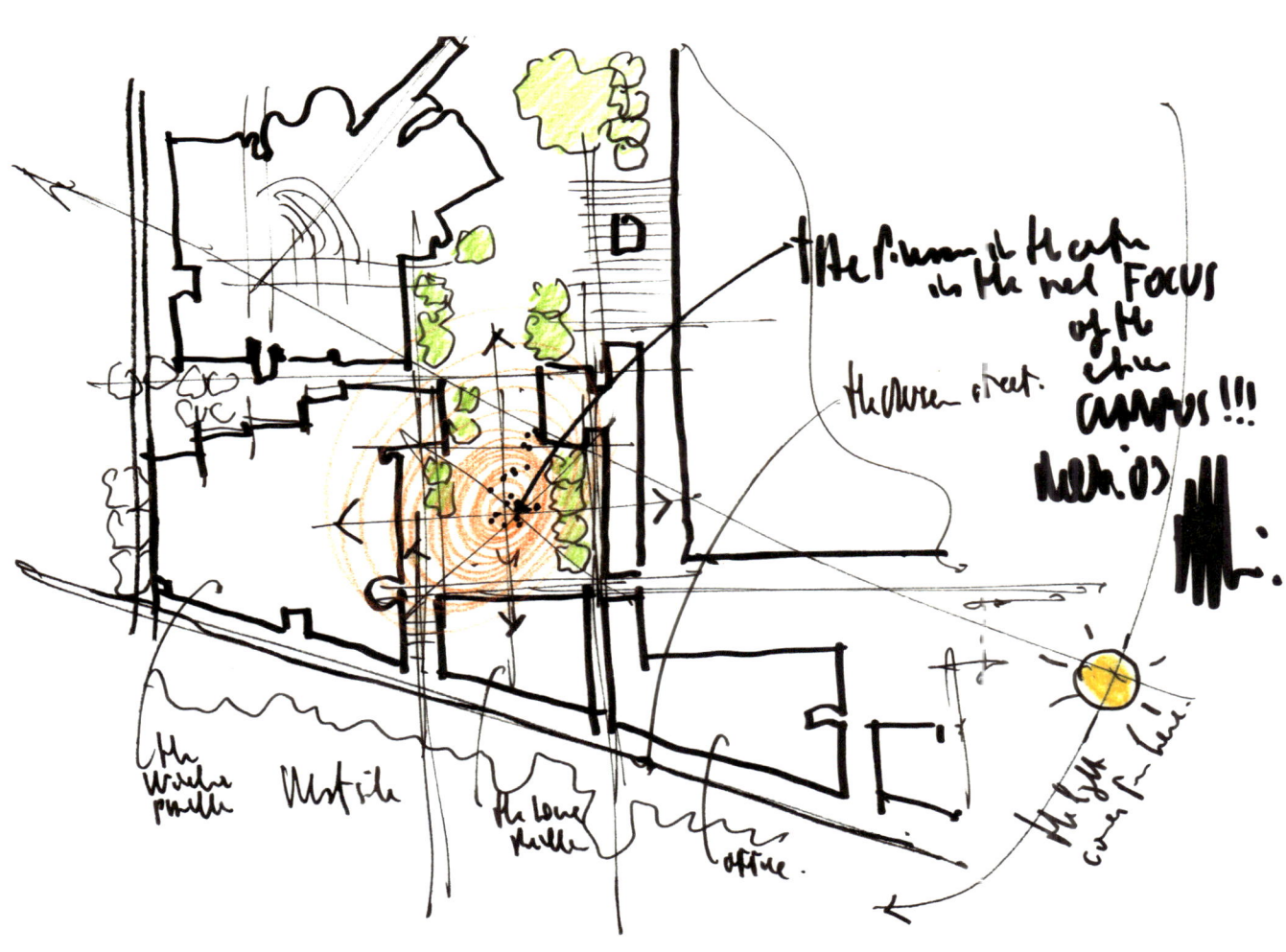

Entwurfsskizze von Renzo Piano / Design sketch by Renzo Piano

Erweiterung des High Museum of Art in Atlanta

Text: Julia Liese
Detail 9/2006

Das Anwachsen der Sammlung und die Einbeziehung privater Stiftungen hatte immer wieder Erweiterungen des ursprünglich 1926 errichteten High Museum of Art erforderlich gemacht (zuletzt 1983 durch Richard Meier). Eine umfassende Neuordnung durch Renzo Piano ergänzt die Anlage nun um drei neue Baukörper zu einem »Dorf für die Künste«. Zentrales städtebauliches Element ist die Plaza, die von den älteren und den neuen Museumsbauten gefasst wird und durch mehrere Zugänge Besucher der umliegenden Straßen anzieht. Zwei neue Ausstellungsgebäude sind über verglaste Fußgängerbrücken mit dem im Zuge der Neuordnung renovierten Flügel von Richard Meier verbunden. Seinen weißen Paneelen stehen die weiß beschichteten Aluminiumbleche der neuen Fassaden respektvoll gegenüber. Ein dritter Neubau Pianos nimmt Räume der Museumsverwaltung auf. Die Erweiterung der Parkgarage und ein Restaurant ergänzen die Neuorganisation des Gesamtareals, das auch das Atlanta College of Arts sowie Konzert- und Theatersäle umfasst. Mit 29 000 m² ist die Museumsfläche nun mehr als verdoppelt und macht das High Museum zum größten Kunstmuseum im Südosten der USA. Wie bereits bei früheren Museen Pianos spielte beim Entwurf der neuen Ausstellungsgebäude die Entwicklung eines besonderen Tageslichtsystems zur natürlichen Belichtung eine wichtige Rolle. 1000 verglaste Elemente auf dem Dach belichten die Abfolge hoher Säle in den Obergeschossen, wo großformatige zeitgenössische Kunst ausgestellt ist. Nach Norden ausgerichtete »Lichtschaufeln« aus Aluminiumblech lassen nur indirektes Sonnenlicht einfallen, eine speziell geformte Decke aus Fertigteilelementen sorgt für gleichmäßige Verteilung in den Räumen. An den Dachrändern geht das markante Profil der Lichtschaufeln in die Fassadenbekleidung über – so prägt deren Detail das Erscheinungsbild des gesamten Ensembles, auch wenn nur die obersten Geschosse vom Tageslicht profitieren.

Extension of the High Museum of Art in Atlanta

Text: Julia Liese
Detail 9/2006

The growth of the collection and the inclusion of private donations had repeatedly required extensions (most recently by Richard Meier in 1983) to the High Museum of Art originally erected in 1926. Renzo Piano's comprehensive reorganisation now adds three new buildings, creating a "village for the arts". Its central urban element is the plaza, which is flanked by the old and new structures and, through several access points, attracts visitors from the surrounding streets. Two of the new buildings are for exhibition purposes and are linked via glazed pedestrian bridges with Richard Meier's tract, which was renovated as part of the reorganisation. Its white panels are now faced by the deferential, white-coated aluminium sheets of the new buildings' facades. The third structure by Piano houses the administration. An expansion of the parking garage and a new restaurant complete the reorganisation of the entire area, which also includes the Atlanta College of Arts as well as concert and theatre halls. At 29,000 m², the museum area has been more than doubled, making the High Museum of Art the largest art museum of the United States' south-east. As in earlier museum projects by Piano, the development of a special daylighting system played an important role in the design of the new exhibition buildings. 1,000 glazed roof elements bring natural light into the sequence of high-ceilinged spaces on the upper floors, where large-format contemporary art is exhibited. North-facing "light scoops" made of sheet aluminium allow only indirect sunlight to enter, which is evenly distributed by specially shaped, prefabricated soffit units. Although only the upper floors receive daylight in this way, the striking form of the "scoops" merges into the facade cladding at the roof's edges and thus shapes the appearance of the entire ensemble.

Schnitte,
Maßstab 1:1500 /
Sections,
scale 1:1,500

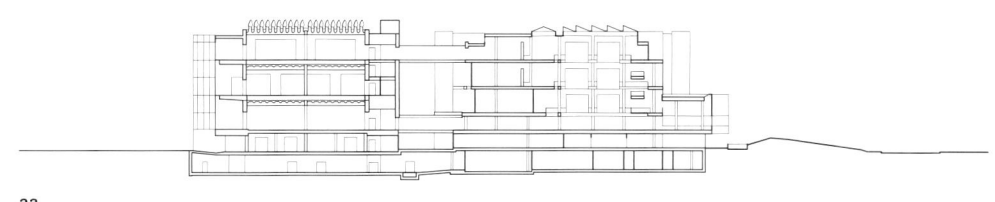

aa

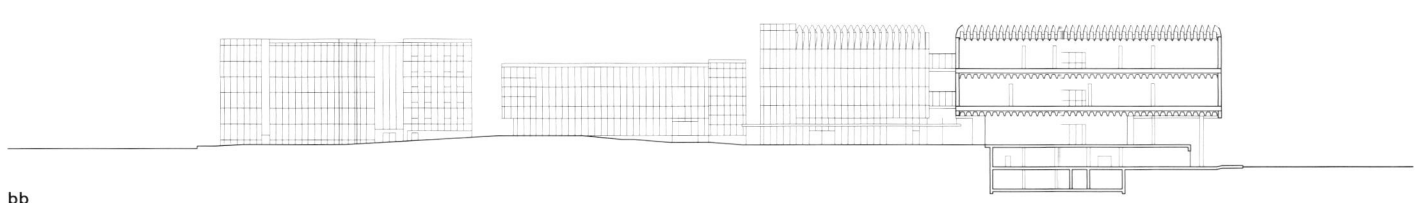

bb

Grundrisse,
Maßstab 1:3000 /
Floor plans,
scale 1:3,000

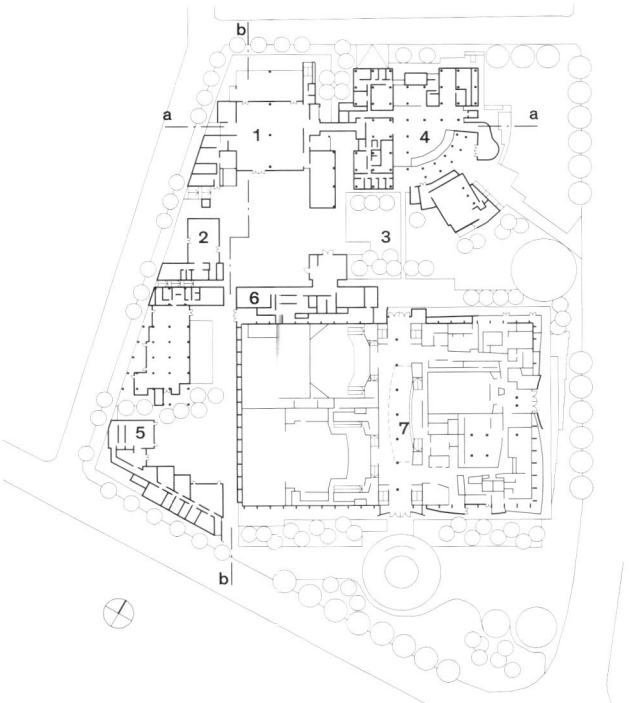

1. Obergeschoss /
First floor

Erdgeschoss /
Ground floor

1	Wieland Pavilion (Renzo Piano)	Wieland Pavilion (Renzo Piano)
2	A. Cox Chamber Wing (Renzo Piano)	A. Cox Chamber Wing (Renzo Piano)
3	Sifly Piazza	Sifly Piazza
4	Stent Family Wing (Richard Meier)	Stent Family Wing (Richard Meier)
5	Verwaltung (Renzo Piano)	Administration (Renzo Piano)
6	Restaurant (Renzo Piano)	Restaurant (Renzo Piano)
7	Memorial Arts Center, College, Konzert- und Theatersäle	Memorial Arts Centre, college, concert hall and theatre complex

Atlanta, 1999–2005

150

High Museum Expansion

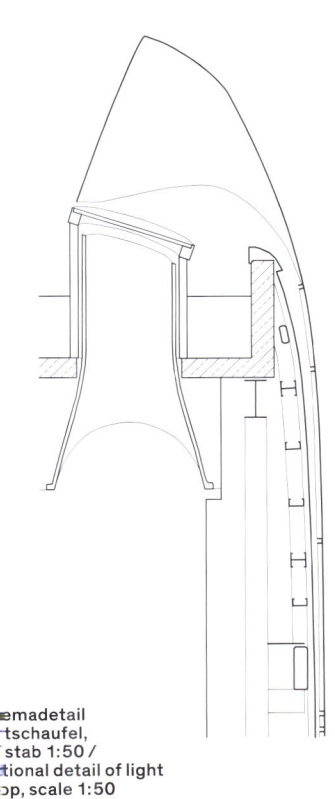

Schemadetail
Lichtschaufel,
Maßstab 1:50 /
Sectional detail of light
scoop, scale 1:50

Atlanta, 1999–2005

High Museum Expansion

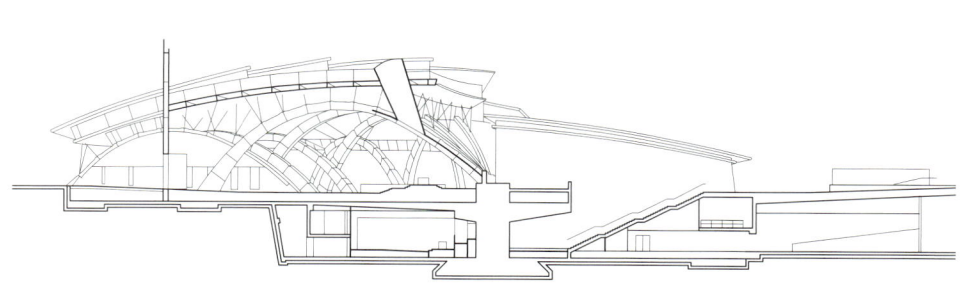

aa

Schnitt,
Maßstab 1:1000 /
Section,
scale 1:1,000

Padre Pio Pilgrimage Church, San Giovanni Rotondo, IT

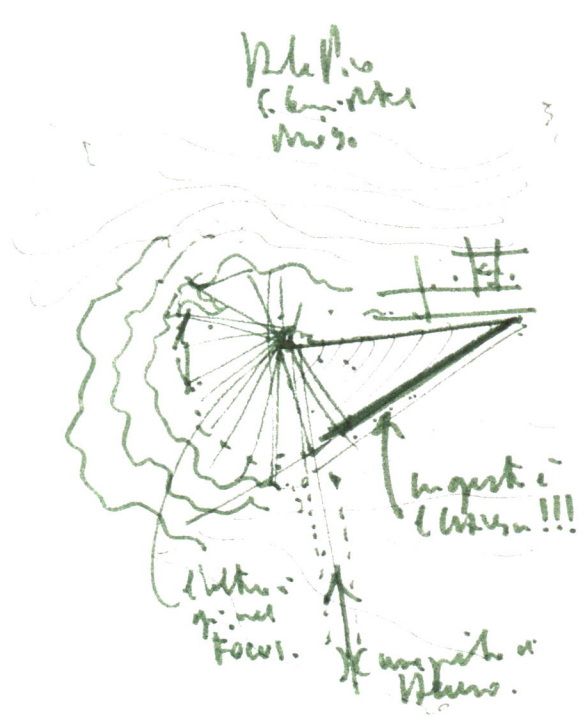

Entwurfsskizze von Renzo Piano / Design sketch by Renzo Piano

Wallfahrtskirche in San Giovanni Rotondo

Text: Julia Liese
Detail 9/2004

Jährlich besuchen einige Hunderttausend Pilger die Heim- und Wirkstätte des 1968 verstorbenen Kapuzinermönchs Padre Pio, dessen Popularität seit seiner Heiligsprechung im Jahr 2002 sprunghaft angestiegen ist. Um die wachsende Besucherzahl bewältigen zu können, entschieden sich die Mönche des Heimatklosters im süditalienischen San Giovanni Rotondo für einen Kirchenneubau unweit des Klosters und der bereits existierenden Kirche aus den 1960er-Jahren. Eine Mauer mit acht integrierten Glocken flankiert den Weg dorthin. Der Besucher passiert zunächst einen riesigen freien Platz im Osten des Neubaus, der die Dimensionen der Wallfahrtskirche relativiert. Die Eingangsfassade ist voll verglast und übernimmt den Großteil der Belichtung des sonst sehr sparsam mit Öffnungen versehenen Raums. Bei Bedarf kann diese geöffnet und so der Platz dem Kirchenraum zugeschlagen werden. Die Kapazität von 6000 Besuchern erhöht sich damit um weitere 30 000. Der spiralförmige Zentralbau besteht aus zwei sich überschneidenen Reihen radial angeordneter Rundbögen. Diese gliedern den Raum von ca. 6000 m² in Kreissegmente unterschiedlicher Höhe.

Nach dem Vorbild gotischer Kathedralen wollte Renzo Piano eine Kirche aus Stein bauen, dennoch sollte die Konstruktion leicht und zeitgemäß sein. Die schmalen Bögen aus apulischen Kalksteinquadern sind im Kern mit durchlaufenden Stahlseilen verspannt, um den häufig auftretenden Erdbeben standzuhalten und die Konstruktion zu stabilisieren. Auf die Bögen ist eine hölzerne Dachkonstruktion mit filigranen Stahlstreben aufgesetzt. Sie zieht sich schuppenförmig tief über die Steinquader. Die inneren Fußpunkte der Bögen laufen im Mittelpunkt kelchförmig zusammen, die Strukturen verdichten und verengen sich, weisen dramaturgisch auf den steinernen Hauptaltar als Zentrum der Liturgie hin. Der Altar ist leicht erhöht auf einem Podest platziert und wird durch eine punktuelle Öffnung der Dachhaut räumlich und inhaltlich hervorgehoben. Das eindringende Licht fällt direkt auf die 40 m hohe Kreuzskulptur des Künstlers Arnaldo Pomodoro. Über eine Treppenanlage auf dem Vorplatz erreicht man das Untergeschoss, in dem sich neben der Krypta ein Gebäudevolumen mit Sakristei, Lagerflächen, 30 Beichtstühlen und mehreren Vortragsräumen befindet, um den Bedürfnissen der Pilgermassen gerecht zu werden – in jeder Hinsicht gigantische Ausmaße für den nur 27 000 Einwohner zählenden Ort.

Pilgrimage Church in San Giovanni Rotondo

Text: Julia Liese
Detail 9/2004

Every year, hundreds of thousands of pilgrims visit the place where Capuchin monk Padre Pio lived and worked until his death in 1968. Since his canonisation in 2002, his popularity has risen dramatically. In response to the growing number of visitors, the monks at his monastery in the South Italian city of San Giovanni Rotondo decided to build a new church near the monastery and the existing church from the 1960s. A wall with eight integrated bells flanks the way there. Visitors first pass a huge free space to the east, which puts into perspective the dimensions of the new pilgrimage church. The entrance facade is fully glazed and brings most of the lighting to the room, which has only few other openings. If necessary, the facade can be opened to link the interior with the adjoining square, thereby increasing the capacity from 6,000 to 36,000 visitors. The huge spiral-shaped central building consists of two intersecting rows of segmental arches, which are laid out in radial form and articulate the roughly 6,000 m² area into circular segments of varying heights.

Renzo Piano wanted to build a church of stone based on the model of Gothic cathedrals, yet with a lightweight, contemporary structure. The slender Apulian-limestone arches, which serve to stabilise the building and to resist the frequent earthquakes, are tensioned internally with continuous steel cables. The exact shape of the different cuboids was computer-calculated because even small deviations would affect the transmission of the compressive loads. The timber roof with filigree steel strutting is fixed over this structure of arches like a series of scales and pulled deeply across the stone cuboid. The inner bases of the arches converge at the centre in the shape of a funnel, the structures condense and constrict and point towards the altar. Raised on a low platform, the stone altar marks the liturgical centre of the church and is accentuated in terms of space and content by light entering through a roof opening above. The penetrating light falls on a 40-metre-high crucifix sculpture by the artist Arnaldo Pomodoro. In the crypt below, the remains of Padre Pio are to be preserved. A staircase on the forecourt leads to the basement, which houses a sacristy, stores, 30 confessionals and a number of lecture rooms to meet the needs of the pilgrim masses – gigantic proportions in every respect for this city of only 27,000 residents.

Grundriss,
Maßstab 1:1000 /
Layout plan,
scale 1:1,000

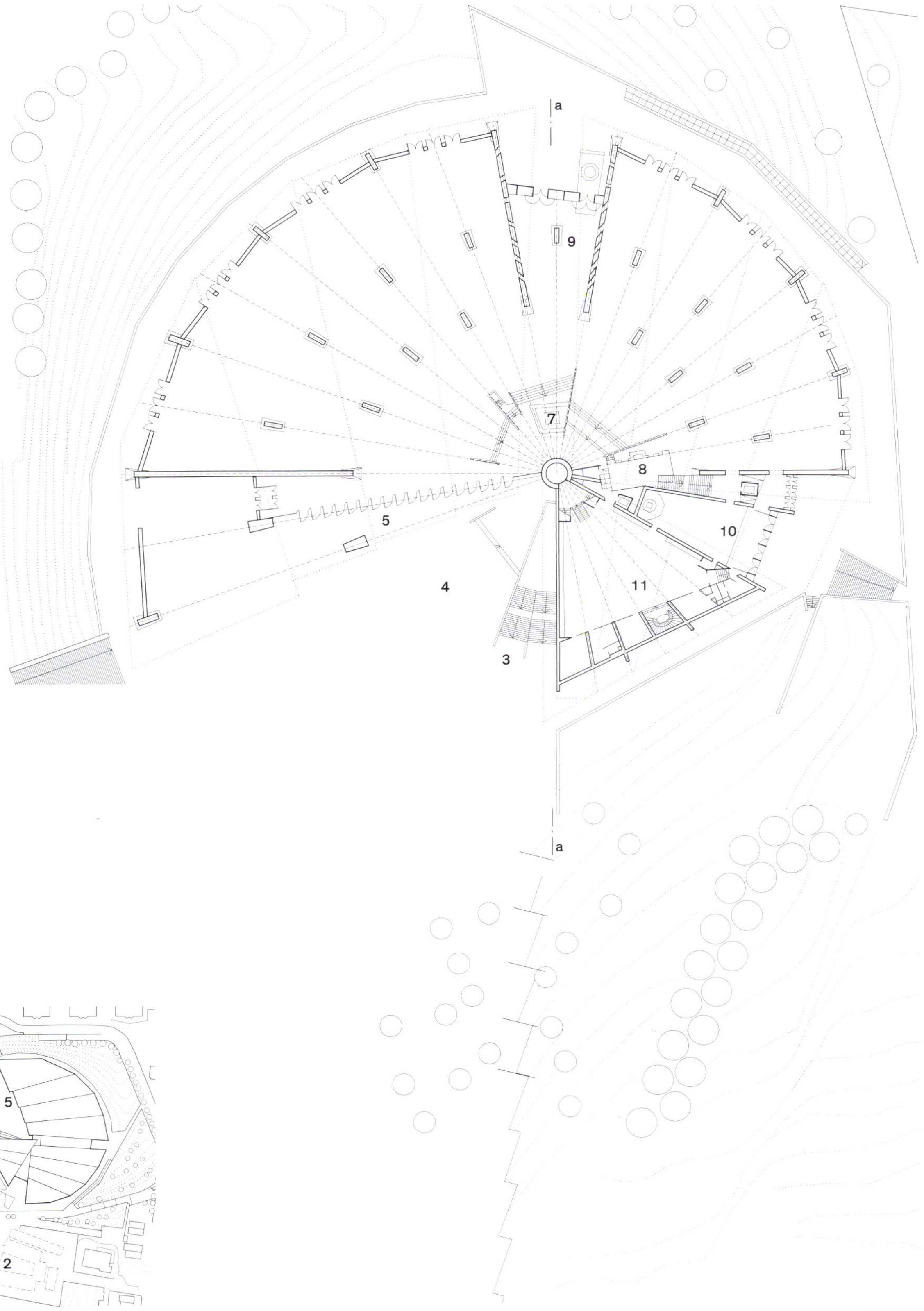

Lageplan,
Maßstab 1:5000 /
Site plan,
scale 1:5,000

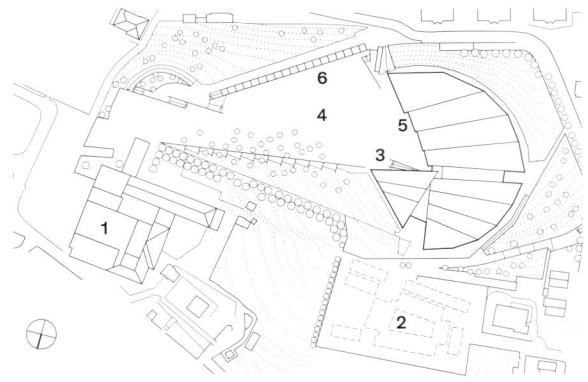

1	Alte Kirche	Old church
2	Kloster (geplant)	Planned monastery
3	Zugang Krypta	Access to crypt
4	Vorplatz	Forecourt
5	Haupteingang	Main entrance
6	Glockenmauer	Wall with bells
7	Altar	Altar
8	Orgel	Organ
9	Taufkapelle	Baptismal chapel
10	Kapelle	Chapel
11	Sakristei	Sacristy

San Giovanni Rotondo, 1998–2004

San Giovanni Rotondo, 1998–2004

Anhang / Appendix

Partner / Partners RPBW Architects

Renzo Piano

Vorstandsvorsitzender. Gründungspartner. Architekt (DPLG) am Standort Paris.
Renzo Piano wurde 1937 in Genua geboren, er stammt aus einer Familie von Baumeistern. Während des Studiums am Polytechnikum Mailand war er im Büro von Franco Albini tätig. 1970 gründete er mit Richard Rogers, mit dem er den Wettbewerb zum Centre Pompidou gewann, das Büro »Piano & Rogers« in London. Später siedelte er nach Paris über. Von den späten 1970er- bis in die 1990er-Jahre arbeitete er mit dem Ingenieur Peter Rice zusammen, mit dem er von 1977 bis 1981 das Atelier Piano & Rice betrieb. 1981 wurde schließlich der »Renzo Piano Building Workshop« gegründet, mit 150 Mitarbeitern und Standorten in Paris, Genua und New York. Piano hat zahlreiche Auszeichnungen und Würdigungen erhalten: die königliche Goldmedaille des RIBA in London (1989), den Kyoto-Preis in Kyoto, Japan (1990), seit 1994 ist er UNESCO-Sonderbotschafter, er erhielt das Praemium Imperiale in Tokio, Japan (1995), den Pritzker-Architekturpreis im White House in Washington (1998), den Goldenen Löwen für sein Lebenswerk in Venedig (2000), die Goldmedaille AIA in Washington (2008) und den Sonning-Preis in Kopenhagen (2009). Seit 2004 ist er zudem für die gemeinnützige Stiftung Fondazione Renzo Piano tätig, die sich durch Bildungsprogramme und -aktivitäten der Förderung des Architektenberufs widmet. Das neue RPBW-Hauptquartier wurde im Juni 2008 in Punta Nave (Genua) eröffnet. Im September 2013 wurde Renzo Piano durch den italienischen Präsidenten Giorgio Napolitano zum Senator auf Lebenszeit ernannt, im Mai 2014 wurde ihm der Ehrendoktortitel der Columbia University verliehen.

Chairman. Founding Partner. Architect DPLG based at Paris Office. Renzo Piano was born in Genoa in 1937 into a family of builders. While studying at Politecnico of Milan University, he worked in the office of Franco Albini. In 1970, he set up the "Piano & Rogers" office in London together with Richard Rogers, with whom he won the competition for the Centre Pompidou. He subsequently moved to Paris. From the end of the 1970s to the 1990s, he worked with the engineer Peter Rice, sharing the Atelier Piano & Rice from 1977 to 1981. In 1981, the "Renzo Piano Building Workshop" was established, with 150 staff and offices in Paris, Genoa, and New York. He has received numerous awards and recognitions among which: the Royal Gold Medal at the RIBA in London (1989), the Kyoto Prize in Kyoto, Japan (1990), the Goodwill Ambassador of UNESCO (1994), the Praemium Imperiale in Tokyo, Japan (1995), the Pritzker Architecture Prize at the White House in Washington (1998), the Leone d'oro alla Carriera in Venice (2000), the Gold Medal AIA in Washington (2008) and the Sonning Prize in Copenhagen (2009). Since 2004 he has also been working for the Renzo Piano Foundation, a non-profit organization dedicated to the promotion of the architectural profession through educational programs and educational activities. The new headquarters was established in Punta Nave (Genoa), in June 2008. In September 2013 Renzo Piano was appointed senator for life by the Italian President Giorgio Napolitano and in May 2014 he received the Columbia University Honorary Degree.

Bernard Plattner

Architekt (DPLG) am Standort Paris. Bernard Plattner wurde 1946 in Bern geboren. Er studierte Architektur an der ETH Zürich und begann seine Karriere mit Piano & Rogers am Centre Pompidou. Seither ist er mit Renzo Piano am Pariser Standort tätig. 1989 wurde er Partner. Zu seinen bekanntesten Projekten gehören das Wohngebäude Rue de Meaux in Paris, das Museum Fondation Beyeler in Basel, die Neuentwicklung des Bereichs um den Potsdamer Platz in Berlin, ein großes Einkaufszentrum in Köln, das Zentrum Paul Klee in Bern und das New York Times Building. Er leitete zudem den Bau des Pathé-Stiftungsgebäudes in Paris. Aktuell leitet er eine Reihe von Großprojekten in Europa wie das neue Gerichtsgebäude in Paris, den neuen Sitz der Pariser Rechtsanwaltskammer, einen Mischnutzungsbereich in Wien, die Hochschule École Normale Supérieure (ENS) Cachan in Paris-Saclay und das Float-Bürogebäude in Düsseldorf. Plattner wurde 2001 zum Vorstandsmitglied ernannt.

Architect DPLG based at Paris Office. Bernard Plattner was born in Bern, Switzerland, in 1946. He studied architecture at ETH in Zürich and started working with Piano & Rogers on the Pompidou Center. Since then, he has continued to work with Renzo Piano in the Paris office. He became a Partner in 1989. A sampling of his notable projects includes: the Rue de Meaux Housing in Paris, the Beyeler Foundation Museum in Basel, the reconstruction of the Potsdamer Platz area in Berlin, a large departement store in Cologne, the Zentrum Paul Klee in Bern and the New York Times Building. He also oversaw the construction of the Pathé Foundation in Paris. He is now responsible for a number of large scale projects in Europe including the new Courthouse in Paris, the new Maison de l'Ordre des Avocats, a mixed-use development in Vienna, the Ecole Normale Supérieure (ENS) Cachan in the suburb of Paris and the Float office building in Düsseldorf. Bernard was appointed member of the board in 2001.

Mark Carroll

Mark Carroll wurde 1956 in Hartford, Connecticut, geboren und absolvierte ein Bachelor- und Masterstudium der Architektur an der Clemson University in South Carolina. 1983 machte er einen Architekturabschluss an der Universität Genua. Ab 1981 war er am Standort Genua tätig, wo er zunächst am Gebäude der Menil Collection in Houston mitwirkte. Als Projektleiter war er anschließend an vielen Projekten beteiligt, wie u. a. dem Aquarium in Genua und dem Werksumbau Fiat Lingotto in Turin. Seit er 1992 Partner wurde, hat er eine breite Palette von Projekten betreut, darunter den Cy-Twombly-Pavillon in Houston, das Aurora-Place-Hochhaus in Sydney, die Erweiterung des High Museum in Atlanta, die neue California Academy of Sciences in San Francisco, die Harvard Art Museums in Cambridge, die Erweiterung des Kimbell Art Museum in Fort Worth und das neue Whitney Museum of American Art in New York. Er hat zudem an der Gestaltung mehrerer bedeutender Masterplan-Projekte mitgewirkt, etwa zum Woodruff Arts Center in Atlanta und zum ehemaligen Falck-Gelände in Mailand. Derzeit arbeitet er am neuen Hauptsitz für JNBY in Hangzhou, China, am Centro Botín in Santander und am Academy Museum of Motion Pictures in Los Angeles. Er war Gastkritiker an vielen Universitäten in Italien, der Schweiz und in den USA und hat eine umfangreiche Vortragstätigkeit. 2013 erhielt er den Architecture Alumni Achievement Award seiner Alma Mater. Carroll wurde 2007 zum Mitglied des Vorstands ernannt.

Born in Hartford, Connecticut, in 1956, Mark Carroll received both his Bachelor of Sciences in Architecture and his Master of Architecture from the Clemson University, South Carolina. He received his Laurea in Architettura from the University of Genoa in 1983. He joined the Genoa office in 1981 working initially on the Menil Collection in Houston. As a project director, he was subsequently involved in many projects including the Aquarium in Genoa and the Fiat Lingotto factory conversion in Turin. Since becoming a partner in 1992, he has overseen a broad range of projects including the Cy Twombly Pavilion in Houston, Aurora Place in Sydney, the High Museum expansion in Atlanta, the new California Academy of Sciences in San Francisco, the Harvard Arts Museums in Cambridge, the expansion of the Kimbell Art Museum in Fort Worth and the new Whitney Museum of American Art in New York. He has also contributed to the design of several significant masterplanning projects including the Woodruff Arts Center in Atlanta and the ex-Falk areas in Milan. He is currently working on the new headquarters for JNBY in Hangzhou, China, the Centro Botín in Santander and the Academy Museum of Motion Pictures in Los Angeles. He has been a visiting critic at many universities in Italy, Switzerland as well as in the USA. He also lectures widely. In 2013 he received the Architecture Alumni Achievement Award from his alma mater. Mark was appointed member of the board in 2007.

Giorgio Grandi

Architekt (DPLG) am Standort Genua. Der 1957 geborene Giorgio Grandi studierte an der Architekturschule in Genua und kam 1984 zum Genueser Büro des RPBW. Er hat an diversen Projekten als leitender Architekt gearbeitet, so auch an der Neuentwicklung des Hafens von Genua im Zuge der Expo '92 zum Leitthema Columbus. 1992 wurde er Partner und hat einige der bedeutendsten Projekte in Italien betreut, wie etwa die Wallfahrtskirche San Pio de Pietrelcina in Foggia, den Hauptsitz der Banca Popolare di Lodi, die Pirelli-Fabrik in Turin und den Masterplan für das kürzlich fertiggestellte ehemalige Falck-Gelände in Mailand. Derzeit leitet er das Projekt zum Notfallzentrum für Kinderchirurgie in Uganda.

Architect DPLG based at Genova Office. Born in 1957, Giorgio Grandi studied at the Genoa School of Architecture and joined RPBW's Genoa office in 1984. He worked as lead architect on various projects including the re-development of the Genoa Harbour for the 1992 Colombus International Exposition. He became a partner in 1992 and was responsible for some of the most significant projects in Italy including the Padre Pio Pilgrimage Church in Foggia, the Banca Popolare di Lodi headquarters, the Pirelli Factory in Turin and the masterplan for the ex-Falck area in Milan recently completed. He is currently in charge of the Emergency Children's surgery Center in Uganda.

Giorgio Bianchi

Architekt (DPLG) am Standort Paris. Giorgio Bianchi wurde 1957 geboren und studierte Architektur in Genua. Er kam 1985 zum RPBW und arbeitete bis 1994 am Standort Genua an den meisten damaligen Großprojekten mit, einschließlich der Neuentwicklung des Alten Hafens von Genua. 1995 wechselte er zum Pariser Standort des RPBW, um am Entwurf des Theaters am Potsdamer Platz in Berlin zu arbeiten. Seit er 1997 Partner wurde, hat er zahlreiche Projekte betreut, darunter die Sanierung des Centre Pompidou, die er weiterhin leitet, die Erweiterung der Morgan Library in New York, ein wichtiges privates Wohngebäude in Colorado und in jüngerer Zeit das Kulturzentrum der Stavros-Niarchos-Stiftung in Athen. Derzeit leitet er das Projekt für ein Hauptquartier von Kum & Go in Des Moines, Iowa. Seit 2000 hat er alle RPBW-Ausstellungen mitgestaltet. Er hat Vorträge an vielen Universitäten gehalten, darunter am Polytechnikum Mailand und an der Graduate School of Architecture der Columbia University. Bianchi wurde 2013 durch den französischen Kultusminister der Orden eines Chevalier des Arts et des Lettres verliehen.

Architect DPLG based at Paris Office. Born in 1957, Giorgio Bianchi studied architecture in Genoa. He joined RPBW in 1985 and was based in Genoa until 1994, working on most of the major projects of that time including the re-development of Genoa Old Harbour. In 1995, he moved to RPBW's Paris office to work on the design of the Stage Theater am Potsdamer Platz in Berlin. Since becoming a partner in 1997, he has been responsible for numerous projects including the rehabilitation of the Centre Georges Pompidou for which he is still in charge for, the Morgan Library expansion in New York, an important private residential building in Colorado and more recently, the Stavros Niarchos Foundation Cultural Center in Athens. He is now leading the Kum & Go headquarters project in Des Moines and the renovation of the Centre Pompidou. He has worked on the design of all RPBW exhibitions since 2000. He has been invited to lecture at many universities including Milan Politecnico and Columbia University's Graduate School of Architecture. Giorgio was also appointed Chevalier des Arts et des Lettres by the French Minister of Culture in 2013.

Emanuela Baglietto

Architektin (DPLG) am Standort Genua. 1960 geboren, studierte Emanuela Baglietto an der Architekturschule in Genua und kam 1988 zum Standort Genua. Sie hat an zahlreichen Projekten und Wettbewerben als leitende Architektin mitgearbeitet, wie etwa am Hauptsitz der Credito Industriale Sardo in Cagliari. 1997 wurde sie Partnerin. Sie hat viele gebaute Projekte in Europa und in den USA betreut, darunter das Mercedes-Benz Design Center in Stuttgart, das Nasher Sculpture Center in Dallas, die Erweiterung des Isabella Stewart Gardner Museum in Boston und das Astrup Fearnley Museum in Oslo. Zu den neuesten Projekten gehören der Entwurf des Centro Botín in Santander, ein großes Wohnprojekt in Sydney und ganz aktuell das Istanbul Modern Museum in der Türkei.

Architect DPLG based at Genova Office. Born in 1960, Emanuela Baglietto studied at the Genoa School of Architecture and joined RPBW's Genoa office in 1988. She worked as lead architect on numerous projects and competitions including the Credito Industriale Sardo headquarters in Cagliari. She became a partner in 1997. She has been responsible for many built projects in Europe and in the USA, including the Mercedes-Benz Design Center in Stuttgart, the Nasher Sculpture Center in Dallas, the expansion of the Isabella Stewart Gardner Museum in Boston and the Astrup Fearnley Museum in Oslo. Recent projects include the design of the Centro Botín in Santander, a major residential project in Sydney, and even more lately, the Istanbul Modern Museum in Turkey.

Antoine Chaaya

Architekt (DPLG) am Standort Paris. 1960 im Libanon geboren, studierte er Architektur an der Université Saint-Esprit de Kaslik (USEK) im Libanon. Nach seinem Abschluss trat er 1987 in das Pariser Büro ein. Er arbeitete an diversen Projekten als leitender Architekt, darunter am Kanak Cultural Center in Neukaledonien und dem Potsdamer-Platz-Projekt in Berlin. Seit er 1997 Partner wurde, hat er viele andere Projekte betreut, einschließlich des »Il Sole 24 Ore«-Hauptsitzes in Mailand, des Broad Contemporary Art Museum (BCAM) und des Resnick-Pavillons am Los Angeles County Museum of Art. Zu seinen aktuellen Projekten gehören die Phase I des neuen Manhattanville-Campus der Columbia University mit vier Universitätsgebäuden, ein Wohnprojekt in Miami und der Hauptsitz der SGBL Bank in Beirut wie auch das Beirut City Museum. Er ist als herausragender Alumni des USEK geehrt worden und Ehrenmitglied des Libanesischen Green Buildings Council (LGBC). Er hat Vorträge in Frankreich, im Libanon und in den USA gehalten, darunter an der Graduate School of Architecture, Planning and Preservation der Columbia University und an der AIA New York. Chaaya wurde 2014 in den Vorstand berufen.

Antoine Chaaya is an Architect DPLG based at the Paris office. Born in Lebanon in 1960, he studied architecture at the Holy Spirit University of Kaslik (USEK) in Lebanon and after graduating joined the Paris office in 1987. He worked as lead architect on a variety of projects including the Kanak Cultural Center in New Caledonia and the Potsdamer Platz project in Berlin.Since becoming a partner in 1997, he has been the partner in charge of many other projects including the "Il Sole 24 Ore" headquarters in Milan, The Broad Contemporary Art Museum (BCAM) and The Resnick Pavilion at the Los Angeles County Museum of Art. Current projects include Phase I of the new Columbia University Manhattanville Campus with four academic buildings, a residential project in Miami, and the headquarters of the SGBL Bank in Beirut, as well as the Beirut City Museum. He has been elected as a distinguished alumni at USEK and as an honorary member at the Lebanese Green Buildings Council (LGBC). He has lectured in France, Lebanon, and the USA, including talks at Columbia University's Graduate School of Architecture, Planning and Preservation, as well as the AIA New York. Antoine was appointed a member of the board in 2014.

Philippe Goubet

Philippe Goubet wurde 1964 in Frankreich geboren und studierte Betriebswirtschaft an der HEC in Paris. Er kam 1989 zum RPBW und war in Genua im Controlling tätig. Von 1988 bis 1992 verbrachte er zudem viel Zeit in Japan und leitete das Tagesgeschäft des Standorts Osaka. 1995 wechselte er zum Standort Paris des RPBW und wurde Partner. Er ist derzeit Geschäftsführer der drei Standorte. Goubet wurde 2000 zum Vorstandmitglied ernannt.

Born in France in 1964, Philippe Goubet studied business administration at HEC in Paris. He joined RPBW in 1989, working in Genoa as a controller. From 1988 to 1992, he also spent a lot of his time in Japan, supervising the Osaka office's day-to-day business. In 1995, he moved to RPBW's Paris office and became a Partner. He is currently the Managing Director of the three offices. Philippe was appointed member of the board in 2000.

Joost Moolhuijzen

Architekt (DPLG) am Standort Paris. Joost Moolhuijzen wurde 1960 in Amstelveen in den Niederlanden geboren. Er studierte Architektur an der Technischen Universität Delft und arbeitete nach seinem Abschluss von 1987 bis 1990 in London bei Michael Squire. Er kam 1990 zum Pariser Büro des RPBW und arbeitete an wichtigen Projekten wie der Entwicklung der Cité Internationale in Lyon. Anschließend war er als leitender Architekt am Potsdamer-Platz-Projekt in Berlin tätig. Seit er 1997 Partner wurde, hat Moolhuijzen eine breite Palette von Projekten betreut, darunter den Modern Wing des Art Institute of Chicago und den Masterplan für den Manhattanville-Campus der Columbia University. Er war, von der ersten Skizze bis zur Fertigstellung, der verantwortliche Partner für das Shard-Hochhaus in London, das 2012 eröffnet wurde. Derzeit betreut er das Fubon-Hochhaus und -Museum in Taipei wie auch die zwei Londoner Projekte Fielden House und Paddington-Bürogebäude. Moolhuijzen wurde 2011 zum Vorstandsmitglied berufen.

Architect DPLG based at Paris Office. Joost Moolhuijzen was born in Amstelveen, Netherlands, in 1960. He studied architecture at the Delft University of Technology and after graduating, he worked in London with Michael Squire from 1987 to 1990. He joined RPBW's Paris office in 1990, working on a number of important projects including the Cité Internationale development in Lyon. He subsequently worked as lead architect on the Potsdamer Platz project in Berlin. Since becoming a Partner in 1997, Joost has overseen a wide range of projects including the Modern Wing of the Art Institute of Chicago and the masterplan for Columbia University's Manhattanville development. He was the partner in charge, from inception to completion, of the Shard in London, completed in 2012. He is now responsible for the Fubon Tower and Museum in Taipei, as well as two projects in London, the Fielden House and the Paddington Office Building. Joost was appointed member of the board in 2011.

Elisabetta Trezzani

Architektin am Standort Genua. 1968 geboren, studierte Elisabetta Trezzani Architektur am Polytechnikum in Mailand, wo sie 1994 ihren Abschluss machte. Sie kam 1998 zum RPBW in Genua und wirkte zunächst am Entwurf des Aurora-Place-Hochhauses in Sydney mit. Anschließend war sie an der Planung und am Bau des Erweiterungsbaus des High Museum in Atlanta beteiligt, wo sie bis zur Vollendung des Projekts 2005 das Baubüro leitete. Nach ihrer Rückkehr nach Genua wurde sie 2011 Associate und Partnerin. Gemeinsam mit Mark Carroll leitete sie die Teams, die am neuen Whitney Museum of American Art in New York und den Harvard Art Museums in Cambridge arbeiteten. Trezzani hat die RPBW-Ausstellungen in Rom, Atlanta, Mailand und New York mitentwickelt. Derzeit arbeitet sie am SoHo-Wohnhochhaus in New York, dem 555 Howard Street Wohn- und Hotelhochhaus in San Francisco, dem Academy Museum of Motion Pictures in Los Angeles sowie an den Whittle School & Studios in Shenzhen, China, und in Washington, D.C. Trezzani wurde 2014 in den Vorstand berufen.

Architect based at Genova Office. Born in 1968, Elisabetta Trezzani studied architecture at the Politecnico in Milan, graduating in 1994. She joined RPBW in Genoa in 1998 working initially on the design of the Aurora Place Buildings in Sydney. She was subsequently involved in the design and construction of the addition to the High Museum in Atlanta, where she ran the site office until the project's completion in 2005. On returning to Genoa, she was made an Associate and a Partner in 2011. Together with Mark Carroll, she led the teams working on the new Whitney Museum of American Art in New York and the Harvard Art Museums in Cambridge. She also worked on the RPBW exhibitions in Rome, Atlanta, Milan and New York. She is currently working on the SoHo residential tower project in New York, the 555 Howard Street tower project in San Francisco, and the Academy Museum of Motion Pictures in Los Angeles, a residential tower and hotel in 555 Howard Street, San Francisco and Whittle School & Studios in Shenzhen, China and in Washington D.C., USA.Elisabetta was appointed member of the board in 2014.

Antonio Belvedere

Architekt (DPLG) am Standort Paris. 1969 geboren, absolvierte Antonio Belvedere ein Architekturstudium an der Universität von Florenz. Er kam 1999 zum Pariser Büro von RPBW und arbeitete an Phase II des Werksumbauprojekts Fiat Lingotto, insbesondere an der Gestaltung des Polytechnikums und der Pinacoteca Agnelli. Anschließend war er leitender Architekt am Masterplan für den Manhattanville-Campus der Columbia University in New York. Nach seiner Beförderung zum Associate in 2004 arbeitete er am Masterplan für das ehemalige Falck-Gelände in Mailand. 2011 wurde er Partner. Ein kürzlich abgeschlossenes Projekt ist das Valletta City Gate in Malta. Derzeit leitet er den Entwurf für das Projekt Bishop Ranch in Kalifornien, für ein Performing Arts Center in Indien und seit Kurzem für ein Kulturprojekt in Russland. Er hat viele Vorträge in Frankreich und Italien gehalten. Belvedere wurde 2015 zum Vorstandsmitglied ernannt.

Architect DPLG based at Paris Office. Born in 1969, Antonio Belvedere graduated in architecture from the University of Florence. He joined RPBW's Paris office in 1999, working on phase two of the Fiat Lingotto factory conversion project, particularly on the design of the Polytechnic and the Pinacoteca Agnelli. He was subsequently lead architect on the masterplan for Columbia University's Manhattanville development in New York. Following promotion to Associate in 2004, he worked on the masterplan for the ex-Falck area in Milan. He became a Partner in 2011. Recently completed projects include the Valletta City Gate in Malta. He is now leading the design of the Bishop Ranch project in California, a Performing Arts Center in India and more recently, a cultural project in Russia. He has also lectured widely, in France and Italy. Antonio was appointed member of the board in 2015.

Projektbeteiligte / Project Credits

2007–2015 The Whitney Museum of American Art at Gansevoort, New York, NY, USA

Bauherr / Client:
Whitney Museum of American Art

Architekten / Architects:
Renzo Piano Building Workshop in collaboration with Cooper Robertson (New York), architects

Entwurfsteam / Design team:
M. Carroll and E. Trezzani (partners in charge) with K. Schorn, T. Stewart, S. Ishida (partner), A. Garritano, F. Giacobello, I. Guzman, G. Melinotov, L. Priano, L. Stuart and C. Chabaud, J. Jones, G. Fanara, M. Fleming, D. Piano, J. Pejkovic; M. Ottonello (CAD operator); F. Cappellini, F. Terranova, I. Corsaro (models)

Fachberatung / Consultants:
Robert Silman Associates (structure); Jaros, Baum & Bolles (MEP, fire prevention); Arup (lighting); Heintges & Associates (facade engineering); Phillip Habib & Associates (civil engineering); Theatre Projects (theatre equipment); Cerami & Associates (audiovisual equipment, acoustics); Piet Oudolf with Mathews Nielson (landscaping); Viridian Energy Environmental (LEED consultant)

Bauleitung / Construction manager:
Turner Construction

2006–2015 Intesa Sanpaolo office building, Turin, IT

Bauherr / Client:
Intesa Sanpaolo

Architekten / Architects:
Renzo Piano Building Workshop

Wettbewerb / Competition:
2006

Entwurfsteam / Design team:
P. Vincent (partner in charge), W. Matthews, C. Pilara with J. Carter, T. Nguyên, T. Sahlmann and V. Delfaud, A. Amakasu; O. & A. Doizy (models)

Entwurfsentwicklung / Design Development:
2006–2015

Entwurfsteam / Design team:
P. Vincent and A. H. Temenides (partner and associate in charge), C. Pilara, V. Serafini, with A. Alborghetti, M. Arlunno, J. Carter, C. Devizzi, V. Delfaud, G. Marot, J. Pattinson, D. Phillips, L. Raimondi, D. Rat, M. Sirvin and M. Milanese, A. Olivier, J. Vargas; S. Moreau (environmental aspects) ; O. Aubert, C. Colson, Y. Kyrkos , A. Pacé (models)

Beratung / Consultants:
Inarco (consulting architect); Expedition Engineering / Studio Ossola / M. Majowiecki (structure); Manens-Tifs (building services); RFR (facade engineering); Eléments Ingénieries / CSTB / RWDI (environmental studies); Golder Associates (hydrogeological consultant); GAE Engineering (fire prevention); Peutz & Associés / Onleco (acoustics); Lerch, Bates & Associates (vertical transportation); SecurComp (security); Cosil (lighting); Labeyrie & Associés (audio/ video equipment); Spooms / Barberis (kitchen equipment); Atelier Corajoud / Studio Giorgetta (landscaping); Tekne (cost consultant); Michele De Lucchi / Pierluigi Copat Architecture (Interior Design); Jacobs Italia (site supervision)

2009–2015 La Valletta City Gate, Valletta, MT

Bauherr / Client:
Grand Harbour Regeneration Corporation

Architekten / Architects:
Renzo Piano Building Workshop in collaboration with Architecture Project (Valletta)

Entwurfsteam / Design team:
A. Belvedere, B. Plattner (partners in charge) with D. Franceschin, P. Colonna, P. Pires da Fonte, S. Giorgio-Marrano, N. Baniahmad, A. Boucsein, J. Da Nova, T. Gantner, N. Delevaux, N. Byrelid, R. Tse and B. Alves de Campos, J. LaBoskey, A. Panchasara, A. Thompson; S. Moreau; O. Aubert, C. Colson, Y. Kyrkos (models)

Fachberatung / Consultants:
Arup (acoustics, civil, structural and MEP engineering); Kevin Ramsey (stone consultant), Daniele Abbado (theatre consultant), Müller BBM (acoustics), Franck Franjou (lighting), Studio Giorgetta (landscaping), Silvano Cova (theatre special equipment)

2006–2014 Jérôme Seydoux-Pathé Foundation, Paris, FR

Bauherr / Client:
Fondation Jérôme Seydoux-Pathé

Architekten / Architects:
Renzo Piano Building Workshop

Entwurfsteam / Design team:
B. Plattner and T. Sahlmann (partner and associate in charge) with G. Bianchi (partner), A. Pachiaudi, S. Becchi, T. Kamp; S. Moreau, E. Ntourlias, O. Aubert, C. Colson, Y. Kyrkos (models)

Fachberatung / Consultants:
VP Green (structure); Arnold Walz (model 3D); Sletec (cost consultant); Inex (MEP); Tribu (sustainability); Peutz (acoustics); Cosil (lighting); Leo Berellini Architecte (interiors)

2007–2013 Kimbell Art Museum expansion, Fort Worth, Texas, TX, USA

Bauherr / Client:
Kimbell Art Foundation

Architekten / Architects:
Renzo Piano Building Workshop in collaboration with Kendall/Heaton Associates, Inc. (Houston), architects

Entwurfsteam / Design team:
M. Carroll (partner in charge), O. Teke with S. Ishida (partner), O. Teke, M. Orlandi, S. Polotti, D. Hammerman, F. Spadini, E. Moore, A. Morselli, Sh. Ishida, D. Piano, D. Reimers, E. Santiago; F. Cappellini, F. Terranova (models)

Fachberatung / Consultants:
Guy Nordenson & Associates with Brockette, Davis, Drake Inc. (structure); Arup with Summit Consultants (services); Arup (lighting); Front (facade consultant); Pond & Company (landscape); Harvey Marshall Berling Associates Inc. (acoustical/audiovisual); Dottor Group (concrete consultant); Stuart-Lynn Company (cost consultant)

Projektleitung / Project Manager:
Paratus Group

2010–2012 Auditorium del Parco, L'Aquila, IT

Bauherr / Client:
Provincia Autonoma di Trento

Architekten / Architects:
Renzo Piano Building Workshop in collaboration with Atelier Traldi (Milan)

Entwurfsteam / Design team:
P. Colonna (associate in charge); C. Colson, Y. Kyrkos (models)

Fachberatung / Consultants:
Favero & Milan (structure and services); Müller-BBM (acoustics); Studio Giorgetta (landscaping); GAE Engineering (fire prevention); New Engineering (security); I.T.E.A. (site supervision)

2000–2009
The Art Institute of Chicago – The Modern Wing, Chicago, IL, USA

Bauherr /
Client:
The Art Institute of Chicago

Architekten /
Architects:
Renzo Piano Building Workshop
in collaboration with Interactive Design Inc. (Chicago), architects

Entwurfsteam /
Design team:
J. Moolhuijzen (partner in charge), D. Rat, C. Maxwell-Mahon with A. Belvedere, D. Colas, P. Colonna, O. Foucher, A. Gallissian, S. Giorgio-Marrano, H. Lee, W. Matthews, T. Mikdashi, J. B. Mothes, Y. Pagès, B. Payson, M. Reale, J. Rousseau, A. Stern, A. Vachette, C. von Däniken and K. Doerr, M. Gomes, J. Nakagawa; Y. Kyrkos, C. Colson, O. Aubert (models)

Fachberatung /
Consultants:
Ove Arup & Partners (structure); Ove Arup & Partners + Sebesta Blomberg (services); Patrick Engineering (civil engineering); Wiss, Janey, Elstner Associates Inc. (structure for bridge interface with Millennium Park); The Talaske Group (A/V consultant); Gustafson Guthrie Nichol Ltd. (landscaping); Morgan Construction Consultants (cost consultant); Carter Burgess (LEED consultant)

2000–2007
The New York Times Building, New York, NY, USA

Bauherr /
Client:
The New York Times /
Forest City Ratner Companies

Architekten /
Architects:
Renzo Piano Building Workshop
in collaboration with FXFowle Architects, P.C. (New York), architects

Wettbewerb /
Competition:
2000

Entwurfsteam /
Design team:
B. Plattner (partner in charge), E. Volz with G. Bianchi, J. Moolhuijzen (partners), S. Ishida, P. Vincent (partners), A. Eris, J. Knaak, T. Mikdashi, M. Pimmel, M. Prini, A. Symietz

Fachberatung /
Consultants:
Ove Arup & Partners (structure and services)

Entwurfsentwicklung /
Design Development:
2000–2007

Entwurfsteam /
Design team:
B. Plattner (partner in charge), E. Volz (associate in charge) with J. Carter, S. Drouin, B. Lenz, B. Nichol, R. Salceda, M. Seibold, J. Wagner and C. Orsega, J. Stanteford, R. Stubbs, G. Tran, J. Zambrano; O. Aubert, C. Colson, Y. Kyrkos (models)

Fachberatung /
Consultants:
Thornton Tomasetti (structure); Flack & Kurtz (services); Jenkins & Huntington (vertical transportation); Heitman & Associates (facade consultant); Ludwig & Weiler (storefront); Office for Visual Interaction (lighting); Gensler Associates (interiors); H. M. White (landscape); AMEC (construction manager)

1998–2006
Maison Hermès, Tokio / Tokyo, JP

Bauherr /
Client:
Hermès Japon

Renzo Piano Building Workshop, architects
in collaboration with Rena Dumas Architecture Intérieure (Paris)

Phase I /
Phase One
1998–2001

Entwurfsteam /
Design team:
P. Vincent (partner in charge), L. Couton with G. Ducci, P. Hendier, S. Ishida (partner), F. La Rivière and C. Kuntz; C. Colson, Y. Kyrkos (models)

Beratende ausführende Architekten /
Consulting executive architect:
Takenaka Corporation Design Department

Fachberatung /
Consultants:
Ove Arup & Partners (structure and services); Syllabus (cost control); Delphi (acoustics); Ph. Almon (lighting); R. Labeyrie (audio/video equipment); K. Tanaka (landscape); Atelier 10/N. Takata (code research); ArchiNova Associates (site supervision)

Skulptur /
Sculpture:
S. Shingu

Phase II /
Phase Two
2002–2006

Entwurfsteam /
Design team:
P. Vincent (partner in charge), F. La Rivière; O. Aubert, C. Colson, Y. Kyrkos (models)

Fachberatung /
Consultants:
GDLC Architectes / L. Couton (consulting architect); Ove Arup & Partners (structure and services); Delphi (acoustics); Ph. Almon (lighting); K. Tanaka (landscape); M. Gonzalez (specifications); ArchiNova Associates (site supervision); Takenaka Corporation Design Department (consulting executive architect)

1999–2005
Zentrum Paul Klee, Bern, CH

Bauherr /
Client:
Maurice E. and Martha Müller Foundation

Architekten /
Architects:
Renzo Piano Building Workshop
in collaboration with ARB Architekten (Bern), architects

Entwurfsteam /
Design team:
B. Plattner (partner in charge), M. Busk-Petersen, O. Hempel (architects in charge) with L. Battaglia, A. Eris, J. Moolhuijzen (partner), M. Prini and F. Carriba, L. Couton, S. Drouin, O. Foucher, H. Gsottbauer, F. Kohlbecker, J. Paik, D. Rat, A. Wollbrink; R. Aebi, O. Aubert, C. Colson, F. de Saint-Jouan, P. Furnemont, Y. Kyrkos (models)

Fachberatung /
Consultants:
Ove Arup & Partners, B+S Ingenieure AG (structure); Ove Arup & Partners, Luco AG, Enerconom AG, Bering AG (services); Emmer Pfenninger Partner AG (facade engineering); A. Walz (geometry studies); Ludwig & Weiler (special structural elements); Grolimund + Partner AG (building physics); Müller-BBM (acoustics); Institut de sécurité (fire prevention); Hügli AG (security); M. Volkart (food service); Schweizerische Hochschule für Landwirtschaft, F. Vogel (planting); Coande (signage)

1999–2005
High Museum of Art Expansion Atlanta, GA, USA

Bauherr /
Client:
High Museum of Art + Woodruff Arts Center

Architekten /
Architects:
Renzo Piano Building Workshop
in collaboration with Lord, Aeck & Sargent Inc. (Atlanta), architects

Entwurfsteam /
Design team:
M. Carroll (partner in charge), E. Trezzani (associate in charge), S. Ishida (partner), S. Colon, D. Patterson, A. Symietz with F. Elmalipinar, G. Longoni, M. Maggi, A. Parigi, R. Sproull, E. Suarez and J. Boon, J. Silvester, S. Tagliacarne B. Waechter, M. Agnoletto, S. Chavez, D. Hlavacek, R. Supiciche, A. Vranz; M. Ottonello, G. Langasco (CAD Operators); D. Cavagna, F. Cappellini, S. Rossi (models)

Fachberatung /
Consultants:
Ove Arup & Partners + Uzun & Case + Jordan & Skala (structure and services); Arup Acoustics (acoustics); Arup Lighting (lighting); HDR / WLJorden (civil engineering); Jordan Jones & Goulding (landscaping); Bergmeyer Associates (interiors/restaurant); Brand + Allen Architects (interiors/retail)

1991–2004
Padre Pio Pilgrimage Church, San Giovanni Rotondo, IT

Bauherr /
Client:
Provincia dei Frati Minori Cappuccini di Foggia

Architekten /
Architects:
Renzo Piano Building Workshop

Phase I /
First phase:
1991–1996

Entwurfsteam /
Design team:
G. Grandi (partner in charge), K. Fraser, V. Di Turi, M. Palmore, C. Manfreddo, M. Rossato, S. Ishida (partner), L. Lin, D. Magnano, P. Bodega, E. Fitzgerald with M. Byrne, B. Ditchbum, H. Hirsch, A. Saheba, G. Stirk; I. Corte, S. D'Atri (CAD Operators); D. Cavagna, S. Rossi (models)

Fachberatung /
Consultants:
Ove Arup & Partners + Co. Re. Ingegneria (structure); Ove Arup & Partners / Manens Intertecnica (services); Müller-BBM (acoustics); STED, Austin Italia (cost consultants); Tecnocons (fire prevention); E. Trabella (planting); Studio Ambiente (urban planning); G. Grasso o.p. (lithurgical advisor)

Phase II /
Second phase:
1997–2004

Entwurfsteam /
Design team:
G. Grandi (partner in charge), V. Grassi (associate) with V. Di Turi, D. Magnano, M. Rossato Piano, S. Scarabicchi and M. Belviso, E. Mijic, C. Pafumi, M. Piazza, G. Robotti, W. Vassal, D. Vespier; I. Corte, S. D'Atri (CAD Operators); D. Cavagna, F. Cappellini, S. Rossi (models)

Fachberatung /
Consultants:
Favero & Milan (structure); Manens Intertecnica (services); Müller-BBM (acoustics); HR Wallingford (roof drainage system); Tecnocons + C. Manfreddo (fire prevention); P. Castiglioni (lighting); F. Origoni (graphic design); D. Lagazzi (stone consultant); N. Albertani (timber consultant); Mons. C. Valenziano (lithurgical advisor); M. Codognato (art consultant); G. Muciaccia (site supervision)

Projektbeteiligte / Project Credits   167

Bildnachweis / Picture Credits

010: Nic Lehoux © RPBW
013 oben / top: Courtesy of Karl Morgen, Friedrich Hilgenstock
013 Mitte / middle: Walz & Krenzer
013 unten / bottom: Courtesy of Karl Morgen, Friedrich Hilgenstock
014: Nic Lehoux © RPBW
015 oben links / top left: Walz & Krenzer
015 oben Mitte / top middle: Walz & Krenzer
015 oben rechts / top right: Courtesy of Karl Morgen, Friedrich Hilgenstock
015 unten / bottom: Courtesy of Karl Morgen, Friedrich Hilgenstock
016 oben / top: Walz & Krenzer
016 unten links / bottom left: Courtesy of Karl Morgen, Friedrich Hilgenstock
016 unten rechts / bottom right: Walz & Krenzer
017 oben links / top left: Walz & Krenzer
017 oben rechts / top right: Courtesy of Karl Morgen, Friedrich Hilgenstock
017 rechts / right: Courtesy of Karl Morgen, Friedrich Hilgenstock
017 unten / bottom: Nic Lehoux © RPBW
018: Nic Lehoux © RPBW
019: Nic Lehoux © RPBW
020: Enrico Cano © VG Bild-Kunst, Bonn 2018
021: RPBW
023: Enrico Cano © VG Bild-Kunst, Bonn 2018
024: Enrico Cano © VG Bild-Kunst, Bonn 2018
025: Enrico Cano © VG Bild-Kunst, Bonn 2018
026 links / left: Enrico Cano © VG Bild-Kunst, Bonn 2018
026 rechts / right: Michel Denancé
028: Enrico Cano © VG Bild-Kunst, Bonn 2018
029: Michel Denancé
031: Enrico Cano © VG Bild-Kunst, Bonn 2018
032 oben / top: Michel Denancé
032 Mitte / middle: Paul Vincent
032 unten / bottom: Raphael Petit
034: Enrico Cano © VG Bild-Kunst, Bonn 2018
035: Enrico Cano © VG Bild-Kunst, Bonn 2018
036: Michel Denancé
037: RPBW
039: Mario Carrieri
040 oben / top: Shunji Ishida © RPBW
040 unten / bottom: Cyril Sancereau
041: Michel Denancé
042: Michel Denancé
043: Michel Denancé
044 oben / top: Michel Denancé
044 unten / bottom: Michel Denancé
045: M. + A. Filiberti
046 oben / top: RPBW
046 unten / bottom: M. + A. Filiberti
048: Michel Denancé
049: Mario Carrieri
050: Michel Denancé
051: RPBW

053: Michel Denancé
054: Michel Denancé
055: Michel Denancé
057 oben / top: Michel Denancé
057 unten / bottom: Michel Denancé
059: Michel Denancé
061: Michel Denancé
063: Michel Denancé
064: Nic Lehoux
065: RPBW
068: Nic Lehoux
069: Nic Lehoux
070: Nic Lehoux
071: Nic Lehoux
073: Nic Lehoux
074: Marco Caselli Nirmal
075: RPBW
078: Marco Caselli Nirmal
080: Marco Caselli Nirmal
081: Marco Caselli Nirmal
082: Marco Caselli Nirmal
083: Marco Caselli Nirmal
084: Marco Caselli Nirmal
086: Nic Lehoux © RPBW
087: RPBW
089 links / left: Nic Lehoux © RPBW
089 rechts / right: Nic Lehoux © RPBW
091 oben / top: Charles Young © RPBW
091 Mitte / middle: Shunji Ishida © RPBW / © Succession Picasso / VG Bild-Kunst, Bonn 2018 / © Alberto Giacometti Estate / ACS, London and ADAGP, Paris 2018
092: Shunji Ishida © RPBW
093: Shunji Ishida © RPBW
094: Thomas Madlener
095: RPBW
097: Michel Denancé
098: RPBW
099: Thomas Madlener
101 oben / top: RPBW
101 unten / bottom: RPBW
105 oben / top: RPBW
105 unten links / bottom left: Serge Drouin © RPBW
105 unten rechts / bottom right: RPBW
106 oben links / top left: RPBW
106 oben rechts / top right: RPBW
106 unten / bottom: Michel Denancé © RPBW
109 oben / top: Michel Denancé
109 unten / bottom: Serge Drouin © RPBW
111 oben links / top left: RPBW
111 oben rechts / top right: Serge Drouin © RPBW
111 unten links / bottom left: David Joseph
111 unten rechts / bottom right: Serge Drouin © RPBW
114: Michel Denancé
115: Serge Drouin © RPBW
117: Michel Denancé © RPBW
119: Michel Denancé © RPBW

120: Serge Drouin © RPBW
123 links / left: picture alliance / Associated Press
123 rechts / right: Dmitri Kessel / The LIFE Images Collection / Getty Images
124 oben / top: Michel Denancé
124 unten / bottom: Michel Denancé
127 oben / top: Thomas Madlener
127 unten / bottom: Thomas Madlener
128: Michel Denancé
129: RPBW
131: Michel Denancé
132: Andrea Wiegelmann
133: Andrea Wiegelmann
134: Michel Denancé
135: Michel Denancé
136: Michel Denancé
137: RPBW
138: Alexander Gempeler
139: Michel Denancé
142: Alexander Gempeler
143: Alexander Gempeler
145: Michel Denancé
146: Michel Denancé
147: RPBW
150 oben / top: Michel Denancé © VG Bild-Kunst, Bonn 2018
150 unten / bottom: Michel Denancé
151 oben / top: Michel Denancé
151 unten / bottom: Elisabetta Trezzani © RPBW
152: Michel Denancé
153: Michel Denancé
154: Michel Denancé
155: Michel Denancé
156: Paul Raftery
157: RPBW
159: Gianni Berengo Gardin
160: Michel Denancé
161 oben / top: Paul Raftery
161 unten / bottom: Michel Denancé

Fotos, zu denen kein Fotograf genannt ist, sind Architektenaufnahmen, Werkfotos oder stammen aus dem Archiv DETAIL. Trotz intensiven Bemühens konnten wir einige Urheber der Abbildungen nicht ermitteln, die Urheberrechte sind jedoch gewahrt. Wir bitten in diesen Fällen um entsprechende Nachricht. / Photographs not specially credited were taken by the architects or are works photographs or were supplied from the DETAIL archives. Despite intensive endeavours we were unable to establish copyright ownership in just a few cases; however, copyright is assured. Please notify us accordingly in such instances.